Theology of Debt

Theology of Debt

HOLLIS PHELPS

CASCADE *Books* · Eugene, Oregon

THEOLOGY OF DEBT

Copyright © 2025 Hollis Phelps. All rights reserved. Except for brief quotations in critical publications or reviews, no part of this book may be reproduced in any manner without prior written permission from the publisher. Write: Permissions, Wipf and Stock Publishers, 199 W. 8th Ave., Suite 3, Eugene, OR 97401.

Cascade Books
An Imprint of Wipf and Stock Publishers
199 W. 8th Ave., Suite 3
Eugene, OR 97401

www.wipfandstock.com

PAPERBACK ISBN: 979 8-3852-3403-5
HARDCOVER ISBN: 979-8-3852-3404-2
EBOOK ISBN: 979-8-3852-3405-9

Cataloguing-in-Publication data:

Names: Phelps, Hollis.

Title: Theology of debt / Hollis Phelps.

Description: Eugene, OR : Cascade Books, 2025 | Includes bibliographical references and index.

Identifiers: ISBN 979-8-3852-3403-5 (paperback) | ISBN 979-8-3852-3404-2 (hardcover) | ISBN 979-8-3852-3405-9 (ebook)

Subjects: LCSH: Debt. | Credit control. | Debt relief. | Atonement.

Classification: HG3701 .P44 2025 (print) | HG3701 (ebook)

Portions of Chapter 5 originally appeared in my article "Overcoming Redemption: Neoliberalism, Atonement, and the Logic of Debt," *Political Theology*, 17 (3) 2016: 264–92. The publisher and copyright holder, Taylor & Francis, has granted permission to republish these portions.

Portions of Chapter 6 originally appeared in my article, "Parasites on Unwilling Hosts: Student Loan Debt and the Generation of Value," *Continental Thought & Theory* 1 (2), 2017. I am the copyright holder of this publication.

To Alden, Jeronimo, Luci, and Sebastian

Contents

Acknowledgments ix

Introduction—The Problem of Debt 1

Chapter 1: Traditions of Usury and Jubilee 11

Chapter 2: Jesus and the Forgiveness of Debt 43

Chapter 3: Paul, Sin, and the Language of Debt 71

Chapter 4: Atonement and the Lord's Prayer in Early Christianity 95

Chapter 5: Anselm's Satisfaction Theory of Atonement 121

Chapter 6: Subjects of Debt 145

Conclusion—The Unsavable Life 166

Bibliography 179

Index 185

Acknowledgments

BOOKS ARE NOT WRITTEN in a vacuum, of course, and this one is no different. I could not have written *Theology of Debt* without the support of numerous people, both inside and outside academia, in various ways. Some of them shall remain anonymous, but I would like to thank in particular Karen Bray, Jeffrey Robbins, Clayton Crockett, Will Schanbacher, Katy Scrogin, Bo Eberle, Ryne Beddard, Colby Dickinson, Jay Forth, Christopher Skinner, and Jordan Miller. The discussions I have had with them over the years have been essential to the development of the argument presented here.

My colleagues at Mercer University have also provided me with numerous resources, support, and loads of encouragement, all of which helped me to complete this manuscript. Priscilla Danheiser, my current Dean, has always supported my work, and my colleagues in the Department of Liberal Studies in the College of Professional Advancement provide the space which allows me to work on such projects, so they deserve mention. Fred Bongiovanni specifically deserves thanks, as does Wesley Barker. Wesley's friendship, penetrating insight, and gentle pushes have been essential to the completion of this manuscript.

I would like to thank Taylor & Francis for permission to publish portions of my article "Overcoming Redemption: Neoliberalism, Atonement, and the Logic of Debt," which appear in chapter 6 of this book.

My kids, Alden, Jeronimo, Luci, and Sebastian always deserve mention and thanks. They have not had a direct hand in anything related to this book, and it is doubtful that they will read any of it. I do not really expect them to. But it is a privilege to be one of their parents. They give my life meaning, and the love that they always show me, along with the love I have for them, is a constant source of inspiration. Because of this, I have dedicated this book to them.

Finally, but certainly not the least, I thank my wife, Paula. She knows all the reasons why, but I could not have completed this book without her unwavering support, encouragement, and love. She has shown me what real joy is, and her companionship is the greatest joy in my life. I am forever grateful for her companionship and my love for her is beyond words. And for what it is worth, she likely will read this book—even though few others ever do. Not because I expect her to, but because she wants to, which is certainly proof that she cares.

Introduction—The Problem of Debt

IN HIS BOOK *DEBT, The First 5,000 Years*, the late David Graeber relates a conversation he had at a garden party at Westminster Abbey with an individual who worked for an organization providing legal support to anti-poverty groups. Graeber discussed with the woman his anti-globalization politics and political action against the International Monetary Fund (IMF), which included calls to abolish Third World Debt. Graeber recounts that the woman responded to his position skeptically, with an air of common sense, insisting that because less economically developed and disadvantaged nations had borrowed money, for whatever reason, they are still obligated to pay their debts. Incredulous, she then rhetorically stated, "Surely one has to pay one's debts."[1] Repaying one's debts seems commonsensical, even natural, a simple fact of life. Graeber's book is a sweeping anthropological and historical response to that assumption, and he shows that debt is not a natural feature of human existence and social arrangements but rooted in power, politics, violence, and a morality that views our being-together in terms of exchange. Although debt appears to go hand-in-hand with such malignancies, Graeber also argues that states and societies have often created "institutions designed to protect debtors."[2] Today, we seem to have this "completely backwards," in that our institutions are "designed to protect not debtors, but creditors."[3]

Repaying one's debts, as mentioned above, seems natural, but so does debt itself—debt appears to coincide with life, with the requirements of living. Most of us carry debt in some form, which also means that we are debtors. Mortgages, home-equity loans, car loans, medical debt, student loan debt, credit card debt, personal installment loans, payday loans, title

---

1. Graeber, *Debt*, 2.
2. Graeber, *Debt*, 18.
3. Graeber, *Debt*, 18.

loans—most of us hold some sort of debt, at least those of us who live in the United States.[4] Some of that debt is certainly considered "good," in that it can be leveraged to increase net worth, property value, income, and overall quality of life and well-being, both now and in the future. But even debt that is "good" is implicated in its own necessity (not many of us can pay cash for a house!) and entails an obligation to repay.

Although debt may in certain instances be "good," it is primarily good for creditors, who use the extension of credit to generate value for creditors, whatever the individual or institutional form. Although "credit" has a better connotation, it is someone's debt—it is positive indebtedness. As Maurizio Lazzarato writes, the relationship between credit and debt is a "power relation. Debt is finance from the point of view of the debtors who have to repay it. Interest is finance from the point of view of the creditors, security-holders who guarantee they benefit from debt."[5] In a neoliberal, finance economy, such as ours, the relationship between creditor and debtor cannot be leveled in any meaningful sense, since it is the precondition of that economy and its horizontal and vertical growth. Lazzarato writes, "Debt is not an impediment to growth. Indeed, it represents the economic and subjective engine of the modern-day economy. Debt creation, that is, the creation and development of the power relation between creditors and debtors, has been conceived and programmed as the strategic heart of neoliberal politics. . . . Debt acts as a 'capture,' 'predation,' 'extraction' machine on the whole of society, as an instrument for macroeconomic prescription and management, and as a mechanism for income redistribution."[6]

Because debt lies at the heart of neoliberalism as a project, debt can be a lever to for disrupting neoliberalism as well. Lazzarato writes, "If debt is indeed central to understanding, and thus combating, neoliberalism, it is because neoliberalism has, since its emergence, been founded on a logic of debt."[7] As a material reality, debt can also be combatted

---

4. Though the claims can be generalized, even if manifested differently in other contexts. Since my primary concern is with subjectivity, I do not discuss national or country specific external debt. Nevertheless, at this time of writing (October 2024), about 80 percent of those in the United States hold some form of household or consumer debt. According to the Federal Reserve Bank of New York, that debt currently totals close to $18 trillion; the figure does not include mortgage debt, which sits at around $12.5 trillion. See, Federal Reserve Bank of New York, "Household Debt and Credit Report."

5. Lazzarato, *Making of the Indebted Man*, 25.

6. Lazzarato, *Making of the Indebted Man*, 24, 29.

7. Lazzarato, *Making of the Indebted Man*, 25.

materially, through the development of strategies and the implementation of concrete, targeted actions.[8] Debt, however, is also a subjective reality: being in debt is to understand and experience oneself as indebted, individually, socially, and metaphysically. As Lazzarato writes, "It is debt and the creditor-debtor relationship that make up the subjective paradigm of modern-day capitalism, in which 'labor' is coupled with 'work on the self,' in which economic activity and the ethico-political activity of producing the subject go hand in hand. Debt breeds, subdues, manufactures, adapts, and shapes subjectivity."[9] To return to Graeber's question, this is one of the reasons we feel obligated to pay our debts. Debt is not just a material reality or economic necessity but, rather, a subjective condition in and through which we understand ourselves and our relationships to others.

To say that debt is also a subjective condition, however, is not to say that it is separate from its concrete economic and sociopolitical instantiations. The two go hand-in-hand, with one supporting the other and vice versa. To disrupt debt, then, we also must disrupt its subjective sense, which includes understanding the various threads that shape indebted subjectivity and envisioning other subjective alternatives, even if only provisionally.

The authors cited above and throughout this book all contribute in their own ways to subjective disruption, but my focus in this book is to draw out some of the significant theological components of indebted subjectivity. As I argue in this book, debt is not just an economic and moral problem but a theological one as well, meaning that disrupting indebtedness qua subjectivity requires disrupting its theological underpinnings. To be sure, the sense of indebtedness cannot be reduced to its theological underpinnings, but it cannot be separated from them either. Many of the authors cited in this book recognize as much as well and have focused on theological notions in relation to debt in various ways. My specific contribution to the literature on debt and subjective indebtedness, however, is to link that sense of indebtedness to the development of a Christian idea of atonement, which develops to understand debt qua sin as a generalized, immaterial condition. Debt, that is, morphs from a material, exploitative condition into a universal, immaterial condition. Debt as sin and atonement as a theological concept remain bound together, so to undermine debt as a subjective mechanism we need to

---

8. McClanahan, *Dead Pledges*, 185–97; Ross, *Creditocracy*, 30–67.
9. Lazzarato, *Making of the Indebted Man*, 38–39.

undermine atonement theory as well, by desacralizing the latter. The goal of this book, then, is to disrupt the sovereignty of debt over the creation and maintenance of subjectivity at the theological level, so that we can think otherwise than and outside of the creditor-debtor relationship, both morally and theologically but also economically. Ultimately, the analysis presented over seven chapters incites us to rethink community and what form social life should take. The argument is, to be sure, ideal and perhaps a bit utopian, and works at an abstract, conceptual level. But given that debt is a multifaceted, overdetermined reality, thinking in such terms is also important for reconceptualizing and dislodging the creditor-debtor relationship. Indeed, in a neoliberal climate that tends to reduce applicability to the pragmatic and easily implemented, thinking may itself be a form of disruption.

Chapter 1 argues that debt and guilt are not necessarily related in certain biblical traditions. To make this claim, I focus on concrete practices of debt limitation and release, specifically prohibitions against usury and the institutions of the Sabbath and Jubilee years. These institutions assume that indebtedness is not a matter of sin and guilt but, rather, one of exploitation. If there is any morality to debt, it falls on the side of the creditor, not the debtor, which is a reversal of the sorts of discourses we find in contemporary neoliberalism. Prohibitions against usury attempt to ward off exploitation in advance and, in what follows, I define usury and discuss it as a metaphysical, theological, and ethical problem. Institutions such as the Sabbath year and the Jubilee work from the backside, so to speak, attempting to redress the economic disparities that build up over time, as creditors, broadly conceived, take advantage of debtors. Although not without problems, prohibitions on usury and commands for the remission of debt, via such institutions like the sabbatical year and the Jubilee year, have in view a broader conception of societal justice.

Chapter 2 traces the ways in which sin and debt become entangled in certain strands that run throughout the Gospels. To do so, in the first section of the chapter, I situate Jesus's mission in relationship to the traditions relating to usury and Jubilee, as discussed in chapter 1. Although Jesus certainly critiques debtor economics and forces thought to conjure alternative social arrangements, we also find slippages between the spiritual and the economic, the immaterial and the material, which ultimately reinforces the position of the creditor over the debtor. So much is evident, especially, in the Lord's Prayer and the Beatitudes, which I discuss at length. The second and third sections of this chapter focus on significant parables, specifically those associated with the forgiveness of debts, scarcity, and abundance. Although the parables retain the economic valence of debt, sin and debt tend to blur into each other, with debt functioning as a stand in for sin. The final section of this chapter discusses debt as it relates to reciprocity and non-reciprocity in relationships. Jesus ultimately admonishes his followers to lend without expecting anything in return, without the specter of debt, but doing so turns us into God's creditors.

In chapter 3 I argue that, although debt and its cancellation have for Jesus some material basis, Paul's thought ignores or, perhaps better said, empties the latter of content, transposing the problem of debt into an ontological condition governed by sin, law, and death on one side, and grace, spirit, and life on the other. The Gospels certainly make use of a dual sense of debt, playing with and crossing its economic and theological valences. Paul, however, drops the economic entirely: debt and sin are directly related to each other and, in the end, function as one and the same under the law. Indebtedness takes on a more general, non-economic, purview, as it becomes associated with terms with a broader scope, one that catches the whole of life. Ultimately, what is in view in Paul's thought is not the materiality of socioeconomic relationships but, rather, a more abstract struggle between sin or flesh and spirit.

Chapter 4 focuses on the relationship among sin, forgiveness, and atonement in early Christianity. Jesus, in these traditions, does not merely offer forgiveness but, rather, makes it possible, insomuch as his death and resurrection enable and instantiate an ontological shift. Christ is not simply a guide or moral teacher but, rather, actually does something that provokes a substantial change—in God, in ourselves, in the interrelationship between the two, and in our relationships with others. Precisely how that change occurs and what it involves, including how it envisions human being, varies among theological traditions, sometimes considerably, and I will not attempt to parse out all the nuances among competing claims here. But, among theories that can claim some orthodox pedigree, all are essentially in agreement that something material happens in and through Christ. Christ is not epiphenomenal but the thing itself, essential to the theological edifice Christianity constructs. Any theological critique, including those that fall under the purview of political and economic theologies, must ultimately wrestle with the question of atonement, specifically what it implies and entails for human being and being as such. I focus on atonement, then, to criticize it and the debtor relationship that, I show, it unavoidably entails. Specifically, I discuss the relationship between atonement and debt in some prominent early theologians, particularly Tertullian, Origen, Augustine, and Gregory of Nyssa. Although these authors make liberal uses of the language of debt in a variety of not all together consistent contexts, they ultimately mark indebtedness as a general, ontological feature of the human condition rather than a specific, deleterious economic condition.

In chapter 5, I focus on the satisfaction theory of atonement, which, although articulated in various forms elsewhere, is largely synonymous with the work of Anselm of Canterbury. I focus on Anselm's satisfaction theory of atonement for three main reasons. First, as I argue in the preceding chapters, Anselm is not the only or even the first thinker in the Christian theological traditions to employ the language of debt to understand the relationship between sin and forgiveness or, more properly speaking, atonement. Nevertheless, he grounds his theory of atonement in the language of debt in a more pronounced, systematic manner than his predecessors. Focusing on Anselm, then, proves the crucial element to understanding the theological elements at work in the creation of indebted subjects. Second, Anselm's understanding of atonement has been the subject of intense criticism among modern and postmodern theologians. Such criticism has usually focused in one way or another on the interrelationship between honor and violence, but comparatively little attention has been paid to the language of debt. I hope that what follows, then, contributes to further criticisms of Anselm's theory. Third, and as I discuss in the following chapters, numerous attempts have been made to rehabilitate Anselm's understanding of the atonement toward the development of a theological-political alternative to contemporary capitalism. The reading provided here at the very least complicates such attempts, in that I read the satisfaction theory as one of the apparatuses that buttresses capitalism, specifically in its neoliberal instantiations. Briefly put, and continuing a line of thought developed in previous chapters, especially the last one, Anselm ontologizes debt as a basic structure of the human condition, from beginning to end.

Following up on all that has been said in the previous chapters, in chapter 6 I draw out the confluence of economic, moral, and theological valences of debt. The main thread that runs throughout this chapter is that debt, understood in economic, moral, and theological senses, functions as a means of subjective control, which is rooted centrally in Christianity because of its emphasis on debt and atonement. One can approach debt variously, to make such a claim; and debt often functions on the subject via sheer force. I am, however, primarily interested in debt as a theological concept, specifically in its relationship to atonement. A theology of debt, then, must trace the contours of its development as a concept, as I have done in previous chapters, but also show how it relates to the moral and economic aspects of debt, especially considering the way in which the latter functions in neoliberal capitalism to generate value. A theology of debt, then, is a political and economic theology, which makes it salient to contemporary sociopolitical concerns surrounding debt and indebtedness. Briefly put, the line that runs throughout the previous chapters regarding debt continues in modern valences of debt, both subjectively and objectively. Under neoliberalism, the indebted subject is also a guilty subject, who owes their creditor not only what is borrowed but their very existence, life itself.

In this final, concluding chapter, I argue that political theology in its constructive mode should abandon the idea of atonement, which amounts to abandoning what is often taken as a central component of the Christian faith. The problem with atonement theories, even ones that attempt to rehabilitate them, is that they still assume debt as a fundamental condition that must be resolved. I want to challenge this assumption, mining theological resources to think about the human condition beyond indebtedness. Abandoning atonement, however, does not mean that we cannot draw on theological and other sources to construct a quasi-religious response to debt. It is the burden of this conclusion to show how this might be the case via the development of a concept of unsavable life, although my attempt to do so is somewhat partial and piecemeal rather than systematic.

A BRIEF NOTE ON THEOLOGY

The term "theology" can be and often is used in numerous ways. At its most basic, literal level and in Christian theological traditions, it is the study of and discourse about God, God's nature, and what God has done and continues to do, all of which includes discussion of concomitant beliefs, doctrines, and practices. So understood, theology is a confessional discipline: although it may have a broader purview, it is done by people of faith for people of faith. Anselm's phrase remains apt here: it is "faith seeking understanding."

Although I draw heavily on theological and confessional sources throughout this book (what else could I draw on!), my approach to these sources, their content, meaning, and implications, is decidedly non-confessional. The readings I provide throughout are not necessarily opposed to confessional, faith-based approaches, even if I am critical of the latter in important, often foundational respects. There is a place for theology *as* theology, along with its corresponding commitments; if I did not think so, I would not have spent my time on it. However, for me theological discourse should not be confined to self-defined horizons; it is far more than an "insider" discourse. Insofar as it constitutes ways to understand being, meaning, and community, theology exceeds the confines of faith. Likewise, it has had and continues to have influence beyond its confessional claims, which should itself warrant various forms of investigation, such as attempted here.

To be more specific, I have two main things in mind when I use the term "theology" to describe this work. First, and simply put, this work is a theology to the extent that it focuses on theological sources. That is, its subject matter is theology, specifically theological sources related to debt, understood as outlined above. Second, drawing on critical theory and liberationist thought, this work is theology in that it engages in both negative and positive criticism of these sources and the concepts contained therein as these are related to debt. Another way to put it is that this book is deconstructive of theology but also intends to be constructive, in a way that allows what the sources analyzed say about debt to be used for non-theological purposes related to debt and subjective and objective debt resistance. I use the language of theology since that is the language that the sources use, but I do so while bracketing its intrareligious truth or value. *Theology of Debt* is non-theological or a-theological.

I also focus heavily on primary sources throughout this work, limiting the extent to which I draw on secondary sources, though I do so when necessary. My goal is to provide a reading of the theological sources throughout through the lens of the problem of debt that I hope is accessible to a more general audience, so I do not want to burden the discussion with scholarly discussions that often have different goals in mind. This is not to say that these are not important, and I may open myself up to criticism here. But constant reference to or a repetition of existing secondary literature can also be limiting, constraining arguments to preset horizons. So much may be especially evident in my discussion of biblical sources. I do not engage contemporary biblical scholarship when reading these sources, preferring instead to read these narratively as they are in their present form. I am not ignorant of contemporary scholarship, but it is also the case that the influence of these texts theologically, socially, and culturally is in their received form, not primarily in academic discussions.

One final note. What follows is not a history or systematic discussion of the development of the notion of debt in relation to sin and atonement in Christian theologies. The reading I provide is more episodic in nature, focusing on relatively defined thematic content, to draw out conceptual issues related to debt. I pull on certain threads in theological traditions to delimit the problem in a specific way. We all have to draw lines somewhere. Nevertheless, I hope that the threads I have chosen illustrate the problem well and allow us to think about debt in a certain way—and beyond.

1

Usury and Jubilee

THE GOAL OF THIS chapter is to show that debt and guilt are not necessarily related in certain biblical traditions. I do so not by tracing the philological development of the concept of sin, as Gary Anderson has aptly done.[1] Rather, I focus on material practices of debt limitation and release, specifically prohibitions against usury and the institutions of the Sabbath and Jubilee years. These institutions assume that indebtedness is not a matter of guilt but, rather, exploitation. If there is any moral responsibility related to debt, it falls primarily on the creditor, not the debtor, which is a reversal of the sorts of discourses we find in contemporary neoliberalism. Prohibitions against usury attempt to ward off exploitation in advance and, in what follows, I define usury and discuss it as a metaphysical, theological, and ethical problem. Institutions such as the Sabbath year and the Jubilee work from the backside, so to speak, attempting to redress the economic disparities that build up over time, as creditors, broadly conceived, take advantage of debtors. Although not without problems, prohibitions on usury and commands for the remission of debt via institutions like the sabbatical year and the Jubilee year, have in view broader conceptions of equity and societal justice, conceptions that take their lead from the material conditions of the marginalized, or the "least of these," as Jesus might put it (Matt 25:45).

---

1. Anderson, *Sin*.

DEFINING USURY

When considering the relationship between sin, guilt, and debt, which form the concept of indebtedness, it is important to emphasize that the relationship between them is not inviolable, historically, theologically, or conceptually. As I discuss in later chapters, although sin and debt eventually become inseparable in subsequent, mainstream theological traditions, there is not necessarily an essential relationship between the two in earlier, less systematically developed documents. Whether we read the biblical texts diachronically or synchronically, it is almost impossible to ascribe to them one, consistent position on any issue. A diversity of materials, genres, authorial viewpoints, and editorial strata lie behind the texts as we now possess them. Even taking their present form as a singular, yet complex, theological text, as I do throughout this book, reveals numerous internal inconsistencies, as any careful reader knows all too well. Whether our political and theological commitments lead us to bemoan or celebrate such heterogeneity, heterogeneity remains, and it should be taken as a matter of fact. Nevertheless, despite the inability to reduce the biblical texts to firm, wholly consistent positions, we can trace certain thematic threads that run throughout, threads that go on to constitute ideas that we can then interrogate. The relationship between sin and debt constitutes one such idea but, considered initially, the two appear as unrelated or disjunct. We must start by treating them separately, then, emphasizing the lack of the other in each: sin without debt and debt without sin.

Contemporary discussions surrounding indebtedness usually and for the most part fall back on individual responsibility regarding one's financial activities. Avoiding debt or, more commonly and desirable for the economy, leveraging debt properly, is simply part of the individual consumer's "financial literacy," for which they are ultimately responsible.[2] A good example of this approach—one that is, moreover, tied explicitly to the theological concepts at issue here—is that advocated by Dave Ramsey through his radio program, seminars, and arsenal of products. Although Ramsey is a conservative, evangelical Christian whose main pitch is to the like minded, his seemingly simple plans to get out of debt and live debt free have garnered him a much broader audience, including many who would disagree with him otherwise. For Ramsey, indebtedness is

---

2. For a critique of "financial literacy" as a fundamentally unjust substitute for collective engagement, see Arthur, *Financial Literacy*.

primarily the result of a behavioral problem, which puts it in the domain of morality. A pitch for his products on his website states, for instance, "Personal finance is 80% behavior and only 20% head knowledge. If you truly want to get out of debt and stay out of debt, you have to treat the *root* of your money issues, not just the symptoms. Even though your choices landed you in a tough spot, you have the ability to fight, kick and claw your way out of debt."[3] Ramsey, moreover, runs together his moralizing approach to debt with biblical and theological statements and themes, which has the effect of equating debt with sin. While providing an overview of some common, but ultimately ineffective, ways people attempt to get out of debt, such as borrowing from friends or family, the same pitch goes on, "The borrower is slave to the lender (see Prov 22:7), and you change the dynamic of a relationship when a loved one loans you money. When you owe someone, suddenly that relative or friend thinks they get to decide how you live."[4]

Ramsey is no doubt correct that the creditor-debtor relationship involves lopsided power dynamics. At the level of the individual, the debtor remains subject to the lender or creditor, who has the freedom to set the conditions of the loan and its repayment. However, the emphasis on debt as symptomatic of a deeper behavioral problem that can only be solved through a concomitant behavioral change ignores the larger, structural problems that create and exacerbate indebtedness. Insofar as the financialized, neoliberal economy is, to a large extent, an economy that runs on individual and collective debt, calls such as Ramsey's for "financial literacy" and individual responsibility function ideologically in support of that very economy. As Chris Arthur argues, consumer financial literacy is not "a solution but a technology that mystifies and supports the very problems that financial literacy education ought to have citizens overcome: exploitation, economic crises, insecurity, alienation, and the further disempowerment of citizens."[5] Ramsey and advocates for the type of financial literacy Arthur critiques offer up a sort of "capitalist theology," whose debt prevention plans assume and reinforce the assumptions of neoliberal economies.[6] If, as Foucault argues, neoliberalism requires

---

3. Ramsey Solutions, "Debt Help that Actually Works"; original emphasis.
4. Ramsey Solutions, "Debt Help that Actually Works."
5. Arthur, *Financial Literacy Education*, xii.
6. Trueba, "Life or Debt." Nor is Ramsey a fan of any left-leaning policies that might help prevent indebtedness in the first place. As Trueba notes, Ramsey equates wealth redistribution with theft, and "the desire to reduce income inequality is one of the seven

that we all be effective "entrepreneurs" of ourselves, then this kind of "financial literacy" is simply part of being a successful, even grateful entrepreneur.[7]

We should acknowledge that one can certainly pull notions from biblical texts in support of such ideological claims, even if economic conditions then and now obviously vary considerably, in both form and content. Ramsey's website cites Prov 22:7, as mentioned above, in support of his claim that borrowers remain subservient to their lenders. Nevertheless, while perhaps literally true when debt is understood individualistically, Ramsey completely ignores that the claim "the borrower is slave to the lender" is not an admonition to the debtor but a condemnation of the rich.

> A good name is to be chosen rather than great riches,
>   and favor is better than silver or gold.
> The rich and the poor have this in common:
>   the LORD is the maker of them all.
> The clever see danger and hide;
>   but the simple go on, and suffer for it.
> The reward for humility and fear of the LORD
>   is riches and honor and life.
> Thorns and snares are in the way of the perverse;
>   the cautious will keep far from them.
> Train children in the right way,
>   and when old, they will not stray.
> The rich rule over the poor,
>   and the borrower is the slave of the lender.
> Whoever sows injustice will reap calamity,
>   and the rod of anger will fail.
> Those who are generous are blessed,
>   for they share their bread with the poor.
> Drive out a scoffer, and strife goes out;
>   quarreling and abuse will cease.
> Those who love a pure heart and are gracious in speech
>   will have the king as a friend.
> The eyes of the LORD keep watch over knowledge,
>   but he overthrows the words of the faithless.

---

deadly sins: 'At the core of this demand is envy.'" The irony, as discussed shortly, is that it is the usurer who has often been considered the thief, not debtors or their advocates.

7. Foucault refers to this variously in *Birth of Biopolitics*. For the connection between self-entrepreneurship and debt, see Lazzarato, *Making of the Indebted Man*, 89–160.

> The lazy person says, "There is a lion outside!
> I shall be killed in the streets!"
> The mouth of a loose woman is a deep pit;
> he with whom the LORD is angry falls into it.
> Folly is bound up in the heart of a boy,
> but the rod of discipline drives it far away.
> Oppressing the poor in order to enrich oneself,
> and giving to the rich, will lead only to loss. (Prov 22:1–16)

If anything, the proverb critiques lending as an oppressive practice, used to exploit the poor; the only "behavioral problem" rests with the lender, not the debtor, who *makes* the latter his slave. Ramsey's ideological sleight-of-hand may make good, ideologically driven copy, but only at the expense of ignoring the obvious sense of the text, which is even clearer if one accounts for the significant preference the biblical texts generally show to the poor, as liberation theologians have long emphasized.[8] This is not to say that the textual traditions are always internally consistent on this matter, nor the theological traditions that develop from them. As Ernst Bloch reminds us, the biblical texts often run at cross-purposes, as they contain genuinely subversive material but also ideological redactions that recommend submission to the status quo.[9] Which material we choose to emphasize and side with often says as much about our commitments as those found in the texts themselves. Ramsey's use of Prov 22:1–6 as a critique of the borrower and borrowing rather than the lender and lending, then, elides the unequal distribution of power at work in the relationship between rich and poor. By putting responsibility on the borrower, whether he intends it or not, Ramsey takes up the position of the rich, who oppress the poor for self-enrichment.

Cognizant of how lending often goes hand in hand with the exploitation of the borrower, specific biblical injunctions attempt to cut off in advance one avenue of exploitation by prohibiting the practice of usury. What is prohibited under the term "usury," however, depends on how we define the term, as the meaning varies in different contexts, in both practice and for ideological reasons. In the broadest scope, the term "usury" refers to a multitude of practices that involve transactions that

---

8. Gutiérrez, *Theology of Liberation*, remains one of the classic statements of this preference for the poor. For a more recent statement of this claim that emphasizes the vital importance of class when considering other types of oppression, see Petrella, *Beyond Liberation Theology*.

9. Bloch, *Atheism in Christianity*, 61.

produce interest. However, usury is not necessarily and always the same thing as interest, even if the two are often easily equated. As Jacques Le Goff emphasizes, usury refers to a set of "forbidden financial practices," which occur in specific situations or circumstances. He writes, "Usury means that a lender receives interest throughout transactions that should not produce interest. And so, usury is not the levying of all interest. Usury and interest are not synonymous, nor are usury and profit. Usury is involved where there is no production or physical transformation of tangible goods."[10]

Nevertheless, confining usury to certain types of interest-bearing transactions can also function ideologically, to justify what could otherwise be understood as oppressive practices. For instance, when the term is used today, usury often refers simply to charging "exorbitant rates of interest," as opposed to charging seemingly fairer, and thus acceptable, rates. The distinction, here, is more practical than anything else, as prohibitions on usury simply do not fit well with the demands of capitalist economies, in whatever phase of development. John Calvin famously, or, depending on one's view, infamously, recognized the problem, which led him to allow for usury in defined circumstances, against longstanding prohibitions surrounding it. He still recognized the dangers of the practice, but saw no need to prohibit it entirely, so long as it was done with a spirit of charity, justice, and in service of the public good. In his *Letter on Usury*, he writes:

> It could be wished that all usury and the name itself were first banished from the earth. But as this cannot be accomplished it should be seen what can be done for the public good. Certain passages of Scripture remain in the Prophets and Psalms in which the Holy Spirit inveighs against usury. Thus, a city is described as wicked because usury is practiced in the forum and streets, but as the Hebrew word means frauds in general, this cannot be interpreted so strictly. But if we concede that the prophet there mentions usury by name, it is not a matter of wonder that among the great evils which existed, he should attack usury. For wherever gains are farmed out, there are generally added, as inseparable, cruelty, and numberless other frauds and deceits.[11]

10. Le Goff, *Your Money or Your Life*, 18.
11. Calvin, *Letter on Usury*, 74.

Calvin concedes that in a better world usury would be banished. The problem is that we do not live in a better world. Thus, he notes that usury "is not wholly forbidden among us unless it be repugnant both to Justice and to Charity."[12] Calvin is not opening some new path, here, as his position in large part reflects the fact that prohibitions on usury had already relaxed considerably by his time, as a burgeoning capitalism demanded. Nevertheless, it is distinct from the suspicion his medieval predecessors cast on it, at least in theory if not always in practice.[13]

USURY AS A METAPHYSICAL PROBLEM

The point of what follows is not to trace a history of usury but, rather, to mark certain conceptual points to better understand its prohibition which, I suggest, coincides with a condition free from the subjective burden of debt.[14] Nevertheless, we can point out that, until the late medieval period, usury, as an economic practice, was for the most part condemned, at least in theory if not always in practice. Indeed, theologically speaking, so much was the practice taboo that without proper restitution, the usurer could expect eternal damnation as their fate. As Jacques Le Goff has pointed out, such condemnation of usury did not merely rest on a moral sense of right—in relation to interpersonal and economic justice—but in metaphysical assumptions about the nature of money and generation. Simply put, usury was considered "unnatural," as it put money to a use for which it was not intended.[15] To condemn usury in such terms, of course, assumes that money has a proper, defined use, and anything outside of that use must be considered illicit by default—against structured, natural laws.

Such concerns over the nature of money or, more specifically, the generation of wealth, go back at least to Aristotle, whose assumptions and style of philosophical reflection provide an indispensable framework for much medieval theological and philosophical speculation. In the *Politics*, Aristotle discusses the art of acquisition or generating wealth, which he divides into two main species: one concerned broadly with

---

12. Calvin, *Letter on Usury*, 74.

13. For a more positive evaluation of this break, see Wykes, "Devaluing the Scholastics."

14. For a history of usury, see Geisst, *Beggar Thy Neighbor*.

15. Le Goff, *Your Money or Your Life*, 17–32.

the requirements of household management, the other with retail trade. Aristotle argues that the acquisition of wealth as a means for proper household management, whether focused on a household as such or, by extension, larger entities such as the state, is natural, an essential component of a good life. Aristotle writes, "Of the art of acquisition then there is one kind which by nature is a part of the management of a household, insofar as the art of household management must find ready to hand, or itself provide, such things necessary to life, and useful for the community of family or state, as can be stored. They are the elements of true riches; for the amount of property which is needed for a good life is not unlimited."[16] The assumption, here, is that acquisition should be based on need. Need, in the context of the acquisition of wealth, should not be equated with mere subsistence, although the basic preservation of life qua life is certainly included in the notion. Rather, for Aristotle need must be understood in relation to what is required for attaining a good life, a life of virtue and sustained contentment. On the other end of the spectrum of mere sustenance, however, is an excess of wealth, which is also not conducive to living a life of virtue on Aristotle's account. In line with his account of the virtues required for living well and our attainment of them, as found in the *Nicomachean Ethics*, proper or "natural" acquisition of wealth lies in a proverbial sweet spot, a median between lack and excess.[17] Hence Aristotle writes, "But there is a boundary fixed, just as there is in the other arts; for the instruments of any art are never unlimited, either in number or size, and riches may be defined as a number of instruments to be used in a household or state. And so we see that there is a natural art of acquisition which is practiced by managers of households and by statesmen, and what is the reason of this."[18]

Aristotle contrasts this natural means of wealth acquisition with retail trade, which is "not a natural part of the art of getting wealth."[19] Most items or things have two uses, one proper to the thing in and of itself, the other secondary to it. Or, as Marx would put it in relationship to the commodity, things have a use-value and an exchange-value.[20] Aristotle notes, for instance, that a shoe can be used as a shoe or it can be exchanged with someone who has need of a shoe for some other desirable item, such

16. Aristotle, *Politics*, 1137 (1256b30).
17. Aristotle, *Nicomachean Ethics*, 952–964 (1102b15–1109b25).
18. Aristotle, *Politics*, 1137 (1256b35).
19. Aristotle, *Politics*, 1138 (1257a18).
20. Marx, *Capital*, 1:125–77.

as food or money. In both cases, the shoe is still a shoe, but only in the former case does its use correspond with its nature, since there is nothing in the shoe that innately corresponds to exchangeability. Aristotle writes, "He who gives a shoe in exchange for money or food to him who wants one, does indeed use the shoe as a shoe, but this is not its proper or primary purpose, for a shoe is not made to be an object of barter."[21] The same can be said of most other items as well, as they function in relation to people and their needs.

Although Aristotle labels this secondary function of a thing in exchange "unnatural," this does not mean that it is useless or corrupt as such. Since, in complex forms of human organization, one's needs usually extend beyond what a household can produce, exchange is inevitable and, indeed, does not immediately obviate the cultivation of a good life. The introduction of money, however, changes matters. Although coin money is first introduced to facilitate exchange, that same introduction inevitably leads to money being sought as such, separate from the actual goods involved in any exchange process. Or, better put, the exchange process, which Aristotle labels retail trade, becomes primarily a means to generate money, above and beyond the usefulness of the things involved. Whether coinage is valuable in and of itself or simply through convention does not so much matter, here. What matters is how the separation of exchange from use corresponds to an art of producing wealth that is unnatural, in the sense that it transgresses limits related to acquisition and desire. Aristotle writes, "For natural riches and the natural art of wealth-getting are a different thing; in their true form they are part of the management of a household; whereas retail trade is the art of producing wealth, not in every way, but by exchange. And it is thought to be concerned with coin; for coin is the unit of exchange and the measure or limit of it. And there is no bound to the riches which spring for this art of wealth getting."[22] One can certainly gain money through such means, but to do so oversteps the boundaries that delimit the contours of "living well," as the excess involved correlates to an excess of desire. He goes on:

> Hence some persons are led to believe that getting wealth is the object of household management, and the whole idea of their lives is that they ought to increase their money without limit, or at any rate not to lose it. The origin of this disposition in men

---

21. Aristotle, *Politics*, 1138 (1257b10).
22. Aristotle, *Politics*, 1139 (1257b20).

is that they are intent upon living only, and not upon living well; and as their desires are unlimited, they also desire that the means of gratifying them should be without limit. Those who do aim at a good life seek the means of obtaining bodily pleasures; and, since the enjoyment of these appears to depend on property, they are absorbed in getting wealth; and so there arises the second species of wealth-getting. For, as their enjoyment is in excess, they seek an art which produces the excess of enjoyment; and, if they are not able to supply their pleasures by the art of getting wealth, they try other arts, using in turn every faculty in a manner contrary to nature.[23]

Aristotle makes it clear that this disordered approach to wealth getting has to do with disordered desire, as it arises out of a concern only with living as such, without reference to the cultivation of virtue. Because of this, the accumulation of wealth for its own sake is only one instance of excessiveness in general: those who find enjoyment in an excess of wealth will also seek excess in other areas of life. Nevertheless, Aristotle says that among the means of generating wealth beyond the delimited usefulness of things, usury is the "most unnatural." The "most hated sort" of the illicit increase in wealth is "usury, which makes a gain out of money itself, and not from the natural object of it. For money was intended to be used in exchange, but not to increase at interest. And this term interest, which means the birth of money from money, is applied to the breeding of money because the offspring resembles the parent."[24] Aristotle considers usury "unnatural" since it entails generation or "offspring" [tokos] where there should be none. He contrasts money, then, with things that are naturally fertile, such as plants, animals, and, of course, human beings. Although *tokos* naturally or ontologically inheres in the latter, coinage is only an inert, material object, which also means that it is and should be sterile.[25]

We should point out that Aristotle's concern regarding usury has to do with what he understands as the nature of money in relation to goods and the well-being of the merchant or usurer, rather than the debtor. Aristotle criticizes usury because it violates certain of his core philosophical and ethical assumptions, rather than what it does to the debtor. Part of this may have to do with the fact that, in his emphasis on retail trade,

23. Aristotle, *Politics*, 1139–40 (1257b40–1258a10).
24. Aristotle, *Politics*, 1141 (1258b5).
25. Noonan, "*Tokos* and *Atokion*," 216.

Aristotle seems to have in mind commercial transactions rather than personal loans, which, as discussed below, is also a distinction at work in biblical texts dealing with usury. Nevertheless, his castigation of usury is of a metaphysical rather than relational nature. Even if we stress the moral component to Aristotle's argument, seen in his distinction between living well and simply living, the concern is with the imagined usurer and what the practice does to them. What usury may do to the debtor is not an issue that comes up in the discussion.

This is not to say that concerns about justice in relation to debt are, in Aristotle, entirely absent. The *Politics*, as a discourse on political actualities and ideals, is concerned with justice, at least as understood variously by Aristotle. Aristotle's delineation of justice as fairness and equality necessitates proportionality, reciprocity and, when required, rectification in relationships, including in exchange. Such requirements would extend to usurious relationships as well. Nevertheless, the emphasis remains on the nature of money and individual virtue, conceived abstractly and in relation to situations that require the invocation of justice as both an ethical and legal principle. Concerning the nature of money, for instance, Aristotle grounds reciprocity in exchange in the idea of money itself, which, for him, is in substance a standardized measure that compares the incomparable in transactions. "Money, then," he writes, "acting as a measure, makes goods commensurate and equates them; for neither would there have been association if there were not exchange, nor exchange if there were not equality, nor equality if there were not commensurability."[26] One can speak, then, of justice in relation to money, but by default usury would be considered unjust, as it is not essentially related to what money is or does. Usury, as mentioned above, seeks generation where there should be none; that is, in putting money to a use for which it is not intended, usury violates the sense of justice that should govern fair and equitable transactions. Simply put, usury makes money more than it measures, which takes it outside the sphere of its proper use.

Although Aristotle insists that justice, in the sense outlined above, must ultimately be codified, buttressed by law to ground it in rational principles rather than individual interests, he also makes it clear that justice is a virtue, a deliberate and sustained "state of character." He writes, "We see that all men mean by justice that kind of state of character which makes people disposed to do what is just and makes them act justly and

---

26. Aristotle, *Nicomachean Ethics*, 1011–12 (1133b).

wish for what is just; and similarly by injustice that state which makes them act unjustly and wish for what is unjust."[27] Such a state of character should, if virtuous, correspond with its social and political counterparts, as justice is intended to "produce and preserve happiness and its components for the political society."[28] When virtue is "complete" in this manner, that is, in the correlation of individual and collective virtue, justice naturally extends outward, from the self to others, which Aristotle characterizes in terms of a relation between and among neighbors. He writes that this sense of justice is "complete because he who possesses it can exercise his virtue not only in himself but towards his neighbor also; for many men can exercise virtue in their own affairs, but not in relations to their neighbor. . . . For the same reason justice, alone of the virtues, is thought to be 'another's good,' because it is related to our neighbor; for it does what is advantageous to another, either a ruler or a copartner."[29] However, the relation among neighbors need not and cannot be one of symmetry, because what is advantageous for any individual and the happiness of society as a whole depends upon predetermined, clearly demarcated roles and standards, which take precedence over the individual as such. That is, one's role determines where and how one can and should act virtuously; virtue does not necessarily determine one's role. Hence, Aristotle writes, "Now the laws in the their enactments on all subjects aim at the common advantage either of all or of the best or of those who hold power, or something of the sort; so that in one sense we call those acts just that tend to produce and preserve happiness and its components for the political society."[30]

USURY AS SIN AND THEFT

Aristotle's concern with usury as unnatural, as contrary to the nature of money, is taken up by medieval theologians, who add a distinctive theological dimension to the discussion, above and beyond the specific biblical stipulations against the practice. I discuss these below, so there is no need to repeat them here, as they function as essential background material for medieval prohibitions on usury. Nevertheless, philosophical

---

27. Aristotle, *Nicomachean Ethics*, 1002 (1129a).
28. Aristotle, *Nicomachean Ethics*, 1003 (1129b).
29. Aristotle, *Nicomachean Ethics*, 1003–4 (1129b–1130a).
30. Aristotle, *Nicomachean Ethics*, 1003 (1129b).

or metaphysical reflections on usury assume, following Aristotle, that the practice goes against the nature of money, making it distinctly unnatural or contrary to natural law. The nature of money, as established in practice, law, and the nature of divine order itself, is for it to be infertile. Thus does St. Thomas Aquinas essentially repeat Aristotle's rationale, when in the *Summa Theologiae* he treats usury as belonging to issues regarding justice. He writes, "Now money, according to the Philosopher (Ethic. v, 5; Polit. i, 3) was invented chiefly for the purpose of exchange: and consequently the proper and principal use of money is its consumption or alienation whereby it is sunk in exchange. Hence it is by its very nature unlawful to take payment for the use of money lent, which payment is known as usury: and just as a man is bound to restore other ill-gotten goods, so is he bound to restore the money which he has taken in usury."[31]

St. Thomas, however, adds depth to Aristotle's argument concerning the nature of money, extending the metaphysical argument against it beyond the notion of generation.[32] St. Thomas argues that, as regards the use of things, "there are certain things the use of which consists in their consumption."[33] This is the case with goods such as wine or wheat which, as drink and food respectively, are consumed in their use. That is, the thing and its use coincide, meaning that, practically speaking, they are one and the same. St. Thomas writes, "Wherefore in such like things the use of the thing must not be reckoned apart from the thing itself, and whoever is granted the use of the thing, is granted the thing itself and for this reason, to lend things of this kin is to transfer the ownership."[34] Charging a fee in addition to use, then, obviates the transfer of ownership involved. As St. Thomas argues, doing so is an attempt to sell "the same thing twice" or "sell what does not exist."[35] Such violations of use are, St. Thomas suggests, to be understood in terms of injustice. He writes that the person who attempts to exploit the relationship between consumption and use "would evidently commit a sin of injustice. On like manner he commits an injustice who lends wine or wheat, and asks for double payment, viz. one, the return of the thing in equal measure, the other, the

---

31. Aquinas, *Summa Theologiae*, II-II, q.78, a.1.

32. See Noonan, "*Tokos* and *Atokion*," 216–18, on which I have relied to reconstruct the argument that follows.

33. Aquinas, *Summa Theologiae*, II-II, q.78, a.1.

34. Aquinas, *Summa Theologiae*, II-II, q.78, a.1.

35. Aquinas, *Summa Theologiae*, II-II, q.78, a.1.

price of the use, which is called usury."³⁶ The same logic applies to money as an object of use. If the purpose of money is primarily to facilitate exchange, then money is used up in the exchange itself. To charge interest on the exchange, then, goes against both exchange and the purpose of money. He writes that money "was invented chiefly for the purpose of exchange: and consequently the proper and principal use of money is its consumption or alienation whereby it is sunk in exchange. Hence it is by its very nature unlawful to take payment for the use of money lent, which payment is known as usury: and just as a man is bound to restore other ill-gotten goods, so is he bound to restore the money which he has taken in usury."³⁷

The usurer, however, does not merely exploit money in such instances but also the borrower. St. Thomas recognizes that the usurious relationship is not entirely voluntary. That is, usury is taken on by a borrower because of a lack of other options; in other words, a borrower only borrows at interest *if* that is the only option available. Indeed, within St. Thomas's framework, one only borrows in the first place out of necessity, from the position of a disadvantageous situation that is not of the borrower's making. Hence, the borrower is, in a sense, compelled into the loan, meaning that they lack freedom in a fuller sense. The usurer attempts to exploit this situation further via the charging of interest. St. Thomas writes, "He who gives usury does not give it voluntarily simply, but under a certain necessity, in so far as he needs to borrow money which the owner is unwilling to lend without usury."³⁸ To argue that usury is not illicit because the borrower freely agreed to it is to argue on the basis of a simplified understanding of choice, which functions ideologically in support of the position and activity of the usurer. According to St. Thomas, an act is only voluntary to the extent that its impetus is internal, that is, from one's own intrinsic inclination.³⁹ However, this is precisely what is lacking in many situations in which one seeks to borrow: in such situations, one does not borrow unless one is compelled by external circumstances to do so. It is in this sense that usury, for St. Thomas, depends on the involuntary, not the voluntary, and is, thus, exploitative.

That usury is the problem, and not indebtedness as such, is clear from St. Thomas's argument that, although lending at interest is sinful,

---

36. Aquinas, *Summa Theologiae*, II-II, q.78, a.1.
37. Aquinas, *Summa Theologiae*, II-II, q.78, a.1.
38. Aquinas, *Summa Theologiae*, II-II, q.78, a.1.
39. Aquinas, *Summa Theologiae*, II-IU, q.6, a.1.

borrowing is not, so long as it is done so with a good end in view. He bases his argument on the assumption that using another's sin for a good purpose does not necessarily immediately entail agreement with or acquiescence to another's sin. He writes:

> It is by no means lawful to induce a man to sin, yet it is lawful to make use of another's sin for a good end, since even God uses all sin for some good, since He draws some good from every evil as stated in the Enchiridion. . . . Accordingly we must also answer to the question in point that it is by no means lawful to induce a man to lend under a condition of usury: yet it is lawful to borrow for usury from a man who is ready to do so and is a usurer by profession; provided the borrower have a good end in view, such as the relief of his own or another's need.[40]

The responsibility for the sin lies with the usurer, not with the borrower or debtor, a point that is reiterated differently in his discussion of the obligation to repay a debt. According to St. Thomas, one is only bound to repayment of the original debt and not the accrual of interest or excess, since the latter is, for St. Thomas, separate from the loan itself. A loan is consumed in its use, and one is only responsible for that use. Any attempt to add anything in addition via interest is to make a claim on something that is not used.

Moreover, even if one does commit to pay in excess of the loan itself, as a way to compensate the lender, the obligation to repay is not worked into the loan itself but, rather, comes from "a debt of friendship, and the nature of this debt depends more on the feeling with which the favor was conferred than on the greatness of the favor itself. This debt does not carry with it a civil obligation, involving a kind of necessity that would exclude the spontaneous nature of such a repayment."[41] The "debt of friendship," however, should spread in both directions since, in such cases, one lends out of friendship as a favor, rather than with the expectation of remuneration.

As stated above, then, usury is sin and the usurer a sinner since the act itself is a species of injustice. As Jacques Le Goff demonstrates, however, medieval prohibitions on usury also viewed the type of sin involved in more specific terms, as a type of theft. Theft, in this instance, involves the attempt to sell a thing twice or what one does not have, as

---

40. Aquinas, *Summa Theologiae*, II-II, q.78, a.4.
41. Aquinas, *Summa Theologiae*, II-II, q.78, a.2.

mentioned in the discussion above. But, more seriously, the usurer is considered a thief of time, which belongs not to him but to God. Thomas of Chobham, for instance, writes that the "usurer sells nothing to the borrower that belongs to him. He sells only time, which belongs to God. He cannot, therefore, make a profit from selling someone else's property."[42] More specifically, what the usurer sells is the gap between lending and repayment, meaning that usury is a claim on the future, one which does not, properly speaking, belong to the usurer. Le Goff quotes a manuscript from the thirteenth century, which combines the critique of usury as false generation, as discussed above, and its equation with theft:

> Usurers sin against nature by wanting to make money give birth to money, as a horse gives birth to a horse, or a mule to a mule. Usurers are in addition thieves, for they sell time that does not belong to them, and selling someone else's property, despite its owner, is theft. In addition, since they sell nothing other than the expectation of money, that is to say, time, they sell days and nights. But the day is the time of clarity, and the night is the time for repose. Consequently they sell light and repose. It is, therefore, not just for them to receive eternal light and eternal rest.[43]

The notion that usury violates nature, that it seeks generation where generation should not take place, brings us back full circle to Aristotle's critique. In addition, however, the usurer trades in expectations, using time itself to generate value. Time does not belong to the usurer, though, and their theft of time is especially egregious in the monetization of night, which should be dead time, a time for rest and repose.[44] Since he sells time, both day, the "time of clarity," and night, the "time for repose," the usurer is cut off from "eternal light and eternal rest."

USURY AS AN ETHICAL PROBLEM

The line that runs from Aristotle through medieval Christianity discussed above prohibits usury for metaphysical reasons, in the sense that usurious practices ascribe to money qualities and uses that are unnatural. Money, in this view, is a neutral object created for the purpose of facilitating

---

42. As quoted by Le Goff, *Your Money or Your Life*, 39.

43. Le Goff, *Your Money or Your Life*, 40–41.

44. For a contemporary discussion of how capitalism seeks to colonize and monetize time, see Crary, *24/7*.

exchange among relatively free actors or entities for needed or desirable things. Profit from exchange is certainly allowed for, but the profit must relate to the surplus contained in the things themselves. Usury shifts the locus of profit-making, ascribing it not to tangible, produced objects but, rather, to money itself. Usury, then, is self-generating money, which violates its nature or substance.

However, although usury abstracts the generation of wealth from the materiality of exchange, it does so not only through self-generation itself but, also, by shifting the focus of the latter. Interest certainly generates wealth, but that generation is not simply related to an abstraction, such as time, but to individuals subject to interest. Usury, that is, relies on the bodies of the indebted, which means that usury extracts life or, more specifically, the time of life, to generate value.[45] Marx imagines this notion in vivid terms, as he refers to usury as a parasitic practice. He writes, "Usury centralizes money wealth where the means of production are dispersed. It does not alter the mode of production but attaches itself firmly to it like a parasite and makes it wretched. It sucks out its blood, enervates it and compels reproduction to proceed under ever more pitiable conditions."[46]

The biblical prohibitions against usury, to which we now turn, are more in line with this way of thinking about usury. That is, for the biblical authors, usury is not considered so much a metaphysical problem as it is a moral and theological problem, in that it relates to the stipulations found in the law, in God's covenant with Israel. This is not to say that metaphysical concerns are entirely absent in one or ethical concerns in the other. It is, rather, a question of priority or emphasis, and the biblical texts fall squarely within a more pragmatic horizon when it comes to the practice of usury.

I discuss debt cancellation or forgiveness in the next section, but prohibitions against usury are preventative in measure, designed to cut off the problem of indebtedness in advance. To understand the need for such legislation on both fronts, it is helpful to briefly discuss the reasons why people fall into debt, via a subtle distinction between credit and debt. As Roland Boer points out, although the two may overlap, credit primarily relies on the presence of "trust," that is, "a complex pattern of

---

45. Usury could in this sense be understood in terms of what Giorgio Agamben terms "bare life." See Agamben, *Homo Sacer*.

46. Marx, *Capital*, vol. 3, ch. 36. Marx's claim dovetails well with Michel Serres's discussion of parasitism. See Serres, *Parasite*, 3–47.

reciprocal relationships within a known community."⁴⁷ So understood, credit is more a structural, organizing principle rather than a moral one, as the word "trust" may imply: as Boer puts it, trust "ensures the mutual allocation and reallocation of all goods within the community."⁴⁸

In contrast, debt is not allocative, as is credit, but primarily extractive, in the sense that the lender seeks to take money, goods, or labor from the debtor, with the purpose of increasing the lender's wealth. Boer points out that debt is extractive in at least three dominant ways. First is via labor, through practices such as "debt slavery" or "indentured labor." In ancient Southwest Asia, for instance, peasants lacking the resources to pay off loans could do so by means of their labor. As Boer points out, a "landlord or the state seeks to ensure that land under its control is worked, and to ensure that those with skills and muscle power to do so are bound by means of debt."⁴⁹ In using labor as a form of debt, the landowner really kills two birds with one stone: it allows the landowner to profit from the debtor himself and the land, which requires said labor to generate value through it. Second, and as should be obvious from the first point, the entire goal of such debt arrangements is to channel wealth upwards to the creditor, whether it be the state, the temple, or the landowner. Boer suggests in a Marxist vein that labor in the sense described above is the original form of such wealth generation, which also means that landowners have little incentive to see debt promptly paid. Interest also functions in this manner, although Boer takes it as a secondary development. Third, and finally, debt ensures economic hierarchy or class divisions in society. Debt, in this sense, is a feature of "class difference and also class conflict."⁵⁰

Returning to usury, the practice is mentioned in various places in the Hebrew Bible, though not frequently. The prohibitions on usury in the Hebrew Bible mostly come from legal materials, though usury is mentioned elsewhere, as in Prov 22, discussed above. Nevertheless, when considering the practice there are really three main passages in the legal materials that are relevant and influential, both in and of themselves and for later authors. Usury is roundly prohibited in these passages, at least for and among certain peoples, namely the Israelites.

47. Boer, *Sacred Economy*, 157.
48. Boer, *Sacred Economy*, 157.
49. Boer, *Sacred Economy*, 159.
50. Boer, *Sacred Economy*, 162.

Given the fact that these prohibitions can be found in different editorial strata, it seems that the prohibition itself was a consistent feature of Israelite society, even if it may have been unevenly applied or followed. There are three relevant legal passages: Exod 22:25–26, Lev 25:35–36, and Deut 23:20–21. Exodus 22:25–26 prohibits treating the poor as a creditor would, that is, to generate financial gain:

> If you lend money to my people, to the poor among you, you shall not deal with them as a creditor; you shall not exact interest from them. If you take your neighbor's cloak in pawn, you shall restore it before the sun goes down; for it may be your neighbor's only clothing to use as cover; in what else shall that person sleep? And if your neighbor cries out to me, I will listen, for I am compassionate.

The fact that the passage mentions the practices of creditors implies that some sort of interest-bearing transactions were not generally prohibited. Under this category would fall commercial lending among relative equals, for instance.[51] The passage prohibits, rather, treating the poor as one would a commercial partner, as a resource for the generation of value. Whereas one may assume a relationship among relative equals in the commercial sphere, lending at interest to the poor takes advantage of their financial straits, which the commandment treats as a violation of that person's dignity vis-a-vis God's covenant. Indeed, God's covenant with Israel requires treating the poor with compassion (Exod 22:25), which is a dominant theme of the biblical texts as a whole, even if it is not without its ambiguities.[52] Attempting to profit from another's poverty or misery via interest is, in this sense, a form of abuse, both against the person involved and God's commandments.[53] Such is the sense behind the injunction to return in the evening a cloak given as collateral. The prohibition against exacting interest from impoverished individuals does not mean a lender could not secure a loan. The extent of such security, however, runs up against the basic needs of the debtor. The former cannot take precedence over the latter, which is the principle expressed in the induction to "restore" a debtor's "cloak before the sun goes down."

Leviticus 25:35–36, the second passage, expresses a similar sentiment: "If any of your kin fall into difficulty and become dependent on

---

51. Hudson, . . . *And Forgive Them Their Debts*, 195.
52. Gutiérrez, *Theology of Liberation*, 162–73.
53. See Geisst, *Beggar Thy Neighbor*, 13–57.

you, you shall support them; they shall live with you as though resident aliens. Do not take interest in advance or otherwise make a profit from them, but fear your God; let them live with you." Leviticus prohibits the exploitation via usury of those who fall into difficulties that would require entering a usurious relationship. The passage goes a step further, however, and commands that those who fall into difficulty should be supported by the better off and treated as they would the resident alien. As Lev 19:33–34 underlines, resident aliens are not to be oppressed but treated as citizens, meaning that the Israelites should "love the alien as yourself, for you were aliens in the land of Egypt: I am the Lord your God."

The third legal passage devoted to usury is Deut 23:20–21: "You shall not charge interest on loans to another Israelite, interest on money, interest on provisions, interest on anything that is lent. On loans to a foreigner you may charge interest, but on loans to another Israelite you may not charge interest, so that the Lord your God may bless you in all your undertakings in the land that you are about to enter and possess." Deuteronomy 23 prohibits all forms of usury, no matter what it is ("money," "provisions," "anything that is lent"), but this only applies on loans from one Israelite to another. The same may be assumed in the other passages, even if it is not explicitly mentioned. As Hudson points out regarding Exod 22:25–26, for instance, commercial lending often would have involved foreign merchants.[54] Any strictures on usury, then, were internal matters, applicable only to and among Israelites. That usury laws would apply only among Israelites is not surprising. Although nothing prevents us from developing more general precepts from the ideas contained therein, Israel was obviously a people among others, meaning that their laws applied to them and them only. As it is today, usury was a common economic instrument among its neighbors, and economic and political viability would have been contingent on its use, at least in part. For better or worse, restrictions on usury and how one treats debtors more broadly, then, were not universal mandates but, rather, covenantal, specific to Israel and thus limited in scope.

Nevertheless, taking these prohibitions together, they primarily have in mind the welfare of the debtor first. Hence, in prohibiting usury, the legal materials discussed above assume it as a common means of exploitation, one that is profitable for the creditor to the debtor's detriment.

---

54. Hudson, . . . *And Forgive Them Their Debts*, 195.

Indeed, the extraction of interest exacerbates poverty under the guise of remedying it. Rather than helping those in need, interest is a mechanism that, as M. Douglas Meeks points out, "leads to poverty and to various forms of slavery."[55] As José Porfirio Miranda emphasizes, the laws against usury are "based on the misery of the exploited man himself," meaning that the prohibitions are intended mainly for the benefit of the dispossessed.[56]

Usury is, thus, an abusive practice, one that latches onto and exploits the poverty of another, for the generation of profit. Miranda argues that the prohibition against usury should be read in light of certain texts that express a suspicion of profit more generally. We can see such suspicion regarding commerce as well. The problem with commerce lies in the surplus value created via exchange, in the excess of the selling price over the purchase price. For Miranda, the problem with this means of acquiring wealth is that it is one of the main sources of what he calls "differentiating wealth," that is, the asymmetrical accumulation of wealth. As Miranda points out, the biblical texts do not, on the whole, prohibit wealth as such.[57] As I have argued elsewhere, the biblical texts do not generally recommend asceticism as the baseline for how individuals and collectives should relate to material possessions, even if certain theological traditions have held voluntary deprivation or poverty in high esteem.[58] Deuteronomy 28:1–14, for instance, equates faithfulness, understood as keeping God's commandments, with abundance, so much so that Israel will have a surplus that it can extend to other peoples as well. Miranda points out that what is at issue are disparities when it comes to wealth, which he, along with the texts in question, simplify by invoking the difference between poor and rich. The very fact that the poor exist while others remain rich is the problem. Differentiating wealth is thus relative wealth, a wealth that accrues to some and not others. Miranda takes the argument a step further, noting that such wealth is illegitimate because there is no legitimate means of acquiring it, since differentiating wealth is created at another's expense. It is always, for Miranda, immoral if not necessarily illegal: "only by illicit means is it possible to reach a higher economic level than that of the majority of the population."[59]

55. Meeks, *God the Economist*, 85.
56. Miranda, *Communism in the Bible*, 149.
57. Miranda, *Communism and the Bible*, 21–56.
58. Phelps, *Jesus and the Politics of Mammon*, 135–68.
59. Miranda, *Communism in the Bible*, 25.

Profit via commerce is one such illicit activity since it is one source of differentiating wealth. Miranda rejects the notion of a "just price" via "market value," as this will always be imposed on the subordinate party in an exchange relationship, whether at the level of labor or consumption. He writes, "The market value must always be the one that allows merchants and managers to take a profit . . . But the differentiating social position of the rich can exist only to the extent that they take a profit. In other words, when we suppose that there is a just price we are committing the fallacy of begging the question—by presupposing that there is a legitimate manner of acquiring differentiating wealth."[60] Commerce exploits this situation, using it as a means to acquire wealth as profit and exacerbate the gap between rich and poor. Indeed, it is in this gap that sin resides, as Miranda quotes Ecclesiasticus as suggesting: "Many have committed sin for gain, and those who seek to get rich will avert their eyes. As a stake is driven firmly into a fissure between stones, so sin is wedged in between selling and buying" (27:1–2).

However, it is important to emphasize that, despite the condemnations of profit, and usury in particular, as abusive, oppressive practices, Israel can portray itself as a creditor to other nations. I mentioned above that Deut 28:1–14 equates faithfulness with abundance, an abundance that, moreover, is well in surplus over Israel's needs. The idea that Israel's abundance extends to others as well is, of course, well expressed in the Abrahamic covenant, as expressed in Genesis 12. There, God says to Abram, "Go from your country and your kindred and your father's house to the land that I will show you. I will make of you a great nation, and I will bless you, and make your name great, so that you will be a blessing. I will bless those who bless you, and the one who curses you I will curse; and in you all the families of the earth shall be blessed" (12:1–3). In Deuteronomy 28, however, such "blessing" to others is expressed in terms of a creditor-debtor relationship. Israel is told, for instance, "The Lord will open for you his rich storehouse, the heavens, to give the rain of your land in its season and to bless all your undertakings. You will lend to many nations, but you will not borrow" (28:12). God commands that Israel's abundance or surplus, expressed here as a "rich storehouse," should be extended to others as well, but in the form of debt. The idea is perfectly consistent with the prohibitions against usury, discussed above, as these apply to Israel in and of itself and not in its relationship to other nations.

---

60. Miranda, *Communism in the Bible*, 27.

Moreover, it is clear from the passage that such lending is not altruistic but, rather, leveraged in Israel's relationship with others. Specifically, it is a means of subordinating other nations to Israel and, thus, a mechanism of differentiation, which is implied in the opposite command not to borrow. Israel should be a lender not a borrower, a creditor and not a debtor, since the latter entails subservience. That the idea of lending is not simply a manner of speaking to emphasize abundance but, rather, an expression of a desire for differentiation is clear in vv. 13–14: "The Lord will make you the head, and not the tail; you shall be only at the top, and not at the bottom—if you obey the commandments of the Lord your God, which I am commanding you today, by diligently observing them, and if you do not turn aside from any of the words that I am commanding you today, either to the right or to the left, following other gods to serve them."

DEBT CANCELLATION AND THE JUBILEE

The legal and philosophical prohibitions discussed in the previous sections put limitations on usury for numerous reasons. Aristotle had argued against usury along metaphysical lines. Money is, for Aristotle, primarily for the facilitation of exchange, which defines the proper sphere of its use. Usury, however, puts money to a use that is unnatural, in that it seeks to generate value from money itself. Medieval theologians, such as St. Thomas Aquinas, largely take up this position, emphasizing in addition the ways in which usury steals time by exploiting the gap between lending and repayment.

Whatever the philosophical objections to the practice may be, a concern with justice is present as well, as it is for the legal materials found in the biblical texts examined in the last section. Proscriptions on usury assume that it is an exploitative practice, in that it seeks to profit off another's misfortune. Although, in a credit-based economy such as ours, usury does not immediately coincide with the economic needs that arise out of sheer desperation, it still assumes a fundamental lack. Usury, in this sense, can still be considered exploitative, in that it makes a claim on the future based on economic lack in the present, whether this lack be for basic, consumer goods or so-called big-ticket items, such as cars, housing and real estate, or even education.

The assumption behind these prohibitions on usury assume that debt is a moral problem, but not primarily on the side of the debtor: it is the creditor who bears ethical responsibility in lending. The proscriptions against usury, whether they take abstract, metaphysical form, or more down-to-earth, moral commands, assume that charging interest is a practice ripe for abuse. Part of the fear is over the way in which usury all too easily leads to exploitation of the borrower and their needs. Prohibitions on usury, then, if not always practical from an economic perspective, at least have in view a broader conception of social justice, one that in theory has an eye toward the less fortunate or, more strongly said, oppressed.

Otherwise put, prohibitions on usury assume that indebtedness is primarily the result of the combination of circumstance and exploitation. One does not become indebted unless one is externally compelled to do so, because circumstances, whatever they may be, demand it. Becoming indebted, then, is not a voluntary act, if we take St. Thomas's definition of the latter seriously, since it lacks intrinsic inclination. That is, one would not take on debt unless one had to, meaning that indebtedness occurs out of necessity. Indebtedness, then, is a forced state or relationship. One could, of course, always refuse the choice of indebtedness, but that would be to resign oneself to one's situation, to acquiesce to one's lack, one's poverty. Refusing indebtedness, in this sense, is to refuse life, meaning that it is to choose death.

The problem, then, has the structure of the Lacanian forced choice, which is really no choice at all. When discussing the being of the subject as alienated or divided in Seminar XI, Lacan uses the example of muggers, who confront their victims with the demand, "Your money or your life!" As Lacan points out, one is condemned no matter which option one chooses, which is why he also refers to this "forced choice" as the "lethal factor" at work in "the play of signifiers." He states, "If I choose money, I lose both. If I choose life, I have life without money, namely, a life deprived of something." It is the same with the option "freedom or death": "Well! You've got the freedom to die. Curiously enough, in the conditions in which someone says to you, *freedom or death!*, the only proof of freedom that you can have in the conditions laid out before you is precisely to choose death, for there, you show that you have freedom of choice."[61] Using the language of St. Thomas, in such situations we are constrained to involuntary acts, acts that lack intrinsic inclination.

---

61. Lacan, *Four Fundamental Concepts of Psychoanalysis*, 212–13.

Usury exploits this situation, as it is an economic practice wielded by the usurer to profit from the other's misfortune. Usury commodifies lack, since it is designed to generate wealth for the usurer from the poverty of the other or, more generally, from the other's lack. Medieval theologians considered usury a theft of time, but underneath such abstractions lie real, flesh and blood individuals. Usury requires the exploitation of individuals to generate wealth, which is also why prohibitions and condemnations of usury focus on the usurer or creditor rather than the debtor. The economic relationship is also a moral relationship, meaning that responsibility, and thus guilt, lies primarily with the usurer or creditor, not the debtor. Indebtedness, understood in relation to biblical and theological injunctions against usury, is a form of exploitation.

Prohibitions on usury may curtail some of its deleterious effects; in this sense, they are an attempt to ward off exploitation in advance. Ameliorating exploitation, however, is also worked into traditions such as the Sabbath year and the Jubilee year, which function to remedy the negative effects of debt after the fact via various debt cancellation mechanisms. Debt cancellation, as outlined in the biblical texts, is not novel in and of itself, nor does it necessarily coincide with a more just sociopolitical vision. Michael Hudson has discussed at length debt cancellation practices in Bronze Age societies, going back to the eighteenth century BCE. Debt cancellation was a well-known, often ritualized practice in such societies, even if it was not necessarily standard. Hudson emphasizes that we should take seriously the context for such practices. Absent faith in a self-regulating market, which is one of the putative bedrocks of modern capitalism, Bronze Age societies often had to make targeted economic interventions to restore equilibrium. We, of course, do the same thing today, even if free-market partisans are loathe to recognize the indispensability of the policies and direct interventions that steer the economy in certain directions and, in times of crises, keep it afloat. Significant contemporary economic interventions, however, are often directed to financial, corporate, or government institutions, on the assumption that stabilizing the economy at this level will "trickle down" to lower strata. What this means is that any sort of substantial, widespread debt cancellation at the individual level is usually completely off the table, as it is considered not only ineffective in the long run but also morally hazardous. That is, cancelling debt would ruin the trust that credit putatively requires.

As Hudson points out, however, such assumptions remain foreign to Bronze Age societies, which often had to make periodic adjustments to restore equilibrium and maintain social cohesion. These adjustments often targeted debtors directly, releasing them from debt obligations to private creditors. It is important to emphasize that this was not necessarily done out of any sort of altruistic concern for the indebted or a desire to establish a more just society. Debt cancellation was more pragmatic. The time and resources spent servicing debts to private creditors took away from public responsibilities, meaning that too much indebtedness went against what was considered the common good. As Hudson puts it, "Rulers saw that if cultivators had to work off their debts to private creditors, they would not be available to perform their public corvee work duties, not to mention fight in the army."[62] Moreover, the benefits of cancellation for the indebted also served to coax loyalty under the guise of freedom. Hudson writes, "By liberating distressed individuals who had fallen into debt bondage, and returning to cultivators the lands they had forfeited for debt or sold under economic duress, these royal acts maintained a free peasantry willing to fight for its land and work on public building projects and canals. . . . By clearing away the buildup of personal debts, rulers saved society from the social chaos that would have resulted from personal insolvency, debt bondage, and military defection."[63] Indeed, transitions from one ruler to the next often involved some form of debt cancellation, as a means for the new ruler to gain popular support.

Debt cancellation, in this sense, was a means of managing scarce resources first, rather than a moral obligation, and inculcating favorable sentiments among the masses toward the ruling classes. We can assume this general background to the Sabbath year and Jubilee traditions, as outlined in the relevant biblical texts. What makes Israelite debt cancellation unique, however, is that it is worked into the law, as a regularized part of covenantal obligations. That is, debt cancellation is not left up to the whims of individual rulers or even contingent social needs. It is, rather, part of the law itself, which signifies its importance as a practice. Saying as much does not mean that it was necessarily followed to the letter, as I discuss below. Nevertheless, absent complete social leveling, it presents debt cancellation as an ideal, essential to any pursuit of justice.

As far as institutions go, the Jubilee is certainly among the more potentially revolutionary that we find in the Hebrew Bible, at least economically speaking. The Jubilee's insistence on the regular return of property

---

62. Hudson, . . . *And Forgive Them Their Debts*, 3.
63. Hudson, . . . *And Forgive Them Their Debts*, 3.

and, more generally, manumission of debts, certainly fits with an overriding concern for justice that runs through certain, at times dominant, strands of the biblical materials. It works such debt cancellation into the law, so that it becomes regular and automatic, at least in theory. Such a concern is not always internally consistent with other thematic and theological tropes that can and often do reinforce dominance and exploitation, as Ernst Bloch has reminded us.[64] We do not need to reduce the biblical materials to a theological desire for consistency, however, to appreciate the significance of the Jubilee, interpreting and interrogating it as an idea relevant for contemporary use.

One of the problems when discussing debt cancellation practices, such as the sabbatical and Jubilee years, is the extent to which they were ever put into practice. The same could, no doubt, be said about other practices as well. The biblical materials that outline legal and ritual requirements and social responsibilities present us with an ideal, rather than a description of reality, of what occurred on the ground, so to speak. The gap between idea and reality is not merely speculative or philosophical but, rather, indicated in the texts themselves. Not only do legal and ritual stipulations assume their violation, in that they arise out of specific circumstances that require them in the first place. Much of the narrative that makes up the so-called Deuteronomic History also exhibits this gap, as the narrator portrays Israel and Judah as consistently failing to live up to the standards God sets for them in the law. The theological presupposition behind this narrative is that such failure ultimately explains the fall of both Israel and Judah.

Nevertheless, scholarly opinions on the question as to what extent debt cancellation practices were ever followed not surprisingly run the gamut from skepticism to belief. How one evaluates the Jubilee, in this respect, often depends on when one dates the legislation, with a later dating usually corresponding to more skepticism. My purpose, here, is not to take sides on this largely historical debate, which would involve getting into complex issues regarding dating. It seems likely that the truth is somewhere in the middle. The fact that certain loopholes, such as the well-known *prozbul*, were established with respect to the Sabbath year, if not the Jubilee itself, would seem to imply that types of debt remission were put into practice. That is, one only tries to find ways to evade the law

---

64. Bloch, *Atheism in Christianity*, 1–15.

if that aspect of the law functions; loopholes are reactive, established out of need, in other words.

As Philip Birnbaum notes, in the first century BCE Rabbi Hillel had, it seems, observed that the prospect of debt cancellation had squeezed access to credit. Without the ability to charge interest, lenders had no incentive to lend if a Sabbath year was on the horizon. Hillel created a mechanism as a remedy. Arguing that the stipulations in the Sabbath year only applied to private individuals or lenders, he created a mechanism, called the *prozbul*, which allowed lenders to transfer their loans to the court. Since the sabbatical year did not affect the court and its holdings, transferred loans, on which the lenders could collect at any time, remained outside the purview of the mandate. As Birnbaum notes, the *prozbul* technically left the "biblical law unchanged by means of a legal fiction, according to which the court, instead of the individual lender, reclaimed the law."[65] By minimizing risk to the lender, the *prozbul* may indeed function to unfreeze credit, but it does so by shifting the subject of the law. Technically speaking, the sabbatical year legislation remains in place, although its intent is largely emptied of significance. Economically speaking, it is perfectly rational that a lender not accept such risk. But if this is the main concern, then it shows that access to credit, resources, and goods is already determined in advance by wealth differentials that favor some over others.

Nevertheless, we can appreciate the idea behind debt cancellation practices separately from the question of to what extent they were applied. Leviticus 25 provides the most extended discussion of debt-cancellation practices in the Hebrew Bible, although they appear in various other texts, if not with any frequency. Ezekiel 46:17, for instance, refers to a "year of liberty," which appears to be the sabbatical year; Jeremiah likewise refers to the freeing of enslaved persons on the seventh year (Jer 34:8–22). Nevertheless, Leviticus 25 begins by outlining stipulations related to the sabbatical year which, as the name implies and mirroring its weekly counterpart, is to occur every seventh year. The law commands that, on analogy with the rest that one observes on the seventh day of each week, every seventh year is to be a Sabbath year. Specifically, the sabbatical year entails the following:

> Six years you shall sow your field, and six years you shall prune your vineyard, and gather in their yield; but in the seventh year

---

65. Birnbaum, "Prozbul," 528.

> there shall be a sabbath of complete rest for the land, a sabbath for the Lord: you shall not sow your field or prune your vineyard. You shall not reap the aftergrowth of your harvest or gather the grapes of your unpruned vine: it shall be a year of complete rest for the land. You may eat what the land yields during its sabbath—you, your male and female slaves, your hired and your bound laborers who live with you; for your livestock also, and for the wild animals in your land all its yield shall be for food. (Lev 25:3–7)

Rest for the land involves ceasing the normal practices that allow for domestic agricultural production, including planting new crops, pruning existing growth, and harvesting or gathering any aftergrowth. The law does, however, permit the consumption of what the land produces on its own during the Sabbath year, meaning that what the text has in mind is the cessation of commercial, agricultural production, whether for the purpose of storage or sale on the market.[66]

The Sabbath year also included stipulations regarding the remission of debts, at least those held by members of the community; the law explicitly does not apply to "foreigners," the logic of which we discussed regarding usury in previous sections. Deuteronomy 15 states:

> Every seventh year you shall grant a remission of debts. And this is the manner of the remission: every creditor shall remit the claim that is held against a neighbor, not exacting it of a neighbor who is a member of the community, because the Lord's remission has been proclaimed. Of a foreigner you may exact it, but you must remit your claim on whatever any member of your community owes you. (15:1–3)

Coinciding with a remission of debts is an increase in generosity, as the law commands a more concerted effort to provide for those in need. Such a command makes sense generally, but also specifically in light of the remission of debts. The released indebted would also be among those most in need, both prior to their bondage and after.

> There will, however, be no one in need among you, because the Lord is sure to bless you in the land that the Lord your God is giving you as a possession to occupy, if only you will obey the Lord your God by diligently observing this entire commandment that I command you today. . . . If there is among you anyone in need, a member of your community in any of your

---

66. Lazonby, "Apply the Jubilee."

> towns within the land that the Lord your God is giving you, do not be hard-hearted or tight-fisted toward your needy neighbor. You should rather open your hand, willingly lending enough to meet the need, whatever it may be. Be careful that you do not entertain a mean thought, thinking, "The seventh year, the year of remission, is near," and therefore view your needy neighbor with hostility and give nothing; your neighbor might cry to the Lord against you, and you would incur guilt. Give liberally and be ungrudging when you do so, for on this account the Lord your God will bless you in all your work and in all that you undertake. Since there will never cease to be some in need on the earth, I therefore command you, "Open your hand to the poor and needy neighbor in your land." (Deut 15:7–11)

The passage commands to give liberally to those in need, but it also anticipates its own objections, commanding care for the poor through and despite such objections. That is, in commanding to give without hesitation even in proximity to the sabbatical year, the law anticipates attitudes that something like the *prozbul* codifies. Although the *prozbul*, then, appears as a technical workaround to the law, it clearly violates its intent and spirit, so to speak.

The sabbatical year also commands the manumission of slaves and bondspersons, who are to be released and granted their freedom.

> If a member of your community, whether a Hebrew man or a Hebrew woman, is sold to you and works for you six years, in the seventh year you shall set that person free. And when you send a male slave out from you a free person, you shall not send him out empty-handed. Provide liberally out of your flock, your threshing floor, and your wine press, thus giving to him some of the bounty with which the Lord your God has blessed you. Remember that you were a slave in the land of Egypt, and the Lord your God redeemed you; for this reason I lay this command upon you today. (Deut 15:12–15).

Such persons should be treated with the same generosity previously mentioned. "Do not consider it a hardship when you send them out from you free persons, because for six years they have given you services worth the wages of hired laborers; and the Lord your God will bless you in all that you do" (Deut 15:18).

Leviticus 25 also provides stipulations for the Jubilee year. Regardless of to what extent it was practiced or not, Lev 25 requires, among other things, a wholesale manumission of debt in every fiftieth year on

Yom Kippur or the Day of Atonement. "And you shall hallow the fiftieth year and you shall proclaim liberty throughout the land to all its inhabitants. It shall be a jubilee for you: you shall return, every one of you, to your property and every one of you to your family" (Lev 25:10).

Thus, the Jubilee year calls for a reset of social relationships, in the sense that it stipulates the redistribution of collective wealth and seeks to address the conditions that make the latter necessary, at least during the year itself. On the one hand, the Jubilee year redresses any disparities that have arisen in relation to property ownership and focuses on the dispossessed: "In this year of jubilee you shall return, every one of you, to your property" (Lev 25:13). Such an emphasis on property, it seems, is not only fully cognizant of the way in which ownership in ancient Israel and the broader world more generally is one of the main preconditions of wealth, differentiating wealth, and debt bondage. It also establishes God as the real owner of the land: "The land shall not be sold in perpetuity, for the land is mine; with me you are but aliens and tenants. Throughout the land that you hold, you shall provide for the redemption of the land" (Lev 25:23–24). Because they are only aliens and tenants, theologically speaking the Israelites remain in a position of servitude toward God. God's claim over the land establishes God's prerogative toward it, which is expressed in God's ability to leverage an excess or surplus of production in fallow years, such as the Sabbath year: "The land will yield its fruit, and you will eat your fill and live on it securely. Should you ask, 'What shall we eat in the seventh year, if we may not sow or gather in our crop?' I will order my blessing for you in the sixth year, so that it will yield a crop for three years. When you sow in the eighth year, you will be eating from the old crop; until the ninth year, when its produce comes in, you shall eat the old" (Lev 25:20–22). God's prerogative toward the land, however, also undercuts any human claims concerning ultimate ownership and, thus, seeks to dissolve the disparate social conditions that simultaneously make possible and emerge from the concentration of wealth in land ownership.

The proclamation of the Jubilee year, however, does not merely focus on human debt but also the relationship between human beings and non-human beings, specifically the land. "That fiftieth year shall be a jubilee for you: you shall not sow, or reap the aftergrowth, or harvest the unpruned vines. For it is a jubilee; it shall be holy to you: you shall eat only what the field itself produces" (Lev 25:11). The Jubilee year thus provides relief for both the land and human beings, which also means that their respective well-being is intertwined with the other. The Jubilee year, in this sense, participates in the logic that governs the observance of the Sabbath, though on a broader scale.

CONCLUSION

The philosophical and legal traditions discussed above serve as theological backdrop for discussions of usury, which was largely proscribed up through the medieval period, even if it occurred in practice. The point of the above discussion, however, is not usury per se but, rather, to emphasize that at no point does the relationship between sin and debt enter the picture. Debt is certainly a moral problem, but not primarily on the side of the debtor: it is the creditor who bears ethical responsibility in lending and ownership. The proscriptions against usury and indebtedness more generally, whether they take abstract, metaphysical form, or more down-to-earth, moral commands, assume that charging interest is a practice ripe for abuse. Part of the fear is over the way in which usury and other debt mechanisms all too easily lead to exploitation of the borrower and their need. Prohibitions on usury and commands for the remission of debt, via such institutions as the sabbatical year and the Jubilee year, have in view a broader conception societal justice.

2

Jesus and the Forgiveness of Debt

As we saw in the last chapter, the prohibition on usury assumes that indebtedness is primarily the result of the combination of circumstance and exploitation. One does not become indebted unless one is externally compelled to do so, because circumstances, whatever they may be, demand it. Becoming indebted, then, is not a voluntary act, if we take St. Thomas's definition of the latter seriously, since it lacks intrinsic inclination. That is, one would not take on debt unless one had to, meaning that indebtedness occurs out of necessity. Indebtedness, then, is a forced state or relationship. One could, of course, always refuse the choice of indebtedness, but that would be to resign oneself to one's situation, to acquiesce to one's poverty or lack. Refusing indebtedness, in this sense, is to refuse life, meaning that it is to choose death. Structurally, one is trapped in a forced choice, which is really no choice at all.

Usury exploits this situation, as it is an economic practice wielded by the usurer to profit from an other's misfortune. Usury commodifies lack, since it is designed to generate wealth for the usurer from the other's poverty, their lack of the resources needed for survival and some amount of satisfaction. Medieval theologians considered usury a theft of time, but underneath such abstractions lie the bodies of real individuals. Usury requires the exploitation of individuals as the raw materials to generate wealth, which is also why the biblical prohibitions on, and condemnations of, usury focus primarily on the usurer or creditor rather than the debtor. Such focus is, of course, in sharp contrast to discourses concerning debt in neoliberal capitalist societies, which throw the weight of responsibility onto the debtor and their ability to repay, on their creditworthiness. The economic relationship is, then, also a moral relationship, meaning that responsibility, and thus guilt, lies primarily with the usurer or creditor, not the debtor. Indebtedness, understood in relation to biblical and theological injunctions against usury, is a form of exploitation and does not necessarily coincide with sin, whether understood as an individual act or state of being. If sin *is* involved, it lies squarely with the usurer, not the debtor, contra today's reigning ideologies.

We see similar concerns in Jesus's activities, which can be construed along the lines of a critique of debtor economics.[1] Nevertheless, scholars who have emphasized that Jesus's mission originally focused on the notion of debt forgiveness often fail to wrestle with the fact that the latter is always wrapped up with sin in developing theological traditions, meaning that the two often work interchangeably, although not necessarily in one direction. Even if we grant that the so-called historical Jesus focused primarily on economic issues, especially debt, which only later became wrapped up with the concept sin via a theologization of his message, problems still arise. The Christian theological tradition, which will go on to relate atonement to debt cancellation, does not take as its foundation the "historical Jesus" but, rather, Jesus as presented in the texts themselves and the interpretations that follow, interpretations which form theological and ecclesiastical traditions. Positing a Jesus behind the texts, a Jesus in and of himself prior to editorial interventions and interpretations, may certainly provide important insights, but these ultimately fail to grapple with the reception of the theological traditions that emerge and go on to shape various forms of life. Historical "corrections" to who Jesus was and is, in the end, have little impact on already existing, sedimented moral and sociopolitical apparatuses. Noting how the latter is, at least in part, based on the coincidence of sin and debt in the texts themselves seems a better, sociocritical approach, in that it allows us to interrupt these apparatuses from within. When I speak of or use the name "Jesus," then, it is the Jesus as presented as a composite in the Gospels, with all the internal tensions therein.

The burden of this chapter is to trace the ways in which sin and debt become entangled in certain strands that run throughout the Gospels. To do so, in the first section of this chapter, I situate Jesus's mission in relationship to the traditions relating to usury and Jubilee, as discussed in the last chapter. Although Jesus certainly critiques debtor economics

---

1. Oakman, *Political Aims of Jesus*; Oakman, *Jesus, Debt, and the Lord's Prayer*.

and forces thought to conjure alternative social arrangements, we also find slippages between the spiritual and the economic, the immaterial and the material, which ultimately reinforces the position of the creditor over the debtor. So much is evident, especially, in the Lord's Prayer and the Beatitudes, which I discuss at length. The second and third sections of this chapter focus on Jesus's parables, specifically those associated with the forgiveness of debts, scarcity, and abundance. Although the parables retain the economic valence of debt, sin and debt tend to blur into each other, with debt functioning as a stand in for sin. The final section of this chapter discusses debt as it relates to reciprocity and non-reciprocity in relationships. Jesus ultimately admonishes his followers to lend without expecting anything in return, without the specter of debt, but doing so turns us into God's creditors.

JUBILEE AND THE LORD'S PRAYER

The sociocultural and religious backgrounds that one chooses to emphasize shape the concomitant portrait of Jesus. That is, how we understand Jesus and his activities largely depends on the context in which is we situate him. There is not necessarily one, correct path to take or set of issues to emphasize because the Gospels, as we have them, are as overdetermined as the context in which they were produced.[2] In what follows, I emphasize economic issues, particularly debt, and its relation to sin in certain passages from the Gospels. Although I draw limitedly on critical, sociocultural biblical studies when necessary, my goal is ultimately not historical. Rather, the point in what follows is to work out the conceptual relationship between sin and debt, as it is presented in the Gospels when they are taken as a whole, as a record of developing theological traditions and the ambiguities and ambivalences therein. Each Gospel is, no doubt, a document with its own viewpoint, but because they rely on a similar set of sources, they also present certain theological ideas with relative consistency. More importantly, from a genealogical perspective, this is how the Gospels were received and still used today. Thus, the relationship between sin and debt as developed in later theological traditions depends on this more holistic approach, as exhibited here.

As they are presented in the Gospels, Jesus's activities—or, in more singular, loaded theological terms, mission or ministry—cannot be

---

2. I draw the language of "overdetermination" from Louis Althusser. See Althusser, "Contradiction and Overdetermination."

reduced to one, specific concern. Part of the issue, here, certainly has to do with the source materials themselves, as critical scholars have long pointed out. Although we see considerable overlap among the Gospels, especially among the so-called Synoptic Gospels (Matthew, Mark, and Luke), each presents its own portrait of Jesus for its own theological and political purposes. The same critical scholars often argue that we can get behind narrative construal to some essential core, via form criticism, for instance, but Schweitzer's observation remains salient: the "historical" Jesus uncovered through such efforts mirrors the desire of the scholar.[3] Another way to put the matter is to say that attempts to uncover what Jesus "really" said and did are irretrievably political. As Craig Martin points out, they say more about the interpreter than the one being interpreted, meaning that interpretations are contemporary endeavors for and about the present—and I unabashedly accept this notion for my own reading, developed here.[4]

Focusing on debt as an overriding theme in Jesus's mission, then, certainly has contemporary concerns in mind, as these relate to indebtedness. The reading that follows is, in this sense, politically motivated, and there's no use denying that, trying to hide behind the pretense of scholarly objectivity. Nevertheless, reading Jesus along the lines of the problem of debt and its relation to sin is only possible to the extent that that relationship arises as a problem in the source materials themselves, that is, in the Gospels and the sources behind them. To read Jesus in light of contemporary concerns surrounding debt also shows that these concerns are not just contemporary. Although subject to different conceptualizations and forms of organization, depending on geographic, political, and historical circumstances, debt as an expression of a fundamental asymmetry in interpersonal social relations persists. At issue is not the focus on debt but, rather, that debt remains an issue.

That more traditional, theological interpretations or modern, critical interpretations of Jesus, from whatever position on the political spectrum, have not often insisted on grounding the issue of debt is perhaps the more interesting observation.[5] The specific focus of an interpretation says just as much as its lack, its absences and occlusions. To ignore the problem of debt, whether intentionally or via its dematerialization—and

---

3. Schweitzer, *Quest of the Historical Jesus*.
4. Martin, *Critical Introduction to the Study of Religion*, 93–116.
5. See Oakman, *Political Aims of Jesus*; and Oakman, *Jesus, Debt, and the Lord's Prayer*, for pertinent exceptions.

here and in subsequent chapters, I discuss such dematerialization at length—is to ignore debt as a problem, here and now but also across different historical and sociopolitical apparatuses. Ultimately, such ignorance turns debt into a theological problem which, in turn, loops back onto the economic sphere, providing moral justification for the creditor-debtor relationship.

To focus on debt, then, as an overriding concern in Jesus's mission, is to intentionally read the record of what he said and did in view of and for the present situation. But doing so is only possible to the extent that there is some overlap in the material with our own material condition, and that overlap takes place via debt as a mode of exploitation. However, although Jesus certainly critiques debtor economics and forces thought to conjure alternative social arrangements, it is also the case that he in significant ways exacerbates the problem. The constant slippage between the spiritual and the economic, the immaterial and the material, ultimately reinforces the position of the creditor over the debtor, granting theopolitical sanction to uneven social relationships. Those invested in traditional theological claims about Jesus may balk at such a suggestion, but from a critical, non-theological perspective concerned primarily with debt, as outlined here, what Jesus said and did as presented as a composite in the Gospels is not and should not be immune from critique. To say as much is not to dismiss Jesus—far from it. It is simply to recognize that the value of his discourse is limited to his own perspective, as is everyone's.

According to Luke's Gospel, Jesus begins his Galilean ministry by setting his mission in continuity with the Jubilee tradition, which I discussed in the last chapter. During the Sabbath at a synagogue in Nazareth, he stands up in front of the congregation and reads from the scroll of the prophet Isaiah the following words:

> The Spirit of the Lord is upon me,
>   because he has anointed me
>   to bring good news to the poor.
> He has sent me to proclaim release to the captives
>   and recovery of sight to the blind,
>   to let the oppressed go free,
> to proclaim the year of the Lord's favor. (Luke 4:18–19)

Although the passage from Isaiah is broader in scope, "the year of the Lord's favor" is an obvious reference to the Jubilee year. As mentioned in the last chapter, the Jubilee year called for the periodic manumission of debt. Its "good news to the poor," here, is also marked as a release from oppression and captivity, and the restoration of health. The metaphorical imagery that Jesus uses in relation to his own mission, such as "sight to the blind," is not simply limited to debt and economic matters more generally but bodily integrity. Such is also the case with later theological reflection, as we will see in the next few chapters, even if the debt metaphor would solidify into an ontological description of the condition of individuals as subject to sin.

Nevertheless, Luke narrates that once Jesus goes on to affirm the immediate fulfillment of the passage in its reading and hearing, he is immediately rejected, in part because the prophetic claim appears as out of step with his established identity (e.g., "They said, 'Is this not Joseph's son?'" [Luke 4:22]). The mocking tone that Jesus uses with those at the synagogue certainly does not help his case, and he is summarily run out of town, a result that appears consistent with his own expectations regarding the situation ("Truly I tell you, no prophet is accepted in the prophet's hometown" [Luke 4:24]).

We should not, however, read the incident only as a rejection of Jesus and his claim to the prophetic mantle. The rejection is also a rejection of the message itself, for the prophet's message is inseparable from their identity. Such a claim applies in general but is particularly apt when it comes to Jesus and his mission. The prologue to the Gospel of John provides one of the clearest, richest expressions of this identity, albeit in the mythopoetic language of a more developed incarnational theology: "In the beginning was the Word, and the Word was with God, and the Word was God. He was in the beginning with God. All things came into being through him, and without him not one thing came into being. What has come into being in him was life, and the life was the light of all people. The light shines in the darkness, and the darkness did not overcome it" (John 1:1–5).

To return to Luke, Jesus also, however, shifts the intended subject of Isaiah's pronouncement, which evokes the ire of those in his presence. The latter would have understood Isaiah's broad, messianic claims of restoration, including specifically the reference to Jubilee, as applying to them, that is, to Israel as then reduced to a mere province of the Roman Empire. Claims of release from captivity and oppression would understandably have been taken as claims for them. Jesus, however, shifts the target of the prophetic utterance, dividing the broader audience from within which, practically speaking, amounts to excluding those immediately present. Jesus's illustrative use of Elisha and Elijah enforces this division.

> But the truth is, there were many widows in Israel in the time of Elijah, when the heaven was shut up three years and six months, and there was a severe famine over all the land; yet Elijah was sent to none of them except to a widow at Zarephath in Sidon. There were also many lepers in Israel in the time of the prophet Elisha, and none of them was cleansed except Naaman the Syrian. (Luke 4:26–27)

The point is that the general promises made to Israel have specific addressees, in this example the outcasts, the excluded (e.g., a widow and a leper). Jesus reverses the exclusion, here, including the excluded and excluding the included. Jesus's thinking has the marks of the idea of the so-called righteous remnant, a body of the faithful within the faithful who can expect restoration.[6] The theme plays an important role in Isaiah 61 itself, but also in Paul's thought, particularly in his Letter to the Romans (cf. Rom 11:1–10). Nevertheless, to reiterate, in rejecting the person of Jesus, those present at the synagogue reject his mission as well, which emerges as a common theme throughout the Gospels.

The incident at the synagogue, which revolves around the proclamation of Jubilee, thus anchors Jesus's ministry as one that is, at least in part, opposed to debt and the social inequities that reinforce it. Although the episode is usually taken as the beginning of Jesus's mission proper, at least according to Luke, we should also read it in light of his wilderness temptation, which occurs immediately prior in the narrative (Luke 4:1–13). Here, the devil tempts Jesus in the wilderness for forty days, offering him, among other things, power, authority, and glory. Jesus rejects the devil's seductions, claiming that his allegiance is to God and God alone. If we put the temptation narrative in dialogue with the synagogue episode, a fundamental tension emerges between worldly power, authority, and glory and freedom from debt. That is, Jesus's announcement of Jubilee is predicated on the explicit rejection of worldly forms of power, authority, and glory. One of the main forms that these worldly forms of power take is debt.[7]

That it is the devil that offers him power, authority, and glory is, thus, related to debt, which I discuss in more detail in chapter 4 in reference to the ransom theory of atonement. Briefly, the latter assumes that

---

6. For a more detailed discussion of this notion, see Brondos, *Fortress Introduction to Salvation and the Cross*, 5–18.

7. For a discussion of the ways in which debt functions as power, see Di Muzio and Robbins, *Debt as Power*.

the devil's sovereignty over the world expresses itself via human indebtedness; Christ's atonement, in effect, pays off this debt, releasing the hold the devil has on us. As the author of 1 Timothy puts it, Christ Jesus "gave himself a ransom for all" (1 Tim 2:6).[8] Nevertheless, Jesus's claim to bring "good news to the poor" via the proclamation and establishment of Jubilee is consistent with the basic message of his main sermon which, in Luke's Gospel, is the Sermon on the Plain. In it, as is well known, Jesus expresses his and God's partiality or preference for the poor, via a set of contrasts that assign blessings and woes.[9]

> Blessed are you who are poor,
> for yours is the kingdom of God.
> Blessed are you who are hungry now,
> for you will be filled.
> Blessed are you who weep now,
> for you will laugh. (4:20–21)
>
> But woe to you who are rich,
> for you have received your consolation.
> Woe to you who are full now,
> for you will be hungry.
> Woe to you who are laughing now,
> for you will mourn and weep. (4:24–25)

What is often referred to as the reversal of values called for here turns around or flips normal expectations regarding societal norms and structural inequities. Jesus bluntly states that the rich have already had theirs and, because of that, their time is up. God's blessings are reserved not for the rich but for the poor, who are the heirs to God's kingdom. God's kingdom, as presented here but also elsewhere, is one of fullness and laughter, one that lacks the lack that characterized their former lives opposite the rich. The poor are not lauded out of any putative moral superiority on their part but simply because they are poor, because they are exploited.

The reversal, along with accrual of blessings and woes, is the same that we see in the story of the rich man and Lazarus (Luke 16:19–31). While the rich man in the parable dwells comfortably in his house all day, with all his needs met, a poor man named Lazarus sits sick and hungry outside the house's gate. Both eventually die, but their respective

---

8. I discuss the notion of "ransom" at length in ch. 5, but see Singh, *Divine Currency*, 136–37, for commentary that dovetails with my own.

9. As mentioned in the last chapter, this notion of "preference" is a key theme of liberationist readings of the Gospels.

post-mortem destinations reverse their earthly lots: Lazarus is "carried away by the angels to be with Abraham" (Luke 16:23) while the rich man finds himself tormented in Hades. The rich man cries out for mercy but there is none to be had, since he knew via "Moses and the prophets" (Luke 16:29) his responsibilities to the poor man, to the poor in general. He has already received any "mercy" he may have thought he was due in his prior, earthly comfort.

If holding debt not only expresses power but is one of the ways in which it is established and maintained, then Jesus's rejection of power translates as well into a rejection of debt. Put in positive terms and in line with liberation theologies, Jesus and his God explicitly side with the poor.[10] The "preferential option for the poor," which, contextually speaking, translates as well into a preferential option for debtors, is one of the defining characteristics of the kingdom of God as opposed to exploitative, worldly economies. We must emphasize, however, that God's explicit partiality for the poor does not rest on a notion of moral worth or virtue, as if what were at stake were matters of personal character. As Gutiérrez, among others, emphasizes, God does not side with the poor because they are, in any way, morally upstanding vis-a-vis their oppressors. God sides with the poor *because* they are poor, which, insofar as poverty expresses injustice, is simply another way of saying that God is a God of justice.[11] To put it in more non-theological language, the issue is structural rather than individual, denoting a system that is built on and breeds injustice irrespective of personal motivations and actions. The former should be taken to frame the latter, meaning that structure overrides the individual, no matter how "good" they may be.

Marx makes essentially the same point, when he insists that we should not understand capitalist drives moralistically, as determined by, for instance, greed, but as a structural component of the economic apparatus itself.

> But, so far as he is personified capital, it is not values in use and the enjoyment of them, but exchange-value and its augmentation, that spur him into action. Fanatically bent on making value expand itself, he ruthlessly forces the human race to produce for production's sake; he thus forces the development of the productive powers of society, and creates those material conditions,

---

10. This is, of course, relatively standard fare in Latin American liberation theology, but see the Gutiérrez, *Essential Writings*, 78–148, for presentations of the theme throughout various of his works. See also Sobrino, *No Salvation Outside the Poor*.

11. See, for instance, Gutiérrez, *Essential Writings*, 144–46.

> which alone can form the real basis of a higher form of society, a society in which the full and free development of every individual forms the ruling principle. Only as personified capital is the capitalist respectable. As such, he shares with the miser the passion for wealth as wealth. But that which in the miser is a mere idiosyncrasy, is, in the capitalist, the effect of the social mechanism, of which he is but one of the wheels. Moreover, the development of capitalist production makes it constantly necessary to keep increasing the amount of the capital laid out in a given industrial undertaking, and competition makes the immanent laws of capitalist production to be felt by each individual capitalist, as external coercive laws. It compels him to keep constantly extending his capital, in order to preserve it, but extend it he cannot, except by means of progressive accumulation.[12]

The capitalist, according to Marx, may certainly be and often is greedy, in that he "has a passion for wealth as wealth." However, that passion is, in his case, the result of "social mechanism," which functions as an external compulsion over and above individual enjoyment. Or, one could say that the enjoyment of wealth is found in that external compulsion, in the structural drive to accumulate. For Jesus, however, that compulsion does not obviate responsibility and, in the end, judgment. Sure, one may be a mere cog in a mechanism who lacks real freedom, as David Harvey puts it,[13] but Jesus pronounces blessings and woes on what sort of cog one is, on the place one occupies in the mechanism. This is why the rich man in the parable of the rich man and Lazarus goes on to judgment, while Lazarus goes on to eternal life. The rich man does not do anything explicitly against Lazarus in the story; rather, his wealth inevitably blinds him to the needs of Lazarus, to the poor.

Nevertheless, the Gospels do not only present this reversal between poor and rich in materialist terms. In the Sermon on the Mount in Matthew, Jesus preaches:

> Blessed are the poor in spirit, for theirs is the kingdom of heaven.
> Blessed are those who mourn, for they will be comforted.
> Blessed are the meek, for they will inherit the earth.
> Blessed are those who hunger and thirst for righteousness, for they will be filled.
> Blessed are the merciful, for they will receive mercy.
> Blessed are the pure in heart, for they will see God.

---

12. Marx, *Capital*, 1:24, 3.
13. Harvey, *Companion to Marx's Capital*, 257.

> Blessed are the peacemakers, for they will be called children of God.
> Blessed are those who are persecuted for righteousness' sake, for theirs is the kingdom of heaven.
> Blessed are you when people revile you and persecute you and utter all kinds of evil against you falsely on my account. Rejoice and be glad, for your reward is great in heaven, for in the same way they persecuted the prophets who were before you. (Matt 5:3-12)

Although Matthew and Luke contain similar content, they are different, in that in Matthew poverty is dematerialized and moralized, turned into a sort of internal attitude or virtue. Jesus does not pronounce blessing on the poor, as he does in Luke, but on the "poor in spirit," which could apply to the economically rich and poor alike. Hunger is not real hunger, the physical need for sustenance, but rather a "hunger for righteousness," which is likewise dematerialized and rendered vague. The mainstream of Christian theological traditions has for the most part interpreted Jesus's criticisms of wealth in precisely these terms, as we will see in later chapters. What matters is not, as discussed in the last chapter, what Miranda calls differentiating wealth as such, as indicative of structural inequity, but one's attitude toward wealth, one's internal disposition with respect to it. The language that Jesus uses in Matthew only reinforces such a reading, which is clear in its emphasis on additional qualities such as meekness, mercy, purity, and peacemaking. Such qualities certainly have their place, but when read moralistically, as inner exhortations, they can have a pacifying effect, one that maintains dominant ideologies.

It is telling, then, that Matthew's Jesus does not pronounce any woes in addition to blessings. The simple fact is that, when read on its own terms, there is no place for woes, at least in any strong sense. Because the blessings primarily refer to the cultivation of immaterial dispositions, understood as moral precepts rather than material realities, they can be taken as universal in scope, applicable to the materially poor and rich alike. Rather than reversing values, Jesus here reinforces existing values via the establishment of a spiritual substrate. Elsewhere in Matthew, we do, of course, see an emphasis on how one treats "the least of these," so to speak. Matthew 25:31–46 famously reads:

> When the Son of Man comes in his glory, and all the angels with him, then he will sit on the throne of his glory. All the nations will be gathered before him, and he will separate people one from another as a shepherd separates the sheep from the goats, and he will put the sheep at his right hand and the goats at the left.

> Then the king will say to those at his right hand, "Come, you that are blessed by my Father, inherit the kingdom prepared for you from the foundation of the world; for I was hungry and you gave me food, I was thirsty and you gave me something to drink, I was a stranger and you welcomed me, I was naked and you gave me clothing, I was sick and you took care of me, I was in prison and you visited me." Then the righteous will answer him, "Lord, when was it that we saw you hungry and gave you food, or thirsty and gave you something to drink? And when was it that we saw you a stranger and welcomed you, or naked and gave you clothing? And when was it that we saw you sick or in prison and visited you?" And the king will answer them, "Truly I tell you, just as you did it to one of the least of these who are members of my family, you did it to me." Then he will say to those at his left hand, "You that are accursed, depart from me into the eternal fire prepared for the devil and his angels; for I was hungry and you gave me no food, I was thirsty and you gave me nothing to drink, I was a stranger and you did not welcome me, naked and you did not give me clothing, sick and in prison and you did not visit me." Then they also will answer, "Lord, when was it that we saw you hungry or thirsty or a stranger or naked or sick or in prison, and did not take care of you?" Then he will answer them, "Truly I tell you, just as you did not do it to one of the least of these, you did not do it to me." And these will go away into eternal punishment, but the righteous into eternal life.

Jesus, in this passage, hinges one's eternal fate to one's treatment of others, particularly the downtrodden (the hungry, the thirsty, the stranger, the naked, the sick, and the imprisoned). However, in framing the problem this way, Jesus reduces justice to individual righteousness, to the singular relationship one maintains with the poor, who reflect Christ himself. Emphasizing eternal punishment or eternal life only solidifies this notion. The passage is, thus, perfectly consistent with the dematerialization we see in Matthew's Sermon on the Mount.

The emphasis on the immaterial over the material in the sermon has everything to do with the way Matthew frames the beginning of Jesus's ministry. Both Matthew and Luke, of course, situate that beginning in relation to John's mission and baptism, but Matthew emphasizes that that baptism is one of repentance. Jesus, likewise, constitutes his ministry via a call to repentance, as he does in Mark's Gospel as well (cf. Mark 1:14–15). Matthew narrates that, after the arrest of John, Jesus leaves Nazareth for Capernaum, where Jesus begins to proclaim his central message, "Repent, for the kingdom of heaven has come near" (Matt 4:17). He calls his first disciples under the aegis of the importance of sharing and spreading that message, as it is prerequisite for receiving the "good news of the kingdom" (Matt 4:23).

Nevertheless, if we return to Luke, we see the importance of the Jubilee theme in the Gospel's version of the Lord's Prayer, which explicitly grounds the importance of debt forgiveness when petitioning God via prayer.

> Father, hallowed be your name.
> Your kingdom come.
> Give us each day our daily bread.
> And forgive us our sins,
> for we ourselves forgive everyone indebted to us.
> And do not bring us to the time of trial. (Luke 11:2–4)

In asking God for sustenance, the prayer expresses reliance on God for one's basic needs. More importantly for our purposes, however, is that the prayer connects the forgiveness of sins with the forgiveness of debts. The connection between the two is possible because of the collusion between the two concepts, which results in the two collapsing into each other: sin takes the form of debt and debt, conversely, takes the form of sin. Just as God forgives one's sins qua debts, so we too should forgive the debts of others qua sins. One could, in fact, push further and aver that one's sin can only be forgiven on the condition that we forgive the debts of others. This certainly seems to be the assumption, since forgiving the debt of others appears as a condition that God should and would forgive one's sins. That the prayer has material debt in mind when it speaks of forgiveness is evident in the phrasing but is, also, explicitly in line with Jesus's mission as one intent on instantiating Jubilee.

Matthew's version of the prayer is even more explicit regarding the relationship between sin and debt, as one's relationship to God is likewise conceptualized in terms of debt:

> Our Father in heaven,
>   hallowed be your name.
>   Your kingdom come.
>   Your will be done,
>   on earth as it is in heaven.

> Give us this day our daily bread.
> And forgive us our debts,
>> as we also have forgiven our debtors.
> And do not bring us to the time of trial,
>> but rescue us from the evil one.
>
> For if you forgive others their trespasses, your heavenly Father will also forgive you; but if you do not forgive others, neither will your Father forgive your trespasses. (Matt 6:9–14)

In Luke's version of the prayer, Jesus links sin and debt by making the forgiveness of material debts a condition for the forgiveness of sins. That is, for one to be forgiven of one's sins, one must also have forgiven others any debts owed to them. Jesus in Matthew's version likewise makes forgiveness conditional, but what is at stake is more ambiguous. The prayer asks God to forgive "our debts" rather than "our sins," as in Luke's version, which is likewise contingent upon forgiving "our debtors." Mark's version of the prayer is essentially the same (cf. Mark 6:9–13). However, it is not entirely clear if it is the debt itself or the debtor that is being forgiven. It could be the latter, given the explanation of the meaning of the prayer that Jesus goes on to give in v. 14. His explanation essentially collapses debt into the language of "trespasses," which is consistent with the more immaterial vision underlying the Sermon on the Mount, as I discussed above.[14] The equation of the two, however, refashions debt as a more general, moral concept, indicating a wrong or violation, a crossing of some drawn line. What is lost, however, is the economic sense or valence of the prayer, which specifies the way in which individual and social relationships express themselves in the form of material debt and its forgiveness.

PARABLES OF SIN AND DEBT

I say more about the collusion between sin and debt in later chapters, where I discuss Paul's notion of sin and the development of the doctrine of atonement. Sticking here with the economic valence of the prayer, we can emphasize that the economy presupposed here is one of universal mutuality. The assumption at work is that everyone, individually and collectively, occupies the position of both creditor and debtor simultaneously. The prayer envisions indebtedness in terms of symbiosis rather

---

14. Cf. Meeks, *God the Economist*, 31. Meeks comes to a similar conclusion in reference to the Lord's Prayer, stating, "The prayer has been spiritualized and privatized, as if it referred mainly to our individual, familial, and small group life."

than the asymmetry of the exchange relationship, but doing so also entails the dissolution of indebtedness: if debt, as described in the last chapter, relies on asymmetry, mutual indebtedness entails the end of debt, at least understood as an instrument of capture.[15] Where asymmetry sneaks back in, however, is with the position of God who, as I discuss more thoroughly in the chapters that follow, comes to occupy the position of an absolute creditor, under whom we all occupy the position of debtor.

Nevertheless, Jesus illustrates in various ways the importance of the forgiveness of debts, using both negative and positive examples. One of the more striking illustrations of this message is the parable of the unforgiving servant, as found in Matthew 18. In the parable, Jesus compares the kingdom of heaven to a king seeking to settle indebted accounts with his slaves. The first slave he calls to him, we are told, owes an astronomical amount (ten thousand talents), which he could never hope to repay. The king orders him, his family, and all his possessions sold, to collect at least some of what he is owed. The slave, however, pleads for more time, throwing himself at the mercy of his master. At that point the king has pity on the slave, and "released him and forgave him the debt" (Matt 18:27). Newly forgiven, the slave then goes on to attempt to collect a debt owed to him from a fellow slave. The slave, unsurprisingly, cannot pay, and similarly pleads for mercy. Rather than canceling the debt, as the king did for him, he instead has his fellow slave thrown into prison, until he could pay the debt. The other slaves grow concerned at this action, and report it to the king, who then summons the original slave back to him, chastising him for his lack of mercy:

> "You wicked slave! I forgave you all that debt because you pleaded with me. Should you not have had mercy on your fellow slave, as I had mercy on you?" And in anger his lord handed him over to be tortured until he would pay his entire debt. So my heavenly Father will also do to every one of you, if you do not forgive your brother or sister from your heart. (Matt 18:33–35)

The parable assumes the sort of relational mutuality we find expressed in the Lord's Prayer with regard to the forgiveness of debts. One's own forgiveness depends upon forgiving others, in a dual sense: the former

---

15. I am drawing the notion of symbiosis here from Michel Serres, which he contrasts with parasitism. He does so in numerous places throughout his writing, but consider the following quotation from Serres, *Natural Contract*, 34: "Thus the former parasites have to become symbionts; the excesses they committed against their hosts put the parasites in mortal danger, for dead hosts can no longer feed or house them. . . . This is history's bifurcation: either death or symbiosis."

should lead to the latter, with the latter, moreover, functioning behind the back, so to speak, to justify the former. We could say that, in a way, forgiveness of debts functions in the future perfect, even if it does not take on the explicit grammatical form: one always will have been forgiven, to the extent that one extends the same to others. The parable also highlights the relative insignificance of the debt owed to the slave when compared with what the slave owes the king: there is no way the slave could ever repay such a sum; yet, the king forgives it anyway, which in the parable becomes a mark of the king's mercy or grace. Although what the other slave owes to the original slave is still a significant amount, it pales in comparison to what he owes to the king, at least in absolute terms. The point is that the slave should be willing to forgive a little when so much has been forgiven him, a point which is also stressed in the parable of the two debtors, discussed below.

However, we should not ignore the violence in this parable. Although the hyperbolic sum of money owed to the king is meant on the surface to buttress the king's generosity, it also shores up the absurdity of the debt, at least as owed to the king. That the king could release the slave from his debt so easily, without any self-concern, shows that the debt matters differently depending on the party involved: it is an economic burden for the slave, but for the king it is a lever of power. What matters for the king is not the money per se but having the power of collection or cancellation. The relationship between the king and the slave is asymmetrical, which extends to how debt functions for each. Although the parable attempts to capture the relationship between the forgiven slave and the other slave within this logic, we must assume that the relationship between the two is more symmetrical, in that both are slaves. Even if we allow for different gradations within the sociopolitical status of "slave," the two remain closer to each other in terms of both status and economic standing than either would ever be in relation to the king. To use a contemporary example that one often hears, economically speaking most people are closer to unhoused persons then they ever will be to billionaires.[16] A hundred denarii is a large sum of money for both slaves, and so more is stake in one forgiving the other his debt. Although the slave's failure to act mercifully with respect to his fellow slave is regrettable, in that it shows a lack of solidarity, we also should be careful not

---

16. I am not sure where the articulation of this notion originates, but a search of something along the lines of "closer to homeless persons than to billionaires in America" yields numerous results in articles and on social media platforms.

to uncritically accept that the slave is in any sense in a position like that of the king. We can only do so to the extent that debt functions symbolically, as a stand in for sin, which is exactly what the parable asks us to do: forgiveness, that is, is a matter "of the heart" (Matt 18:35). Indeed, in its narrative context, Jesus gives the parable in response to Peter's question about forgiveness, which has to do with sin: "Then Peter came and said to him, 'Lord, if another member of the church sins against me, how often should I forgive? As many as seven times?' Jesus said to him, 'Not seven times, but, I tell you, seventy-seven times'" (Matt 18:21–22). The economic condition of indebtedness functions metaphorically as a stand-in for sin; however, the metaphorical substitution works toward emptying indebtedness of its material reality.

The slippage between sin and debt can be found in the parable of the two debtors as well, which Jesus tells to illustrate the forgiveness of sins. A Pharisee named Simon asks Jesus to dine at his house. Hearing that Jesus was at Simon's house, a woman, whom the text refers to as a "sinner," comes to the house with a jar of ointment, which she then uses to anoint Jesus. Simon gets angry at this act, not so much at the woman but, rather, at Jesus, for letting the woman anoint him. He mutters to himself, "If this man were a prophet, he would have known who and what kind of woman this is who is touching him—that she is a sinner" (Luke 7:39). Jesus then asks Simon the following question, which takes the form of a short parable: "A certain creditor had two debtors; one owed five hundred denarii, and the other fifty. When they could not pay, he canceled the debts for both of them. Now which of them will love him more?" (Luke 7:40–41). Simon answers that the former will love his creditor more, on the assumption that his creditor had canceled more debt, at least as understood in absolute terms. Jesus affirms Simon's answer, but responds by applying the parable to the woman, which he does by using debt as an analogy for sin:

> Do you see this woman? I entered your house; you gave me no water for my feet, but she has bathed my feet with her tears and dried them with her hair. You gave me no kiss, but from the time I came in she has not stopped kissing my feet. You did not anoint my head with oil, but she has anointed my feet with ointment. Therefore, I tell you, her sins, which were many, have been forgiven; hence she has shown great love. But the one to whom little is forgiven, loves little. (Luke 7:45–47)

Jesus then forgives the sins of the woman, which provokes the ire of the other guests.

In the story, debt is not necessarily sin and sin not necessarily debt, but the two are close enough conceptually to be used analogously, in reference to each other, without any interpretive leap. The relationship between the two, however, only runs one way. That is, Jesus does not use the concept of sin to illustrate the concept of debt but, rather, the converse: debt, which in the parable is material, economic debt, illuminates the concept of sin. The direction of this substitution, however, ultimately subsumes material, economic debt under the concept of sin. On a side note, which will become important when we discuss Anselm's satisfaction theory of atonement, it is worth pointing out that the analogy assumes that not all sins are equal. That is, just as one can owe more debt than another to one's creditor, so too can one have more sins, quantitatively and qualitatively, in need of forgiveness.

Whereas the parable of the unforgiving servant paints a picture of the perils of not forgiving debt and, by extension, sin, as commanded, the parable of the dishonest manager provides a more positive example, even if it is not as straightforward. The parable tells the story of a certain estate manager accused by his employer, a rich man, of "squandering his property" (Luke 16:1). Called to give an account of his mishandlings of the property, the threat of dismissal from his position is imminent. Unable, he thinks, to do much else (he says, "I am not strong enough to dig, and I am ashamed to beg" [16:4]), he devises a plan, so that when "dismissed as manager, people may welcome [him] into their homes" (16:5). Without his employer's knowledge, he calls the rich man's debtors to him, offering a significant cut to the amount of debt owed if they render payment immediately.

> "How much do you owe my master?" He answered, "A hundred jugs of olive oil." He said to him, "Take your bill, sit down quickly, and make it fifty." Then he asked another, "And how much do you owe?" He replied, "A hundred containers of wheat." He said to him, "Take your bill and make it eighty." (Luke 16:6–7)

Even though it is a good deal for the debtors, the manager's actions are not the result of generosity or compassion; they are admittedly self-serving. When his actions come to the rich man's attention, he praises the once-disgraced manager for acting "shrewdly." The parable then concludes with the following, more general admonishment: "For the children of this age are more shrewd in dealing with their own generation than are the children of light. And I tell you, make friends for yourselves by means of dishonest wealth so that when it is gone, they may welcome you into the eternal homes" (Luke 16:8–9).

The parable provides a positive example of the petition for forgiveness in the Lord's Prayer, in that it makes forgiveness mutual. The manager gets back in his employer's good graces and has his debts essentially forgiven by forgiving the debts of others, at least a portion of them. Jesus then uses the actions of the manager as exemplary without, however, criticizing the manager's motivations. Indeed, he does the opposite: he commends the dishonesty of the manager, largely for pragmatic reasons, as a means of securing one's eternal home.

Immediately after he tells the parable, Jesus goes on to invoke the contrast or disjunction between God and mammon.

> Whoever is faithful in a very little is faithful also in much; and whoever is dishonest in a very little is dishonest also in much. If then you have not been faithful with the dishonest wealth, who will entrust to you the true riches? And if you have not been faithful with what belongs to another, who will give you what is your own? No slave can serve two masters; for a slave will either hate the one and love the other, or be devoted to the one and despise the other. You cannot serve God and wealth. (Luke 16:10–14)

I have discussed elsewhere how to connect the parable with the claim that one cannot serve God and wealth, or mammon, simultaneously, in relation to a more general critique of money.[17] Here, it is important to point out that, if we line up the actors in the parable with the above quotation, it seems clear that the rich man is on the side of wealth or mammon, while the dishonest manager, who stands in for the faithful, is on the side of God. As his actions in the parable make clear, this has nothing to do with his moral character; indeed, he is unambiguously dishonest. It has to do, rather, with him dealing "shrewdly" with his employer's wealth, which is concretely expressed in the notion of debt cancellation. Debt cancellation or forgiveness, then, is a means of serving God rather than wealth, against mammon, and it lines up with how Jesus defines his mission in Luke's Gospel, as discussed above. What is also striking about these passages is that they lack the moralization of debt via the invocation of the concept of sin. Invoking the concept of sin, in this context, would

---

17. Phelps, *Jesus and the Politics of Mammon*, 13–44.

empty the importance that dishonesty plays as a virtue in the parable, but it would also undermine the clear disjunction Jesus establishes between God and wealth, between God and mammon. This is not to say that one cannot provide a more immaterial reading of the parable, reading the disjunction and, by extension, forgiveness of debts, more metaphorically, as a matter of internal disposition rather than material relationship. Nevertheless, debt forgiveness, as understood via the parable, lines up with serving God, not wealth, even if one extends such forgiveness via intentions that are not necessarily pure.

MYTHS OF SCARCITY AND ABUNDANCE

Although they do not mention debt explicitly, we should read Jesus's parables concerning the abundance associated with the kingdom of God in light of debt cancellation and debt's injustice. This is because the notion of debt is wrapped up with myths of scarcity, which result in the asymmetrical accumulation of money, resources, and goods. The extension of credit to others within such conditions becomes a way to profit off this asymmetry, which only increases the gap between creditor and debtor. All of this is done, of course, under the guise of supposed economic laws and necessity, but these can only be viewed as such based on putative scarcity, which includes the absolute right to property.[18]

In the parable of the rich fool (Luke 12:16–21), a member of the crowd listening to Jesus asks him to compel his brother to divide the family's inheritance with him. Jesus responds that he is no "judge or arbitrator," but admonishes the man, "Take care! Be on your guard against all kinds of greed; for one's life does not consist in the abundance of possessions" (12:14–16). Jesus then goes on to illustrate the point by telling a parable about a rich landowner who produced an overabundance of crops. Since he did not have enough space to store them, he devises a plan to tear down his smaller, existing barns to build larger ones, adequate to the long-term storage of his surplus. Doing so would, he thinks, provide him with comfort and security; as he says, "I will say to my soul, Soul, you have ample goods laid up for many years; relax, eat, drink, be merry" (12:19). Rather than praised for his acumen and foresight, Jesus labels him a fool. "But God said to him, 'You fool! This very night your life is being demanded of you. And the things you have prepared, whose will

---

18. Duchrow and Hinkelammert, *Property for People, Not for Profit*, 5–27.

they be?' So it is with those who store up treasures for themselves but are not rich toward God" (12:20–21).

Jesus goes on to contrast the actions of the rich man in the parable by urging his followers not to worry about their needs, which come directly from God. It is worth quoting what Jesus says here at length.

> He said to his disciples, "Therefore I tell you, do not worry about your life, what you will eat, or about your body, what you will wear. For life is more than food, and the body more than clothing. Consider the ravens: they neither sow nor reap, they have neither storehouse nor barn, and yet God feeds them. Of how much more value are you than the birds! And can any of you by worrying add a single hour to your span of life? If then you are not able to do so small a thing as that, why do you worry about the rest? Consider the lilies, how they grow: they neither toil nor spin; yet I tell you, even Solomon in all his glory was not clothed like one of these. But if God so clothes the grass of the field, which is alive today and tomorrow is thrown into the oven, how much more will he clothe you—you of little faith! And do not keep striving for what you are to eat and what you are to drink, and do not keep worrying. For it is the nations of the world that strive after all these things, and your Father knows that you need them. Instead, strive for his kingdom, and these things will be given to you as well." (12:22–31)

Rather than acting like the rich man, who stores up his abundance for future use for himself, not others, Jesus encourages his followers to live like birds, which "have neither storehouse nor barn," and flowers, which "neither toil nor spin." The kingdom of God is such that all needs are provided, even over and above the accumulated riches of the world, for even "Solomon in all his glory was not clothed like one of these." The contrast between this vision and the rich man's actions in the parable clearly focus on one's attitude to the role that resources play in life. The rich man accumulates the surplus of his goods, keeping them for himself, out of a need for security, which is another way of saying out of fear of scarcity. The birds and the flowers, who become models for denizens of God's kingdom, do not so accumulate, because their security comes from God, which is another way of saying that scarcity is not operative in such a vision. One could read the contrast between the two in line with Georges Bataille's distinction between restrictive economy and general economy:

while the former limits economic activity to productivity and scarcity, the latter focuses on expenditure and surplus.[19]

If we bring the notion of debt into this contrast, we see that debt operates in the gap opened in the disjunction between the two perspectives. Debt, as mentioned above, relies on the asymmetrical accumulation of resources, but this occurs through the colonization or theft of abundance or surplus—and abundance and surplus Jesus names the kingdom of God. Accumulation, in other words, creates scarcity, which is then leveraged via the extension of credit to induce indebtedness, which further exacerbates the asymmetry. However, while acknowledging the practical limits of the theological language, if we take Jesus seriously, there is nothing natural about such a system. Scarcity, on which debt operates, is a self-referential construction, and can only thrive so long as it ignores other ways of conceptualizing and actualizing economy and social relationships.

In Matthew's Gospel, Jesus likewise recommends to his followers to live like birds and flowers, accumulating nothing and relying on God for their needs (Matt 6:25–24). The passage occurs in light of general admonishments not to worry by storing up "treasures on earth" (Matt 6:19), but it immediately follows Jesus's statement of the disjunction between God and wealth, or mammon. "No one can serve two masters; for a slave will either hate the one and love the other, or be devoted to the one and despise the other. You cannot serve God and wealth" (Matt 6:24). Wealth, as a means of accumulation over against the lack of others, thus puts one in opposition to God.

Envisioning abundance in contrast to a restricted economy can also be seen in the stories of Jesus feeding the multitudes. In Matthew's Gospel, after John's assassination at Herod's command, Jesus attempts to withdraw to a remote location, but is followed by the crowds that usually attend him. He heals the sick among them but, close to nightfall, his disciples urge him to send the crowds away, to buy food from the local villages. Apparently, the location was far enough away from said villages that traveling to them would require both light and time. Jesus tells his disciples to give them something to eat, so that they can stay. The disciples, however, note that there is "nothing here but five loaves and two fish," certainly not enough for the thousands present. Jesus asks his disciples to bring him the loaves and "then he ordered the crowds to sit down on the grass. Taking the five loaves and the two fish, he looked

19. Bataille, *Accursed Share*, 19–26.

up to heaven, and blessed and broke the loaves, and gave them to the disciples, and the disciples gave them to the crowds. And all ate and were filled; and they took up what was left over of the broken pieces, twelve baskets full. And those who ate were about five thousand men, besides women and children" (Matt 14:18–21).

Mark's version (Mark 6:30–34) and Luke's version (Luke 9:10–17) are essentially the same, save for narrative framing and a few minor details. Nevertheless, under the guise of miracle, the story illustrates the abundance that God's kingdom instantiates. Insofar as the they seek to send the crowds away for their own security and safety, the disciples act analogously to the rich man who stored up the surplus of his goods. Jesus, however, urges them to act otherwise, and essentially treats those present as so many birds and flowers, manifesting God's provision for their sustenance and well-being.

NON-RECIPROCITY AND THE LAW

Theological discussions of sin often define it as "missing the mark" or "erring,"[20] but we can grasp it in terms of debt as well. A key passage, in this regard comes from Luke 17, directly after Jesus famously telling his disciples that if they had "faith the size of a mustard seed, you could say to this mulberry tree, 'Be uprooted and planted in the sea,' and it would obey you" (Luke 17:6). The implication, of course, is that they do not possess such faith. Jesus then states:

> Who among you would say to your slave who has just come in from plowing or tending sheep in the field, "Come here at once and take your place at the table"? Would you not rather say to him, "Prepare supper for me, put on your apron and serve me while I eat and drink; later you may eat and drink"? Do you thank the slave for doing what was commanded? So you also, when you have done all that you were ordered to do, say, "We are worthless slaves; we have done only what we ought [*opheilomen*] to have done!"'(Luke 17:7–10)

In the passage above, "we ought" translates *opheilomen*, which is the imperfect active indicative of *opheilo*. The verb literally means "to owe" and, thus, is directly related to the notion of debt, though it can be used metaphorically, as in the passage above, to refer simply to duty or doing what

---

20. Cf. Biddle, *Missing the Mark*.

one ought to do. The passage implies, however, that doing one's duty, making good on one's obligation or debt, is not enough in and of itself.

Rather, one must act in excess of what is commanded, which elsewhere Jesus considers the essence of the law. Such sentiment is clearly expressed in Matt 5, where Jesus says during his Sermon on the Mount:

> Do not think that I have come to abolish the Law or the Prophets; I have not come to abolish them but to fulfill them. For truly I tell you, until heaven and earth disappear, not the smallest letter, not the least stroke of a pen, will by any means disappear from the Law until everything is accomplished. Therefore anyone who sets aside one of the least of these commands and teaches others accordingly will be called least in the kingdom of heaven, but whoever practices and teaches these commands will be called great in the kingdom of heaven. For I tell you that unless your righteousness surpasses that of the Pharisees and the teachers of the law, you will certainly not enter the kingdom of heaven. (Matt 5:17–20)

Jesus goes on to give concrete examples of this fulfillment of the law, which in essence makes the law more difficult to follow. Regarding murder, for instance, it is not enough simply not to murder; anger itself is subject to judgment. Likewise with adultery: it is not enough to not commit adultery, for "anyone who looks at a woman lustfully has already committed adultery with her in his heart" (Matt 5:28). What Jesus does, in effect, is "superegotize" the law, to borrow a term that Slavoj Žižek uses.[21] The law is not simply an external imposition that one is bound to follow to the letter but, rather, must manifest itself in its intention, in its spirit (cf. 2 Cor 3:6).

The spirit of the law thus internalizes the law, expanding its reach to one's disposition with respect to the law, to one's intentions. But it also expands the external scope of the law, in that it applies it beyond any sort of parochialism. Jesus says, for instance, "You have heard that it was said, 'Love your neighbor and hate your enemy.' But I tell you, love your enemies and pray for those who persecute you, that you may be children of your Father in heaven. He causes his sun to rise on the evil and the good, and sends rain on the righteous and the unrighteous" (Matt 5:43–45).

Michel Henry reads the command to love one's enemies as well as one's neighbor in terms of "a general critique of the law of reciprocity

---

21. Žižek, *Fragile Absolute*, 100. Žižek here uses it primarily in reference to Paul, but it applies as well to Jesus's claims in the Sermon on the Mount.

of feelings in human relationships."[22] That is, human relationships are largely founded on reciprocity. For instance, we love those close to us, perhaps even our neighbors, but not so with our enemies: their hostility to us is reciprocated in our hostility to them. The relationship between creditor and debtor is also reciprocal, even asymmetrical in terms of power since the creditor loans money expecting repayment from the debtor. The debtor has a responsibility to return what has been given to him, because reciprocity demands it. Henry, however, suggests that Jesus affirms non-reciprocity, which is located in one's immediate relationship with God which, in turn, extends to others. Such a relationship manifests itself concretely in the overturning of values, which entails that we act toward others in excess of expectations. Henry quotes Luke 6:34 to solidify this point, which makes the connection to debt explicit: "Love your enemies, do good, and lend, *expecting nothing in return*. Your reward will be great, and you will be children of the Most High; for he is kind to the ungrateful and the wicked."[23]

However, what Henry overlooks is that non-reciprocity still entails some expectation, even if it is transposed on a different, immaterial plane. One may lend without expecting anything in return from the lendee, but one always does so under the expectation of heavenly reward. Jacques Derrida, in his reading of this passage, notes that the line demarcating the earthly from the heavenly is precisely where the "heart" comes in. "God asks," he writes, "that one give without knowing, without calculating, reckoning, or hoping, for one must give without counting, and that is what takes it outside of sense."[24] What matters is where one saves their real treasure, whose depository lies "beyond the economy of the terrestrial visible or sensible, that is, the corrupted or corruptible economy that is vulnerable to moth, rust, and thieves."[25] One's "heart," in this sense, resides where one saves their treasure: in the earthly domain or in the heavenly domain, the separation of which constitutes God's economy over-against established economies.

Whether one's conscious motivation stems from the anticipation of the reward matters little, as the reward itself always functions in the background, blurring the lines between the reciprocal and the

---

22. Henry, *Words of Christ*, 32.
23. As quoted in Henry, *Words of Christ*, 32; emphasis is Henry's.
24. Derrida, *Gift of Death*, 97.
25. Derrida, *Gift of Death*, 98.

non-reciprocal.²⁶ Derrida, in line with Henry, notes that the division between the material and the immaterial, the celestial and the earthly, implies "breaking with exchange as a simple form of reciprocity."²⁷ But we also should not ignore Derrida's claims elsewhere on the impossibility of the gift, the upshot of which is the constant entanglement of the reciprocal and the non-reciprocal, exchange and gift.²⁸

What is, perhaps, more interesting to point out is that investing in the here and now for heavenly reward puts the faithful in the position of lender or depositor. One in effect functions as a creditor to God, with full expectation that the conditions of the relationship will be met. Such a claim may appear at first glance to be preposterous, especially considering later-developed theological doctrines that emphasize God's self-sufficiency and the assumption that faith lies in belief, in creedal affirmation. However, Gary A. Anderson has convincingly argued that almsgiving or charity is closely related to faith, in the sense that it fosters dispositions to oneself, others, and God. Belief is not absent in such transactions, especially those involving debt. The extension of credit to another is, in a reciprocal economy, based on the belief that the loan will be repaid; hence lending takes a speculative form, in that it evaluates and projects the prospect of future repayment as condition for the extension of credit itself. The relationship between acts of lending, whether for purely personal gain or more laudably for charity, cannot be reduced to moral proclivities but, rather, is a sign of one's obedience to God. As Anderson notes, "Though the Bible makes several laws regarding the making of loans, its concern is with the way in which such financial arrangement is handled (forbidding the exacting of interest), not with an obligation to provide a loan in the first place (e.g. Exod 22:24–26)."²⁹ Indeed, in Ben Sira, lending in this sense is considered a form of almsgiving.

> The merciful lend to their neighbors;
> by holding out a helping hand, they keep the commandments;
> Lend to your neighbor in his time of need;
> repay your neighbor when a loan falls due.
> Keep your promise and be honest with him,

---

26. Derrida, *Gift of Death*, 100.
27. Derrida, *Gift of Death*, 101.
28. Derrida explores this in numerous ways in, for instance, *Given Time*.
29. Anderson, *Charity*, 43.

and on every occasion you will find what you need. (29:1–3)[30]

Anderson cites other passages expressing similar sentiments (cf. 29:14–20), but his overall point is that, for Ben Sira, lending is a type of charity: "Ben Sira does not link the obligation to give alms to any . . . legal precedents; rather he understands the gift of alms as a sort of loan."[31]

Anderson concludes that, in light of the link between almsgiving and charity, the relationship between creditor and debtor was not entirely exploitative, though he does not really consider the overall systemic apparatuses that would require lending because of asymmetrical access to wealth and resources more generally. Creditors could, then, be considered generous within such a system, since they provide material support to the "welfare system of antiquity."[32] Nevertheless, what is most important for our immediate purposes is Anderson's observation that lending to the poor, in the manor described above, is really doing business with God.[33]

One of the key passages from the Christian Scriptures, in this respect, is found in Matthew 6, which occurs almost immediately after the Lord's Prayer: "Do not store up for yourselves treasures on earth, where moth and rust consume and where thieves break in and steal; but store up for yourselves treasures in heaven, where neither moth nor rust consumes and where thieves do not break in and steal. For where your treasure is, there your heart will be also" (19:21–21). The passage clearly relates to the mandate, discussed above, concerning lending without the expectation of return. One lends primarily out of some accumulated excess, so lending is a way to put that excess into circulation for the benefit of others; it is one way, in other words, not to store wealth. But lending on the material plane functions as credit on the heavenly: almsgiving is a means to "store up for yourselves treasures in heaven." Since how we treat the poor is how we treat God, almsgiving to the poor is, in essence, "making a loan to God."[34] Anderson references Prov 19:17 to buttress his point: "Whoever is kind to the poor lends to the Lord, and will be repaid in full." If this is true, then a significant part of faith is the expectation that credit extended to God via deposits in the heavenly treasure will be

---

30. As quoted in Anderson, *Charity*, 42.
31. Anderson, *Charity*, 46.
32. Anderson, *Charity*, 50.
33. Anderson, *Charity*, 52.
34. Anderson, *Charity*, 186.

repaid, in the form of eternal life.[35] One's kindness to the poor, in effect, turns God into one's debtor, and God makes good on that debt via the repayment of eternal life.

CONCLUSION

One way to understand Jesus's mission is to emphasize its concern with debt and indebtedness. This is especially the case with Luke's Gospel, in which Jesus connects the beginning of his ministry to biblical traditions concerned with debt cancellation, specifically the tradition of Jubilee. As I discussed in chapter 1, the Jubilee and Sabbath year traditions attempt to redress uneven socioeconomic relationships through the periodic manumission of debts. Debt, in this line of thought, is understood as exploitative: indebtedness is not understood in relation to sin but is, rather, the result of the creditor taking advantage of structural inequities. Such is the assumption behind prohibitions on usury, and if anyone is to be labeled sinful, it is the usurer, the creditor, and not the debtor. Jesus's mission, then, has a very real material reality in mind—indebtedness—to which he devotes considerable attention, including the parables discussed above.

However, we can also find instances in the Gospels of the dematerialization of debt, of making indebtedness a moral or spiritual condition. The forgiveness of debts, in this sense, functions as a metaphor for and coincides with the forgiveness of sin, with the debtor occupying the position of the latter. Although the material reality of debt as related to conditions of and relationships based on scarcity, abundance, reciprocity, and non-reciprocity are never lost in the Gospels, we see shifts back and forth between the material and the spiritual. The latter emphasis comes to predominate in theological reflection on sin and atonement, as I discuss in subsequent chapters. In sum, whereas debt in the biblical and Jubilee traditions is related to exploitation, in the Gospels we find it in addition functioning metaphorically to understand sin and forgiveness. In the next chapter, we see how a version of the latter plays out in Paul's thought, especially in relation to his discussion of law, sin, death, and the subject.

---

35. Brown, *Ransom of the Soul*, provides a good overview of the theological development of this notion in early Christianity.

3

Paul, Sin, and the Language of Debt

IN WHAT FOLLOWS, I read Paul conceptually, with an eye toward philosophical and theological concerns related to debt and indebtedness. My reading, in this sense, is more in line with contemporary attempts to mine Paul's thought for philosophical and political insight, than the historical-critical studies in which biblical scholars trade.[1] Thus, as I have indicated in previous chapters, I am more interested in the conceptual reception of Paul's thought, especially in regard to debt, rather than establishing any original sense to his thought, to the extent that would be possible. Although I focus mainly on Romans and Galatians, as have other, recent philosophical readings, I also draw on letters not normally attributed to Paul. The theological traditions that emerge after Paul take up and interpret these letters and the thought contained therein as Pauline, so it only makes sense to focus on these as well, given the emphasis of the chapter on reading Paul in concert with his reception.

I read Paul, then, through a set of problematics he has given theological traditions, but my reading of Paul is not as positive as recent, philosophical readings.[2] Although I do not deny that one may find some radical potential in his letters, we also should not ignore the problems

---

1. Badiou, *Saint Paul*; Agamben, *Time That Remains*; Žižek, *Fragile Absolute*; Žižek, *Ticklish Subject*; Breton, *Radical Philosophy of Saint Paul*; Taubes, *Political Philosophy of Paul*; Blanton, *Materialism for the Masses*; van der Heiden et al., *Saint Paul and Philosophy*; Caputo and Alcoff, *Saint Paul Among the Philosophers*.

2. For a convincingly trenchant reading of Paul and attempts to provide a positive, philosophical valuation and extension, see Concannon, *Profaning Paul*.

surrounding the interconnection of sin, law, debt, and slavery. Whereas, as I argued in the last chapter, debt and its cancellation have for Jesus some material basis, Paul's thought ignores or, perhaps better said, empties the material of content, transposing the problem of debt into an ontological condition governed by sin, law, and death on one side, and grace, spirit, and life on the other. The Gospels certainly make use of a dual sense of debt, playing with and crossing its economic and theological valences. Paul, however, drops the economic entirely: debt and sin are directly related to each other and universalized; in the end, they function as one and the same under the law. Indebtedness takes on a more general, non-economic, purview, as it becomes associated with terms with a broader scope, one that catches the whole of life. Ultimately, what is in view in Paul's thought is not the materiality of socioeconomic relationships but, rather, a more abstract struggle between sin or flesh and spirt.

THE PROBLEM OF LAW

Although contemporary biblical scholars have sought to correct supersessionist readings of Paul when it comes to his relationship to the law,[3] it is hard to avoid the conclusion that he is, indeed, harsh on the law, at least when the latter is construed in a certain way. Paul's criticism of the law has nothing to do with the popular Protestant notion that the law was, in design, impossible to keep. Paul certainly did not think so, at least if we take his own admissions about his relationship to the law at face value. Paul seems to take the opposite view, boasting without boasting, "If anyone else has reason to be confident in the flesh, I have more: circumcised on the eighth day, a member of the people of Israel, of the tribe of Benjamin, a Hebrew born of Hebrews; as to the law, a Pharisee; as to zeal, a persecutor of the church; as to righteousness under the law, blameless" (Phil 3:4–6). Like Jesus, his Christ, Paul elsewhere praises the law as encapsulating the basic command to love one another: "For the whole law is summed up in a single commandment, 'You shall love your neighbor as yourself'" (Gal 5:14). Clearly, then, Paul has some good things to say about the law and does not seem to consider it annulled and

---

3. The literature on this topic is vast, but for a philosophically informed discussion of it that also attempts to retrieve Pauline thought to develop a contemporary materialism, see Blanton, *Materialism for the Masses*. His previous work is relevant on this point too, especially when it comes to the reception of Paul in modern and postmodern biblical studies and philosophy. See Blanton, *Displacing Christian Origins*.

its implementation unworkable, which is similar in this respect to Jesus himself.

Such positive claims as these, however, sit uneasily with more vitriolic claims, such as when he refers to the law as the "law of sin and of death" (Rom 8:2). I discuss numerous, similar examples below, but what are we to make of this apparent disconnect, especially the more negative portrayals of the law as they appear throughout his letters? Stanislas Breton has pointed out that Paul's objection to the law "cannot be reduced to a fastidious ritualism, as is sometimes thought."[4] It is not just mere "works" and their multiplication that piques Paul's ire when it comes to the law, as many a Christian have assumed. Breton quotes Paul in affirmation of this point, "For the one who has loved the other has fulfilled the Law" (Rom 13:8). According to Breton, what provokes Paul is the disconnect between its ever-expanding, particularly focused prescriptions and proscriptions and its tacit universalism. Breton writes:

> The exorbitant importance we accord to the Law is out of proportion with the limited reach of its jurisdiction, if, that is, we make of its borders the egocentric curve of an election. Indeed, it is not *universal*. The Gentiles remain outside its influence. . . . Paul tacitly affirms from this non-universality that the law is neither necessary nor fundamental. A more radical authority preceded it: faith in the promise, concealed by the Law under a veil of forgetfulness.[5]

Much of Paul's thought, then, is concerned with working out the relationship between Jews and gentiles and what this conceptually and practically entails regarding the law for the putative universality of Paul's gospel. Such is, at least, how the Christian theological tradition, along with its modern and postmodern philosophical counterparts, has normally read Paul. Whether one is Jew or Greek—which, as Badiou points out, functions rhetorically to identify what Paul takes as the dominant discursive options available to his audiences[6]—one still is subject to God's law and, in turn, God's judgment. Paul writes:

> All who have sinned apart from the law will also perish apart from the law, and all who have sinned under the law will be judged by the law. For it is not the hearers of the law who are

---

4. Breton, *Radical Philosophy of Saint Paul*, 87.
5. Breton, *Radical Philosophy of Saint Paul*, 88; emphasis in original.
6. Badiou, *Saint Paul*, 40–54.

> righteous in God's sight, but the doers of the law who will be justified. When Gentiles, who do not possess the law, do instinctively what the law requires, these, though not having the law, are a law to themselves. They show that what the law requires is written on their hearts, to which their own conscience also bears witness; and their conflicting thoughts will accuse or perhaps excuse them on the day when, according to my gospel, God, through Jesus Christ, will judge the secret thoughts of all. (Rom 2:12–16)

We can see here how demanding Paul is. It is not uncommon to read Paul and Jesus along different, oftentimes divergent lines, and one can take the supposed opposition between the two for good or ill. Badiou, for instance, considers Paul's doctrinal focus an asset over-against the "exploits" of the Gospels. For Badiou's Paul, "Jesus' teachings, like his miracles, are splendidly ignored. Everything is brought back to a single point: Jesus, son of God . . . and Christ in virtue of this, died on the cross and was resurrected."[7] One can certainly emphasize the differences between Paul and Jesus as the latter is presented in the Gospels, and those who do so are certainly correct to point to the lack of biographical information about Jesus in Paul's letters. Nevertheless, this is not surprising and may be less important than Badiou and the like assume. Although it may seem banal to point out, Paul's letters are, in fact, letters, and pretend to be nothing more; his readers would likely have known at least some of the stories behind Paul's theological claims. It would be surprising if they did not, surprising if Paul would have to recount Jesus's exploits to the initiated.

That said, morally speaking, Paul is closer to Jesus than is sometimes assumed, and that includes the deployment of a conceptual apparatus based on debt, as I show throughout this chapter. Nevertheless, to refer to the previous chapter, like Jesus, it is not enough for Paul to merely follow the law in works; one's intentions matter, one's "secret thoughts" count. Paul's understanding of human subjectivity may certainly be somewhat different from ours, but he still places weight on one's internal state, so to speak, where one's heart really lies.[8] Paul uses the example of

---

7. Badiou, *Saint Paul*, 33.

8. Many contemporary theological readings of Paul, especially so-called postliberal readings, emphasize the difference between Paul's vision of the individual and community and modernity's, the latter of which is seen as a decline. For an important criticism of and correction to this view, which emphasizes Paul's Greekness, see Ruprecht, *Afterwards*, 127–62.

circumcision, which he considers an outward expression of a more real, inward state: "For a person is not a Jew who is one outwardly, nor is true circumcision something external and physical. Rather, a person is a Jew who is one inwardly, and real circumcision is a matter of the heart—it is spiritual and not literal. Such a person receives praise not from others but from God" (Rom 2:28–29).

In stating as much, Paul does not seek to diminish the place Jews have vis-a-vis God, which is expressed materially in the particularities of their law, which is also, of course, his and his Christ's law. Rather, what Paul seeks to emphasize is that, whether one falls inside or outside the law's specific purview, one remains "under the power of sin" (Rom 3:9). Being inside or outside the law does not change the fact that one remains accountable to God. The law, in this sense, does not add anything regarding culpability. All that the law adds is "knowledge of sin" (Rom 3:20).

If the law adds knowledge of sin, how, then, do those outside the law know sin? How do they experience or understand their culpability and express their accountability to God? For Paul, the human condition, if we can use such a universalizing phrase, is characterized by "ungodliness" and "wickedness." In their pride, human beings *became* idolatrous "fools," as "they exchanged the glory of the immortal God for images resembling a mortal human being or birds or four-footed animals or reptiles" (Rom 1:23). Notice here, to start, that the language Paul uses implies a previous, untainted state, a posited state that would prove crucial to the development of the doctrine of the fall and original sin. If human beings *became* idolatrous, then this implies a lapse from a prior state, one governed by the "glory of the immortal God," which we, for Paul, exchanged. Paul's language recalls the drama of Genesis, where human beings, male and female, are created in God's image but eventually "fall," to use Christian terminology, via pride to their own, corruptible state (cf. Gen 2–3). But he frames that fall in transactional terms, terms that imply the base exercise of freedom in a seeming religious marketplace.

Paul's understanding of the human condition under sin is negative, to say the least. Having exchanged God's glory for corruptibility and left to their own devices, human beings appear, to put it bluntly, as horrible creatures, completely debased to the core of their being. He writes, for example:

> They were filled with every kind of wickedness, evil, covetousness, malice. Full of envy, murder, strife, deceit, craftiness, they are gossips, slanderers, God-haters, insolent, haughty, boastful,

> inventors of evil, rebellious toward parents, foolish, faithless, heartless, ruthless. They know God's decree, that those who practice such things deserve to die—yet they not only do them but even applaud others who practice them. (Rom 1:29–32)

God may be kind and gracious, but God does not take such things lightly. As Barth put it in his commentary on this passage, "The true nature of our unbroken existence is here unrolled before us. Our ungodliness and unrighteousness stand under the wrath of God. His judgement now becomes judgement and nothing more; and we experience the impossibility of men as the real and final impossibility of God."[9] Indeed, engaging in the acts mentioned in this passage is deserving of nothing less than death, which is what Paul means when he states, using a monetary metaphor, that sin's wages are death (Rom 6:23). We are, then, ultimately responsible for our acts, which qua sinful are offenses to God—we are the ones, for Paul, who exchanged our glory for idolatry. We are subject to death, debtors to death. As I discuss momentarily, Paul frames the identification of sin and our responsibility for it in terms of being subject to law, which also means being subject to debt.

Paul uses the language of monetary exchange, particularly debt and the wage relationship, to adjudicate our accountability before God: "For he will repay according to each one's deeds: to those who by patiently doing good seek for glory and honor and immortality, he will give eternal life; while for those who are self-seeking and who obey not the truth but wickedness, there will be wrath and fury" (Rom 2:6–8). Paul frames responsibility and its consequences, whether positive or negative, in terms of a typical exchange relationship. That is, one is recompensed in accordance with one's deeds, a recompense that functions as judgment, as debt, on said deeds. To those who seek the good, who seek God's glory, honor, and immortality, then one's wages are eternal life. The wicked, however, can expect nothing less than God's wrath, God's punishment—again, the wages of sin are death.

Philosophical interpreters of Paul, such as Alain Badiou and Giorgio Agamben, tend to ignore this side of Paul, as they attempt to recover his thought for the construction of a contemporary, more radical politics. For Badiou, despite his religion, his gospel, Paul remains "a poet-thinker of the event, as well as one who practices and states the invariant traits of what can be called the militant figure. He brings forth the entirely

---

9. Barth, *Epistle to the Romans*, 53–54.

human connection, whose destiny fascinates me, between the general idea of a rupture, an overturning, and that of a thought-practice that is this rupture's subjective materiality."[10] Paul, that is, constructs an "absolutely new" discourse based on the resurrection-event, one that occurs in light of, but establishes itself diagonally to, what Badiou labels Greek and Jewish discourses. Against these figures of what Badiou understands as particularity and mastery, Paul founds a new type of universalism, albeit one that is anti-philosophical in nature, because it reduces all truth to the particularity of the Christ-event. For Agamben, Paul's letters have the "status of the fundamental messianic text for the Western tradition."[11] Although swept under the rug by two thousand years of anti-messianic translation and commentary, Paul's letters in themselves, in defining and working through the aporias of messianic time, remain essential for thinking new forms of community.[12]

I do not want to deny that Paul may, indeed, have something to contribute to present, political concerns. Indeed, elsewhere I have provided readings of Paul along these lines.[13] But it is important to emphasize that his vision of grace, whether read in terms of universalism or messianism, is predicated upon the evaluation of the human condition mentioned above, a fact that often goes ignored among recent, revisionist readings. Contemporary readings of Paul, such as Badiou's and Agamben's, certainly tend to downplay this element in Paul's thought, for the sake of recovering the latter for egalitarian ends. However, although it may seem too banal to mention, it still must be stressed: divine grace, however we interpret it, is only a necessity so long as human beings are judged sinful, not just in their acts but to their core.[14] The problem, ignored by Badiou and Agamben, ultimately lies in wrapping this evaluation of human beings as sinful up in the language of exchange and debt. Such is exactly where law comes in, in that it adds knowledge of sin, as I discuss below.

Nevertheless, to return to Paul, those who follow the law instinctually have it "written on their hearts," but this does not in and of itself entail actual knowledge of sin qua sin. For Paul such knowledge is gained through Christ Jesus who, "apart from law," has disclosed the

---

10. Badiou, *Saint Paul*, 2.
11. Agamben, *Time That Remains*, 1.
12. See also, for instance, Weaver, *Scandal of Community*.
13. See Phelps, *Alain Badiou*, 121–68.
14. Konstan's *Before Forgiveness* remains important in this respect, as he shows that the moral notions that require forgiveness and grace are by no means universal.

"righteousness of God" (Rom 3:21–22). The result of that disclosure is a wholesale leveling of the distinction between those inside and outside the law, between the Jew and the Greek.[15] Paul writes:

> For there is no distinction, since all have sinned and fall short of the glory of God; they are now justified by his grace as a gift, through the redemption that is in Christ Jesus, whom God put forward as a sacrifice of atonement by his blood, effective through faith. He did this to show his righteousness, because in his divine forbearance he had passed over the sins previously committed; it was to prove at the present time that he himself is righteous and that he justifies the one who has faith in Jesus. (Rom 3:22–26)

He emphasizes this lack of distinction in more positive terms in his letter to the Galatians, when speaking of how it is a manifestation of the unity of those "baptized into Christ": "There is no longer Jew or Greek, there is no longer slave or free, there is no longer male and female; for all of you are one in Christ Jesus. And if you belong to Christ, then you are Abraham's offspring, heirs according to the promise" (Gal 3:29–29). Paul, in these passages, provides a rough, though unsystematic, conceptualization of atonement, of the work that Christ's death does on behalf of those who believe. Paul's understanding of atonement, however, is less focused on the individual than the collective, the community that constitutes itself based on faith. Such is the sense of Paul's emphasis on the way that Christ's death and the faithful's baptism into that death break down common distinctions, disrupting the parochial ties that normally bind communities together.

Some recent readers of Paul, such as Badiou, emphasize the importance of Christ's resurrection for Paul over-against Christ's death. Badiou bluntly states that, for Paul, the "event is not death, it is resurrection."[16] That is, for Badiou, suffering plays no salvific role in Paul's theology; his preaching includes "no masochistic propaganda extolling the virtues of suffering, no pathos of the crown of thorns, flagellation, oozing blood, or the gall-soaked sponge."[17] Christ's death, for Badiou's Paul, functions

---

15. Hence, as Taubes argues in *Political Theology of Paul*, 25, Paul's notion of the law should be taken in the broadest sense possible. His "critique of law is a critique of a dialogue that Paul is conducting not only with the Pharisees—that is, himself—but also with his Mediterranean environment."

16. Badiou, *Saint Paul*, 66.

17. Badiou, *Saint Paul*, 68.

merely as a site for the real event's emergence, the resurrection of the crucified. Death plays no role in and of itself and is, thus, absolutely disjunct from resurrection, which signifies life and grace.

The role that death plays for Paul constitutes the disagreement between Badiou and Žižek over what remains significant in Paul's thought, insomuch as Christ's death coincides with the death drive.[18] I return to this reading below, but as much as I agree with Badiou's distaste for the divinization of suffering that has plagued important streams of the Christian theological tradition and in general, this does not obviate the fact that Jesus's death does, in fact, play a more important role for Paul than Badiou allows. Not only is it wholly consistent with Paul's dour estimation of human sinfulness, as discussed above. Jesus's death, as sacrifice, marks a turning point from sin to justification as well. Via his death, we are redeemed; such grace is gift, but it also shows God's righteousness, God's justice. This dual concern remains essential for understanding the human being as indebted and, as we will see in later chapters, forms the crux of atonement theories.

Nevertheless, despite the leveling of distinctions between Jews and gentiles, Paul insists that it does not involve replacing the law or overthrowing it. One is not justified by the law, but this does not mean that the law is invalid or inconsequential, at least for Jews. The law remains the material manifestation of God's particular relationship with Israel, but the law itself does not immediately translate into faith, which is what Paul emphasizes as essential. The law is not necessarily opposed to faith; indeed, it can certainly function as a sphere in which faith operates. But faith cannot be reduced to that specific sphere, as if it could only operate therein. Paul uses the example of Abraham, who was justified in God's eyes by faith, not so-called works.

> What then are we to say was gained by Abraham, our ancestor according to the flesh? For if Abraham was justified by works, he has something to boast about, but not before God. For what does the scripture say? "Abraham believed God, and it was reckoned to him as righteousness." Now to one who works, wages are not reckoned as a gift but as something due. But to one who without works trusts him who justifies the ungodly, such faith is reckoned as righteousness. (Rom 4:2–5)

---

18. Žižek, *Ticklish Subject*, 149–50.

Paul distinguishes between what is due or owed and gift, which is only accessible via a faith that is in excess over the law, or what one does.[19] Abraham, in the passage above, is the prototype here, since he was justified in God's sight apart from the law and, indeed, in excess of his works. As discussed in the last chapter, we find the same idea at work in Jesus's claim that doing one's duty or following through on one's obligation is not enough, in and of itself. What matters, for lack of a better term, is the intention behind it, that which drives action. The latter translates into acting in excess of the law, which can be seen most starkly in Abraham's willingness to sacrifice his son, Isaac, as Kierkegaard and, more recently, Derrida, have emphasized.[20] As Paul argues later on, if we stick at the level of what is owed, at the level of reciprocity, then what is owed is death; for, as he puts it, "the wages of sin is death, but the free gift of God is eternal life in Christ Jesus our Lord" (Rom 6:23).

Paul illustrates this point with respect to circumcision. Abraham does, of course, "receive the sign of circumcision," which marks him as Israel's forbearer and Israel as God's own. But Abraham is counted as righteous prior to circumcision, which for Paul means that circumcision is only a material manifestation of righteousness and not the thing itself. So too with the promises made to Abraham that all nations would be blessed through him; these are given to him prior to circumcision, which means they can be received outside of circumcision as well, that is, outside the specific sphere governed by the law: "For the promise that he would inherit the world did not come to Abraham or to his descendants through the law but through the righteousness of faith. If it is the adherents of the law who are to be the heirs, faith is null and the promise is void. For the law brings wrath; but where there is no law, neither is there violation" (Rom 4:13–15).

Gentiles thus participate in the promises given to Abraham, but they participate in the same way as do Jews: via faith. For Paul, it is Jesus who makes this possible, specifically his death and resurrection. If the "wages of sin is death," as mentioned above, then Jesus gets what is owed to us as debt, in the sense that his death is the result of our trespasses, our sin. As Paul states, "It will be reckoned to us who believe in him who raised Jesus

---

19. The language of gift is, of course, central to Derrida's own reading of Abraham and the "sacrifice" of Isaac in *Gift of Death*, as discussed in the last chapter. For a Derrida-inspired reading of Paul in terms of gift, see Barclay, *Paul and the Gift*.

20. See Derrida, *Gift of Death*, 82–115 and Kierkegaard, *Fear and Trembling*, 54–67.

our Lord from the dead, who was handed over to death for our trespasses and was raised for our justification" (Rom 4:24–25).

Justification transposes enmity toward God into peace with God, hence Paul's famous claim: "Therefore, since we are justified by faith, we have peace with God through our Lord Jesus Christ, through whom we have obtained access to this grace in which we stand; and we boast in our hope of sharing the glory of God" (Rom 5:1–2). He goes on to state:

> For while we were still weak, at the right time Christ died for the ungodly. Indeed, rarely will anyone die for a righteous person—though perhaps for a good person someone might actually dare to die. But God proves his love for us in that while we still were sinners Christ died for us. Much more surely then, now that we have been justified by his blood, will we be saved through him from the wrath of God. For if while we were enemies, we were reconciled to God through the death of his Son, much more surely, having been reconciled, will we be saved by his life. But more than that, we even boast in God through our Lord Jesus Christ, through whom we have now received reconciliation. (Rom 5:6–11).

Statements such as these will go on to play an important role in medieval theories of atonement and their successors, in that Paul implies that reconciliation with God occurs from on high, so to speak. That is, God certainly loves us, hence "while we were still sinners Jesus died for us." But reconciliation is not just about us and our condition before God but also God's relationship to us and our condition. We do not, in other words, exist in a sinful state before a passive, unaffected God; our state and the actions which flow from it, our sins, always occur in relation to God, who is the dominant party. We must be reconciled to God, but God must also be reconciled to us. It is hard to interpret the notions of the "wrath of God" and the fact that we are "God's enemies" in any other way unless we twist Paul's claims beyond recognition. If we are God's enemies, subject to wrath, then it is a change in God that needs to occur, in addition to the change required in us. Another way to put the matter, in line with the language of debt, is to say that it is only the lender who has the power to cancel debt, which means that a change must occur in the lender with respect to the debtor. As we saw in the last chapter, the change that must occur in the lender is one of the senses of the parable of the unforgiving debtor, in which the king, who stands in for God, moves from a retributive posture to one of pity, thereby forgiving the debt of his slave. Nevertheless, the use of the passive voice in the aforementioned quotation reinforces the notion here: we *have received* reconciliation. We are only recipients, meaning that any sort of forgiveness lies squarely in the hands of God.

The theological basis for the necessity of forgiveness via atonement ultimately rests here. We are, as I have emphasized, subject to sin, which includes acting on all the base desires mentioned above, desires to which God has given us up. Such sinfulness, however, does not emerge out of nowhere, by fiat, which also means it is not a natural condition, strictly speaking. Sin, which chains or indebts us to death, is the ultimate result of one man, Adam, whose transgression makes not only him but subsequent generations guilty before God. Adam's sin, that is, subjects us not just to sin, irrespective of any immediate cause on our part, but also to the law. The two go hand in hand, even if they remain disjunct diachronically in Paul's reading of history.

> Therefore, just as sin came into the world through one man, and death came through sin, and so death spread to all because all have sinned—sin was indeed in the world before the law, but sin is not reckoned when there is no law. Yet death exercised dominion from Adam to Moses, even over those whose sins were not like the transgression of Adam, who is a type of the one who was to come. (Rom 5:12–14)

Through Adam, sin entered the world, subjecting us to death, but it is only at the institution of the law proper, signified in the person of Moses, that sin can be understood as sin. The law retroactively assigns sin on the basis of itself, which, as I discuss shortly, also means that the law posits its own transgression.

Paul juxtaposes the entrance of death into the world to the grace of God's justification. The latter takes the same structure of the former, but it does so via reversal or recapitulation, to use the language of Irenaeus.[21] For, whereas death enters the world through the actions of one man, Adam, the actions of one man, Jesus Christ, transpose death into eternal life. Adam condemns us, while Christ justifies us. Paul writes:

---

21. Irenaeus, *Against Heresies*. Irenaeus uses the language of recapitulation throughout *Against Heresies*, but the notion is perhaps most simply expressed in *Against Heresies* 3:21.9–10: "And he recapitulated in himself the work originally fashioned, because, just as through the disobedience of one man sin came in, and through sin death prevailed (Rom 5:12, 19), so also through obedience of one man justice was brought in and produced the fruit of life for men formerly dead."

> But the free gift is not like the trespass. For if the many died through the one man's trespass, much more surely have the grace of God and the free gift in the grace of the one man, Jesus Christ, abounded for the many. And the free gift is not like the effect of the one man's sin. For the judgment following one trespass brought condemnation, but the free gift following many trespasses brings justification. If, because of the one man's trespass, death exercised dominion through that one, much more surely will those who receive the abundance of grace and the free gift of righteousness exercise dominion in life through the one man, Jesus Christ. Therefore just as one man's trespass led to condemnation for all, so one man's act of righteousness leads to justification and life for all. For just as by the one man's disobedience the many were made sinners, so by the one man's obedience the many will be made righteous. But law came in, with the result that the trespass multiplied; but where sin increased, grace abounded all the more, so that, just as sin exercised dominion in death, so grace might also exercise dominion through justification leading to eternal life through Jesus Christ our Lord. (Rom 5:15–21)

Christ's death thus reverses and undoes the postlapsarian condition, shifting us away from death and toward life via his unity with us in his death. If Christ's death mirrors our own, then the same can be said concerning Christ's resurrection: it signals what we, too, can expect.

> For if we have been united with him in a death like his, we will certainly be united with him in a resurrection like his. We know that our old self was crucified with him so that the body of sin might be destroyed, and we might no longer be enslaved to sin. For whoever has died is freed from sin. But if we have died with Christ, we believe that we will also live with him. We know that Christ, being raised from the dead, will never die again; death no longer has dominion over him. The death he died, he died to sin, once for all; but the life he lives, he lives to God. So you also must consider yourselves dead to sin and alive to God in Christ Jesus. (Rom 6:5–11)

All of this does not, however, mean that we can sin without impunity. Christ's death certainly transposes his and our death into life, and the transposition takes the form of gift or grace. Nevertheless, faith is required on our part, and to continue to sin amounts to rejection. Ultimately, for Paul, it is a question of serving two masters—not God and mammon but, rather, sin and righteousness. Hence the metaphor of slavery that runs throughout Paul's claims here.

> When you were slaves of sin, you were free in regard to righteousness. So what advantage did you then get from the things of which you now are ashamed? The end of those things is death. But now that you have been freed from sin and enslaved to God, the advantage you get is sanctification. The end is eternal life. For the wages of sin is death, but the free gift of God is eternal life in Christ Jesus our Lord. (Rom 6:20–22)

If, however, sin is only known through the law, then the same can be said for grace via faith: in the end, the law enables knowledge of both. The law is the mediating factor in the relationship between the two.

THE CONFLICTED SUBJECT

What, then, is the experience of the subject under the *knowledge* of the law? For Paul the experience is characterized as fundamentally conflictual, which we cannot resolve on our own. On the one hand, the law provides guidance in the form of commandments, so we know, intellectually speaking, what is required of us, in terms of both positive and negative acts. On the other hand, such knowledge in and of itself is not enough for us to act in accordance with the law. Sin uses the law as an opportunity for transgression, which is not something we necessarily assent to but, rather, are driven toward. Paul portrays the battle, here, as one between flesh and spirit, which can only be remedied through Jesus Christ.

> For we know that the law is spiritual; but I am of the flesh, sold into slavery under sin. I do not understand my own actions. For I do not do what I want, but I do the very thing I hate. Now if I do what I do not want, I agree that the law is good. But in fact it is no longer I that do it, but sin that dwells within me. For I know that nothing good dwells within me, that is, in my flesh. I can will what is right, but I cannot do it. For I do not do the good I want, but the evil I do not want is what I do. Now if I do what I do not want, it is no longer I that do it, but sin that dwells within me. So I find it to be a law that when I want to do what is good, evil lies close at hand. For I delight in the law of God in my inmost self, but I see in my members another law at war with the law of my mind, making me captive to the law of sin that dwells in my members. Wretched man that I am! Who will rescue me

from this body of death? Thanks be to God through Jesus Christ our Lord! (Rom 7:15–25)

This passage from Romans has generated a good deal of psychoanalytically informed commentary, of which Žižek's is perhaps the most well-known, contemporary example. Žižek's interpretation of the passage also constitutes the basis of his disagreement with Badiou's interpretation of Paul, as mentioned above. For Žižek, the law "divides the subject and introduces a morbid confusion between life and death: the subject is divided between (conscious) obedience to the Law and (unconscious) desire for its transgression generated by the legal prohibition itself."[22] The confusion of the divided subject *is* the death drive or, to use theological language, sin. Thus, for Žižek, the fundamental problem Paul confronts is how the subject can break out of this seemingly endless cycle of law and transgressive desire, which generates guilt.[23]

Nevertheless, I also want to draw attention to Elettra Stimilli's interpretation of the passage, as she grounds the experience of the subject in terms of indebtedness at both ends of the spectrum.[24] Stimilli argues that what distinguishes human beings qua human beings lies in this specific relationship to the law. Unlike other beings, whose actions coincide with their being, human freedom is found in the possibility of transgression, in the freedom *not* to do what one is commanded. That is, for human beings, following the law is not natural but, rather, intentional, related to an act of will, meaning that human beings constitute themselves as subjects in the gap or disjunction between being and doing. Being and doing do not and cannot immediately coincide, otherwise there would be no space for freedom, no place for human beings to be human. Human freedom thus shows itself at the most basic level, not in doing per se but in the capability of not doing, in the possibility to not act in accordance with the law. Human freedom is thus shot through with negativity or lack.

For Stimilli this is how we should read Adam's disobedience, whose refusal to follow the divine command, according to Christianity, precipitates humanity's enslavement to sin. Paul, however, makes this sense of freedom before the law more acute, since for him one would not even know transgression except via the law. The possibility of not following the law, that is, is contingent on the law itself, the institution of which

---

22. Žižek, *Ticklish Subject*, 149.
23. Žižek, *Ticklish Subject*, 149. See also Žižek, *Fragile Absolute*, 113, 143.
24. Stimilli, *Debt of the Living*, 49–82.

creates its own transgression. As Paul puts it, "If it had not been for the law, I would not have known sin" (Rom 7:7). Paul's claim, here, should not be read as a simple identification of sin with the law: the two are not convertible to each other, which Paul emphasizes in his claim that the law is "by no means" sin (Rom 7:7). The law, rather, exposes sin, brings it out into the open. Sin, as a contingent human condition, produces sinful action, but the sinfulness of the action only becomes apparent in the law, in the commandment which, once in place, multiplies sin via its own exposition. The relationship between the two is thus "more complex," as Stimilli emphasizes, which Paul expresses in his own way using the example of covetousness: "I would not have known what it is to covet if the law had not said, 'You shall not covet.' But sin, seizing an opportunity in the commandment, produced in me all kinds of covetousness. Apart from the law sin lies dead. I was once alive apart from the law, but when the commandment came, sin revived and I died, and the very commandment that promised life proved to be death to me. For sin, seizing an opportunity in the commandment, deceived me and through it killed me" (Rom 7:7–11).

For Stimilli what is at issue in such a claim is the possibility of not following the law, a possibility attendant on the law as convention rather than nature. The institution of the law, then, creates the space for its own violation, since it necessarily entails freedom, understood as the gap between being and doing, as mentioned above. Because one cannot follow the law, following the law is also not sufficient in and of itself. As Stimilli puts it, "According to Paul, the *possibility of not* executing a given order that is inherent to human action and constantly exposes one to punishment and condemnation is at one with the impossibility of immediately translating commandments into 'works.' This condition lies at the very origin of the nature of action where the latter cannot find its accomplishment in the form of 'works.'"[25] Otherwise put, the inherent possibility of not following the law is, in the end, freedom from the law, which means that what is at issue for the subject cannot be found in the law but in the self. The self, in its freedom, is subject to itself rather than the law. However, because as Paul says the law is "holy," the same freedom should also coincide with the law, not out of any necessity but, rather, of its own

---

25. Stimilli, *Debt of the Living*, 57; emphasis in original.

accord. Stimilli writes, "The experience of freedom from the law coincides here with a form of total loyalty to the law on the part of everyone's life."[26]

Such an "economic" experience of the relationship between law and life coincides for Paul with grace. As Stimilli suggests, grace should not be understood in opposition to the law but rather in terms of its excess. Grace does not cancel the law but, rather, transposes it into life, meaning that it closes the gap between being and doing. Grace, writes Stimilli, "suspends all judgment and works pertaining to it; its suspension knows no appeal; it is the realization of a justice adequate to the law of faith and exceeds all works and obligations that link them to the precept."[27] Nevertheless, it is in this excess of faith over the law that life takes the form of debt. Under grace, life finds its fulfillment not in something other but, rather, in itself, which means that life takes the form of an investment in oneself. However, because life cannot find fulfillment in law, such investment can never be fulfilled. Stimilli thus notes, "The gift of grace outstrips all due service and, in faith, identifies a productive kind of administration of life that deactivates all extrinsic obligations and thus all effective chances of compensation." Simply put, "The price paid by Christ turns the guilt and sin identified by the law into a debt that, as such, cannot be repaid."[28]

The subject, then, is spread out between two poles, both of which force the subject into a state of indebtedness. Paul speaks of the subject in terms of an inner conflict, of knowing the good but not doing it because of the indwelling of sin. He speaks of this conflict as occurring at the level of, or in, the flesh.

> For those who live according to the flesh set their minds on the things of the flesh, those who live according to the Spirit set their minds on the things of the Spirit. To set the mind on the flesh is death, but to set the mind on the Spirit is life and peace. For this reason the mind that is set on the flesh is hostile to God; it does not submit to God's law—indeed it cannot, and those who are in the flesh cannot please God. (Rom 8:5–8)

Flesh, then, stands in for hostility and lack of submission—for indebtedness to death—none of which can and does please God.

---

26. Stimilli, *Debt and Guilt*, 113.
27. Stimilli, *Debt of the Living*, 57.
28. Stimilli, *Debt of the Living*, 58.

Paul opposes the flesh, in turn, to Spirit, which is not, however, conflictual in itself like flesh but, rather, the source of freedom, the source of life. Spirit, then, is not one more conflict but, rather, ostensibly the end of conflict itself, the cessation of the internal struggle to do the good. Spirit frees individuals from the condemnation of sin and death. Paul writes, "There is therefore now no condemnation for those who are in Christ Jesus. For the law of the Spirit of life in Christ Jesus has set you free from the law of sin and of death" (Rom 8:1–2). The law, Paul maintains, could not do this on its own, since it had been "weakened by the flesh." Hence the need for God to send God's son who, taking sin on its own terms, dealing with it as one of us in the flesh, condemns "sin in the flesh." Christ, here, does not annul the law but, rather, fulfills it, so that "the just requirement of the law might be fulfilled in us, who walk not according to the flesh but according to the Spirit" (Rom 8:4). The transposition from death to life via Christ thereby erases the hostility we have on the side of flesh to God.

There is no in-between point here for Paul, no lukewarmness, to use a phrase from the book of Revelation (cf. Rev 3:16). The relationship between flesh and Spirit is disjunct, meaning that one can fall on one side or the other but not occupy a position in both camps simultaneously. As mentioned above, whereas Jesus distinguishes between God and mammon, Paul displaces this disjunction, putting it on the more abstract disjunction between flesh and Spirit. In doing so, however, indebtedness takes on a more general, non-economic, purview as it becomes associated with terms with a broader scope, ones that catch the whole of life. He writes,

> But you are not in the flesh; you are in the Spirit, since the Spirit of God dwells in you. Anyone who does not have the Spirit of Christ does not belong to him. But if Christ is in you, though the body is dead because of sin, the Spirit is life because of righteousness. If the Spirit of him who raised Jesus from the dead dwells in you, he who raised Christ from the dead will give life to your mortal bodies also through his Spirit that dwells in you. (Rom 8:9–11)

As this passage makes clear, the disjunction takes the form of a supplement, given the nature of the claim. That is, Spirit displaces flesh in our bodies, so that our mortal bodies may no longer be condemned to death but saved, to life.

Another way to put the matter, as Paul does, is to say that the flesh is the site of one form of indebtedness. Living according to the flesh is to live as a debtor, as subject not only to the flesh but, also, to death itself. Death, here, functions as the flesh's creditor, extracting the ultimate payment, which, as said above, Paul elsewhere conceives of as wages. Spirit, however, ostensibly erases this debt to the flesh, to death.

> So then, brothers and sisters, we are debtors, not to the flesh, to live according to the flesh—for if you live according to the flesh, you will die; but if by the Spirit you put to death the deeds of the body, you will live. For all who are led by the Spirit of God are children of God. For you did not receive a spirit of slavery to fall back into fear, but you have received a spirit of adoption. When we cry, "Abba Father!" it is that very Spirit bearing witness with our spirit that we are children of God, and if children, then heirs, heirs of God and joint heirs with Christ—if, in fact, we suffer with him so that we may also be glorified with him. (Rom 9:12–19)

As we can see here, however, debt is not really erased but, rather, transposed onto a different plane. We may no longer be debtors to death but, rather, debtors to Spirit. One debt becomes another, although it is ostensibly put in more positive terms. It is characterized by a "spirit of adoption," we are "children of God," "heirs" and "joint heirs with Christ." We will see this double-indebtedness return with Anselm's theory of atonement, discussed in chapter 5.

This is where Badiou is wrong that "becoming-son," as he puts it, entails the end of mastery, of any form of slavery. For Badiou, both Jewish and Greek discourses constitute figures of mastery, or slavery. They are, in the end, "discourses of the Father."[29] The event of Christ's resurrection breaks open this figure of mastery, establishing a new discourse diagonal to the old. The new, Christian discourse, he argues, puts an end to mastery. Badiou writes, "The sending (birth) of the son names this rupture. That it is the son, not the father, who is exemplary, enjoins us not to put our trust any longer in any discourse laying claim to the form of mastery."[30]

Yes, Paul here does contrast debt, or a "spirit of slavery," with life in the spirit as God's progeny.[31] But elsewhere Paul clearly conceptualizes

---

29. Badiou, *Saint Paul*, 42.

30. Badiou, *Saint Paul*, 43.

31. Although I do not quote him directly in this section, the following discussion is clearly indebted to Agamben's *Time That Remains*, 19–43, particularly on questions of slavery.

righteousness in terms of another type of slavery, one that contrasts with slavery to sin but is a type of slavery no less.

> What then? Should we sin because we are not under law but under grace? By no means! Do you not know that if you present yourselves to anyone as obedient slaves, you are slaves of the one whom you obey, either of sin, which leads to death, or of obedience, which leads to righteousness? But thanks be to God that you, having once been slaves of sin, have become obedient from the heart to the form of teaching to which you were entrusted, and that you, having been set free from sin, have become slaves of righteousness. I am speaking in human terms because of your natural limitations. For just as you once presented your members as slaves to impurity and to greater and greater iniquity, so now present your members as slaves to righteousness for sanctification. (Rom 6:14–18)

The notion of slavery is not in question here, but merely to whom or what one is enslaved. One can, on the side of the flesh, be enslaved to sin, but freedom from sin entails becoming "slaves to righteousness." Paul, of course, does concede that he is speaking in "human terms," so we should not, perhaps, overstate the matter based only on his rhetoric. The problem, though, is that he has numerous other terms available to him, terms that do not involve the transference of slavery from one plane to another. Indeed, he already uses the language of "adoption" and "sonship" elsewhere, as mentioned above, which would putatively be free of any compulsion to slavery, even if the terms still entail hierarchy.

Paul conceives of both ends of the spectrum, here, in terms of enslavement. It is not a question of being enslaved to God or to sin but, more precisely, having a split allegiance: the subject is spread out between spirt or mind and flesh. Paul writes, "So then, with my mind I am a slave to the law of God, but with my flesh I am a slave to the law of sin" (Rom 7:25). I said previously that Paul's discussion of sin has structural similarities to the disjunction Jesus uses between God and mammon. By dividing the subject from within, Paul complicates any sort of one-way allegiance: absent Christ, one is always committed to both simultaneously, which also means that one is never entirely committed to either. The language of commitment, here, may seem inappropriate, as it implies moral decision, but for Paul, we are driven in this direction from within, which Žižek reads in terms of the death drive, as mentioned above. Although Paul complicates the disjunction, he also, however, empties it of its specific, economic content. What is in view in Paul's thought is not the materiality of social-economic relationships but, rather, a more abstract, ontological struggle between sin or flesh and spirit.

Later on in Romans Paul does discuss the importance of love as the principle of relationality, and conceives of it in terms of a lack of indebtedness. He writes:

> Owe no one anything, except to love one another; for the one who loves another has fulfilled the law. The commandments, "You shall not commit adultery; You shall not murder; You shall not steal; You shall not covet"; and any other commandment, are summed up in this word, "Love your neighbor as yourself." Love does no wrong to a neighbor; therefore, love is the fulfilling of the law. (Rom 13:8–10)

Love, in this sense, fulfills the law and replaces debt; or, better put, love becomes debt, that which one owes to every other. Such is, I take it, consistent with Stimilli's observations concerning the functioning of grace as indebtedness.

Nevertheless, we should not ignore Paul's letter to Philemon when discussing the demands of love, in which the demands of love and slavery initially clash but ultimately coincide as related concepts. While imprisoned, Paul has become a "father" to a man named Onesimus, whom Paul considers his "own heart" and "useful" for his work in advancing his gospel. The problem is that it seems Onesimus belongs to Philemon, a Christian, and so Paul feels obligated to send him back to his owner. Paul appeals to Philemon's sense of charity, urging him to treat Onesimus, who had converted to Christianity while with Paul, as he would any other brother.

> I wanted to keep him with me, so that he might be of service to me in your place during my imprisonment for the gospel; but I preferred to do nothing without your consent, in order that your good deed might be voluntary and not something forced. Perhaps this is the reason he was separated from you for a while, so that you might have him back forever, no longer as a slave but more than a slave, a beloved brother—especially to me but how much more to you, both in the flesh and in the Lord. (Phlm 13–16)

Paul even goes on to leverage the language of debt and indebtedness to make his plea: "So if you consider me your partner, welcome him as you would welcome me. If he has wronged you in any way, or owes you anything, charge that to my account. I, Paul, am writing this with my own hand: I will repay it. I say nothing about your owing me even your own self" (Phlm 17–19). Paul writes that he will pay back anything that Onesimus may owe Philemon, in effect taking on Onesimus's debts and obligations as his own. Yet he does so by appealing, under the guise of not appealing, to what Philemon owes Paul, which is his very "own self." As Thomas R. Blanton IV has argued, Paul's appeal to Philemon in this respect is a common rhetorical strategy used by Paul, through which he inverts the "normal patron-client relationship." Blanton writes, "Paul effectively subordinates as clients even moderately wealthy individuals such as Philemon, who is construed as bound to the apostle by an un-repayable debt. . . . Paul's deployment of the language of authority reflects his superior position in a hierarchical relation with Philemon. . . . By characterizing his appeal as a request based on 'love,' Paul provides the means for Philemon to avoid the humiliation of being publicly commanded to do his duty."[32]

But at no point does he challenge Philemon's authority over Onesimus, that is, the figure of mastery involved. Paul's unwillingness to do so is consistent with other statements he makes in this respect. Paul does, of course, famously claim in Galatians, "As many of you as were baptized into Christ have clothed yourselves with Christ. There is no longer Jew or Greek, there is no longer slave or free, there is no longer male and female; for all of you are one in Christ Jesus" (Gal 3:27–28). But the seeming radicality of such statements is severely tempered by other, less conciliatory claims made in the letters attributed to him. For instance, in Titus, a letter whose moralism runs deep, Paul—or someone claiming to be Paul—demands the obedience of slaves. He writes, "Tell slaves to be submissive to their masters and to give satisfaction in every respect; they are not to talk back, not to pilfer, but to show complete and perfect fidelity, so that in everything they may be an ornament to the doctrine of God our Savior" (Titus 2:9–10). Submissiveness in the context of slavery is not just a duty but, rather, a witness to God. The same sentiment is expressed in Ephesians, which is Pauline in sentiment and received as such, even if the letter itself cannot be directly attributed to Paul:

> Slaves, obey your earthly masters with fear and trembling, in singleness of heart, as you obey Christ; not only while being watched, and in order to please them, but as slaves of Christ,

---

32. Blanton, *Spiritual Economy*, 36–37.

doing the will of God from the heart. Render service with enthusiasm, as to the Lord and not to men and women, knowing that whatever good we do, we will receive the same again from the Lord, whether we are slaves or free. (Eph 6:5–8)

Indeed, Paul expresses a great deal of ambivalence regarding one's material status, which is evident in the following passage.

> However that may be, let each of you lead the life that the Lord has assigned, to which God called you. This is my rule in all the churches. Was anyone at the time of his call already circumcised? Let him not seek to remove the marks of circumcision. Was anyone at the time of his call uncircumcised? Let him not seek circumcision. Circumcision is nothing, and uncircumcision is nothing; but obeying the commandments of God is everything. Let each of you remain in the condition in which you were called. Were you a slave when called? Do not be concerned about it. Even if you can gain your freedom, make use of your present condition now more than ever. For whoever was called in the Lord as a slave is a freed person belonging to the Lord, just as whoever was free when called is a slave of Christ. You were bought with a price; do not become slaves of human masters. In whatever condition you were called, brothers and sisters, there remain with God. . . . I mean, brothers and sisters, the appointed time has grown short; from now on, let even those who have wives be as though they had none, and those who mourn as though they were not mourning, and those who rejoice as though they were not rejoicing, and those who buy as though they had no possessions, and those who deal with the world as though they had no dealings with it. For the present form of this world is passing away. (1 Cor 7:17–24, 29–31)

Agamben reads this passage in messianic terms. Paul's use of *hos me* or "as not," which Agamben takes as a technical term in the Pauline lexicon, indicates the meaning of messianic life as *klesis*, that is, calling or vocation. For Agamben *klesis* is not the messianic repetition of factical conditions or a calling to something more authentic or higher. *Klesis*, under the pressure of the *hos me*, is rather the "revocation of every vocation," in the sense that "it revokes the factical condition and undermines it from within without altering its form."[33] Such is the sense of Paul's "weeping as not weeping," "rejoicing as not rejoicing," "buying as not possessing," "using the world as not using it up" (1 Cor 7:29–31). So understood the

---

33. Agamben, *Time That Remains*, 23, 24.

messianic *hos me* coincides with profanation.³⁴ Like the act of profanation with respect to the sacred, messianic *klesis* does not destroy factical conditions but reworks them from within through their neglect, which renders them inoperative. In Agamben's reading of Paul, the *hos me* indicates the "generic potentiality" that *klesis* pries open and it itself is, a potentiality that, again like profanation with respect to the sacred, allows factical conditions to be put to a new use, a use subtracted from proper ends. Agamben, however, largely ignores the other passages mentioned above regarding slavery, which limits the extent of his positive messianism in material terms. Agamben, that is, falls prey to the same abstractions as does Paul, which leads him to pass over the materiality of factical conditions.

CONCLUSION

Paul is, of course, a product of his time. Judging him by contemporary standards engages in anachronism and may, even, fail to show charity to other, more palatable aspects of his thought. Nevertheless, my claim is that such statements go to the core of what Paul says about indebtedness and redemption, meaning that we cannot dismiss less palatable claims so easily without also obviating the core of his thinking. His thinking remains shot through with the notion of indebtedness, which is both a condition of the flesh and a condition of the Spirt, though the latter occurs on the side of love. Love thus takes the form of indebtedness, but, if we take Paul's discussions of and use of slavery seriously, also fails to fully empty indebtedness on the side of the flesh.

My point, here, is not to challenge Paul's basic existential assumptions concerning the subject as conflicted and the presence of death but, rather, the framework in which these are set. That framework, I argued above, envisions life in terms of indebtedness. Indebtedness itself, however, is not imposed from without but, rather, constituted from within and generalized as a basic, human malady, common to all. Following Stimilli, we can say that Paul conceives of life in economic terms, at both ends of the spectrum. But he transposes the specific, economic sense of indebtedness into a more abstract, ontological condition. The division that we find in the Gospels between the indebted and the holder of the debt, which corresponds to the division between God and mammon, is a properly economic distinction that the substitution of flesh and spirit dissolves, which applies to everyone.

34. Agamben, *Profanations*, 73–92.

4

Atonement and the Lord's Prayer in Early Christianity

IN THE LAST CHAPTER, I focused on Paul and the way in which debt is intertwined with death, sin, and the flesh. We can certainly find similar entanglements in the Gospels, as I discussed, but in them we still see a concern with the material, economic condition of indebtedness. Paul, however, elides this concern with material indebtedness, setting indebtedness within the continuum between flesh and spirit. Another way to put the matter is to say that indebtedness, for Paul, is an internal and vertical matter, shorn of any external constraint. Even if one resolves this situation via grace, grace still entails a certain form of indebtedness, albeit one with seemingly more positive connotations.

Christianity prides itself on being a religion of forgiveness, of ourselves and others. But before there is forgiveness, Christianity is first and foremost a religion of atonement, which is also to say that it is a religion of debt. We see this inchoately in Paul's thought, as I also discussed. Nevertheless, and speaking generally from the vantage point of later Christian thought, forgiveness certainly plays a prominent role in Christianity, but forgiveness assumes atonement; without the latter, the former remains empty and impossible, at least in any substantial sense.

The centrality of Jesus Christ for Christianity rests as well on atonement, not forgiveness. If all that Christianity offers is forgiveness—God's forgiveness of us and, by extension, our forgiveness of others and ourselves—then Jesus is, ultimately, inessential, and insignificant in the long run. Jesus could, in such a schema, function perhaps as a moral exemplar, a model that we could, even should, follow. Such is the common reading of Peter Abelard's so-called moral-influence theory of atonement, for instance, although it is important to emphasize that even he does not do away with the necessity of atonement.[1] But nothing about such a schema requires Jesus as such, his specific individuality. What Jesus teaches us, morally speaking, is not necessarily unique, and could be found in numerous other places, whether contemporary with him, us, or some other time. It is not entirely clear why, in such a schema, we would need forgiveness to act morally, in line with what Jesus said and did. But, even if we did need forgiveness, God could always extend it to us outside a grand, historical plan, outside of so-called salvation history. That is, if it is simply forgiveness that is on offer, it could be had in numerous other ways, ways that do not require Jesus or any comparable figure.

Christianity, of course, teaches otherwise. Although many threads run throughout the various theological traditions that make up what we refer to as Christianity, they all tend to agree that more than forgiveness is required. The problem does not lie primarily in the reformation of our actions, although repentance certainly requires as much. The problem is, rather, that the condition in which we find ourselves needs to be changed first before any real change in our actions can take place. That is to say, the problem with human beings in Christianity is ontological before it is ethical: we need to be reconciled at the level of our *being* first. All else follows from this fundamental claim. Again, we saw this inchoately in Paul, where our collective baptism into Christ breaks down worldly barriers, disrupting the parochial ties that normally bind communities together. Similar lines of thought will be seen in this chapter, as we discuss the basic outlines of early understandings of atonement.

Hence the necessity of Jesus Christ and his atonement. Jesus does not merely offer forgiveness but, rather, makes it possible, insomuch as his death and resurrection enable and instantiate an ontological shift. Christ is not simply a guide or moral teacher but, rather, does something that provokes a substantial change: in God, in ourselves, in the interrelationship between the two, and in our relationship with others. Precisely how that change occurs and what it involves, including how it envisions human *being*, varies among theological traditions, sometimes considerably, and I will not attempt to parse out all the nuances among competing

---

1. Kotsko, *Politics of Redemption*, 150–70.

claims here. But, among theories that can claim some orthodox pedigree, all are essentially in agreement that something material happens in and through Jesus Christ. He is not epiphenomenal but the thing itself, essential to the theological edifice Christianity constructs.

I bring this up not for apologetic reasons but the opposite: any theological critique, including those that fall under the purview of political and economic theologies, must ultimately wrestle with the question of atonement, specifically what it implies and entails for human being and being as such. I focus on atonement, then, to criticize it and the debtor relationship that, I show, it unavoidably entails. The first section of this chapter focuses on the relationship between atonement and debt in some prominent early theologians, particularly Tertullian, Origen, Augustine, and Gregory of Nyssa. Although these authors make liberal uses of the language of debt in a variety of (not all together consistent) contexts, they ultimately mark indebtedness as a general, ontological feature of the human condition rather than a specific, deleterious economic condition.

ATONEMENT AND DEBT IN TERTULLIAN, ORIGEN, AUGUSTINE, AND GREGORY OF NYSSA

When considering atonement, it is not so much a question of which theory is "right." It should go without saying that even if one believes in atonement, no theory could ever be proven, whatever that might mean for a theological claim; nor could it be exhaustive, given the variety of and among source materials. Rather, what is important here is what a theory of atonement assumes and does, and what it implies about God, the human condition, and the need for salvation from within the scheme. As Gustav Aulen puts it, "The subject of Atonement is absolutely central in Christian theology; and it is directly related to [the subject of] the nature of God. Each and every interpretation of the Atonement is most closely connected with some conception of the essential meaning of Christianity, and it reflects some conception of the Divine nature."[2]

Aulen famously categorized atonement along three narrative lines: objective, subjective, and dramatic, which latter he also names the Christus Victor model. Although Aulen certainly irons over the particularities of individual authors, for analytic purposes, his classification schema remains helpful for marking the basic differences among how Christians

---

2. Aulen, *Christus Victor*, 241.

have thought of Christ's salvific work over time and continue to do so in the present. Aulen associates the objective view of atonement primarily with Anselm's satisfaction theory of atonement, as he articulates it in *Cur Deus Homo?* I devote the next chapter to a close reading of Anselm's satisfaction theory since, on my account, it is crucial for the creation of modern indebted subjectivities. But put briefly, the satisfaction theory has God as its object, rather than humanity. Humanity is, of course, mired in sin and guilt, in need of deliverance. But what needs to be reconciled is not, primarily, humanity to God but God to humanity. As Aulen puts it, in the satisfaction theory, "God is the object of Christ's atoning work, and is reconciled through the satisfaction made to His judgment."[3] The subjective view, in contrast, is usually associated with Abelard and the so-called moral influence theory. As Adam Kotsko notes, Abelard does not so much reject the satisfaction theory as supplement it with "the motive of love."[4] Nevertheless, in Aulen's classification, for Abelard atonement works on the side of humanity, via a fundamental change of orientation in ourselves and in relation to others. It is in this sense that Aulen labels it as subjective because atonement takes place on the side of human beings rather than God as such.

Aulen lumps subsequent theories of atonement under these two headings. The two lines, objective and subjective, run throughout preceding and proceeding theological traditions, with few exceptions. Although, as stated above, lumping atonement theories under such sweeping categories runs the risk of ignoring the particularities involved, it marks generally the two main lines or options, at least as Aulen sees them. Atonement either occurs on the side of God or on the side of humanity; it is either subjective or objective. One could, of course, argue that it is some mix between the two, that atonement is relational rather than concentrated in one side or the other.[5] But doing so still assumes the fundamental actors in play, that is, God and humanity, meaning that more relational theories still retain objective and subjective elements.

Aulen, as is well known, favors a different model, one that, on his reading, the two categorical options elide. Neither subjective nor objective, in the sense in which he uses those terms, the model is "dramatic," which means that it takes the form of narrative, rather than theological or philosophical argumentation. Of this view, which he also labels "classic,"

---

3. Aulen, *Christus Victor*, 95.
4. Kotsko, *Politics of Redemption*, 158.
5. Cf. Sölle, *Christ the Representative*.

he writes, "Its central theme is the idea of the Atonement as a Divine conflict and victory; Christ—Christus Victor—fights against and triumphs over the evil powers of the world, the 'tyrants' under which mankind is in bondage and suffering, and in Him God reconciles the world to Himself."[6] The dramatic, or Christus Victor, view assumes a certain dualism as prerequisite for atonement, in that it portrays the cosmos and the human condition as caught in a struggle between good and the forces of evil. The latter gets personified in the figure of the devil, but the apocalypticism that frames its plot clearly has in mind earthly, sociopolitical evil as well or, more generally, anything perceived as hostile to God's will.[7] Aulen stresses that the model is not simply focused on salvation but, in addition, reconciliation. He writes:

> This constitutes Atonement, because the drama is a cosmic drama, and the victory over the hostile powers brings to pass a new relation, a relation of reconciliation, between God and the world; and, still more, because in a measure the hostile powers are regarded as in the service of the Will of God the Judge of all, and the executants of His judgement. Seen from this side, the triumph over the opposing powers is regarded as a reconciling of God Himself; He is reconciled by the very act in which He reconciles the world to Himself.[8]

Although the model portrays salvation as occurring via a triumph of good over the forces of evil, Aulen makes it clear that the forces of evil do, "in a measure," obtain their legitimacy from God, which obviates a hard, metaphysical dualism between the two. Otherwise put, although evil rules the world, God provides the space for that rule, meaning that God, from beginning to end, remains omnipotent. Aulen cements this point, noting that the dramatic theory of atonement "represents the work of Atonement or reconciliation as from first to last a work of God Himself, a continuous Divine work."[9] This is in contrast, Aulen argues, to the objective view, which he labels as "discontinuous," since it occurs as an offering *to* God on humanity's behalf. But it is also in contrast to the subjective view, which views the change wrought by atonement as moral change, occurring at the level of the individual. The dramatic view "describes a complete change in the situation, a change in the relation between God

---

6. Aulen, *Christus Victor*, 199.
7. See Kotsko, "Persistence of the Ransom Theory of Atonement," 277–94.
8. Aulen, *Christus Victor*, 132.
9. Aulen, *Christus Victor*, 144.

and the world, and a change also in God's own attitude."[10] Christus Victor, then, is the "drama of a world's salvation."[11]

Adam Kotsko provides a helpful gloss on the differences among objective, subjective, and dramatic models, which latter he refers to as ransom theories, the sense of which I discuss below. He notes that "objective" views of atonement are, essentially, "religious" views, in that they emphasize, in one way or another, divine retribution. "Subjective" views, in contrast, understand atonement in moral terms, as they dictate one's individual actions toward others via love. Both, however, share an emphasis on the importance of "individual transformation," as opposed to Paul's more collective vision. The ransom theory, however, falls outside or between the dichotomy. Rather than being "objective" or "subjective," the ransom theory is "intersubjective and social." The ransom theory is, in this sense, intentionally and irretrievably political, in the sense that it focuses on "the structures of power and legitimacy within which humanity lives."[12] Kotsko argues that the ransom theory has functioned as normative for all subsequent accounts of redemption, which is why I focus on it so heavily in what follows. Such is the case not only with articulations of redemption that draw on and extend the logic of ransom but also among those who react to it, arguing against it to construct an alternative, as I show in the next chapter.[13]

I would add that the ransom theory is also, because of this, ontological in orientation, because it involves an actual change of being with respect to the human condition. "Objective" views focus on God's change with respect to humanity (from anger to compassion, judgment to mercy, offense to pardon, and so on); "subjective" theories, instead, focus on a change in the individual at the moral level. The ransom theory, however, assumes a change in the status of human beings in the world and, moreover, the world itself. As discussed below, atonement signifies a shift from human enslavement to evil to good, but this is not simply a shift of allegiance: evil is defeated through the action of Christ's death and resurrection.

Dramatic understandings of atonement, such as the ransom theory and, more broadly, Christus Victor, often portray such defeat via Christ's descent into hell between the time of his death and resurrection. If we

10. Aulen, *Christus Victor*, 144.
11. Aulen, *Christus Victor*, 144.
12. Kotsko, "Persistence of the Ransom Theory of Atonement," 278.
13. Kotsko, "Persistence of the Ransom Theory of Atonement," 279.

take the narrative line of the model seriously, if not necessarily literally, such a descent makes sense, considering hell as the quintessential image of evil's abode, of death itself. Hilarion Alfeyev has traced the origin and development of the doctrine in detail in scriptural, apocryphal, theological, and liturgical texts in early Christianity through the patristic era, showing its ubiquity.[14] Although the details at times differ and the doctrine becomes more abstract as it develops, Origen provides a good example, both in terms of the content of his claim and the focus of this chapter. Echoing Paul (cf. Phil 2:1–7), he writes, for instance:

> Christ emptied himself . . . and took upon himself the form of a servant, suffered the dominance of the tyrant and became obedient unto death. By this death he destroyed him who possessed the power of death, that is the devil, in order to liberate those held by death. For, having bound the strong man and having conquered him by the cross, he entered into his house, which is the house of death, or Hades, and spoiled his goods, that is, liberated the souls which death held. It is precisely this that the Gospel enigmatically refers to when saying, "How can one enter a strong man's house and plunder his goods, unless he first binds the strong man?" He first bound him on the cross and then entered his house, that is, Hades, and from there "ascended on high" and "led a host of captives," namely, those who were risen with him and entered the heavenly Jerusalem. This is why the Apostle rightly says: "Death no longer has dominion over him."[15]

Christ, for Origen, suffers death to destroy the power of death, a power personified in the devil. Christ's descent into hell liberates those over whom death, the power of the devil, had sway. Christ's death means, then, that death no longer has power, has dominion over humanity.

As we will see in the next chapter, Anselm's so-called satisfaction theory of atonement empties the dramatic element of early theological reflection on atonement of any ultimate significance. Anselm dismisses such accounts as theologically suspect and naive. In portraying the salvation of humankind in terms of what to many a theologian looks like a shady transaction between God and the devil—which comes to the fore in, say, Gregory of Nyssa—God comes out looking deceptive and the devil too powerful. Advocates of the ransom understanding of atonement had,

---

14. Alfeyev, *Christ the Conqueror of Hell*.
15. Quoted in Alfeyev, *Christ the Conqueror of Hell*, 51.

no doubt, already anticipated and dealt with many of these objections. Nevertheless, Anselm's supposedly more rational satisfaction theory would come to predominate, which also had the effect of putting debt front and center to understand the relationship between God and human beings, both pre- and post-redemption.

Debt, as I discuss below, also plays an important role in the ransom theories, but two points are worth emphasizing from the start. Debt is not the only metaphor used to describe Christ's salvific work, but when it is used, it is often related to the power of evil, that is, the devil. Early theological reflections on the soteriological significance of Christ's resurrection certainly couch it in terms of indebtedness, then, but they also employ other metaphorical tropes.[16] One of the most prominent is, no doubt, that of health, which conceives of Christ's action in terms of healing from sickness. Like the language of debt, such language is found in the biblical texts themselves and illustrated particularly through numerous of Jesus's miracles. In Matthew 9, for instance, Jesus states, "Those who are well have no need of a physician, but those who are sick" (9:12). The language of sickness and health is, however, also not without its problems. Arguably, the discourse on health recapitulates the logic of the immunity paradigm, whose genealogy and conceptual parameters Roberto Esposito has outlined and critiqued.[17] Nevertheless, it is a good reminder of the relative diversity of soteriological language in early theological reflections.

Debt language in the early theological traditions, those associated with the so-called church fathers, is certainly not monolithic, then, as one specific theory of atonement had yet to be established. As I discuss below, discussions of atonement during the time took place under dominant assumptions and themes, but atonement itself had yet to be codified or systematized under one overriding metaphor. By the time we get to Anselm, sin is conceived primarily as a debt owed to God, but in earlier theological traditions the use of debt language was more fluid, shifting among subjects, objects, and occurring as one among a variety of metaphors.

16. Some of these tropes include metaphors related to sickness and health, victory and defeat, life and death, and even fishing, as I discuss later on. My point is not to provide an exhaustive list, but to make clear that multiple metaphors constituted early Christian theological reflection on the nature of Christ's work, before it was systematized. Even after the latter, these metaphors still function *metaphorically* but not *literally*, as we find in Anselm in the next chapter.

17. See Esposito, *Immunitas*.

We can now turn to some specific ways in which debt gets articulated, sometimes differently, among some of the early thinkers of the church, particularly Tertullian, Origen, Augustine, and Gregory of Nyssa. In chapter 3, I noted that lending without expectation of return, as Jesus commands, disrupts the logic of reciprocity on the material plane but repeats it on the immaterial plane. Such is how we can understand the notion of storing up treasures in heaven, which is accomplished via charity and good works toward the poor on earth.[18] The logic expressed in such notions overturns the position of creditor and debtor: in exchanging the material for the immaterial via the poor, one in effect credits God. God, in this context, can be understood as in debt to the faithful, owing the latter eternal life. Although the notion may seem odd, especially when judged from the position of the classical theological attributes ascribed to God, God is, at times, portrayed as a debtor to human beings.

For example, in the second chapter of *On Repentance*, Tertullian discusses the relationship between sin and repentance at length, but he explicitly characterizes God as a debtor, rather than human beings. Noting that God is both the acceptor and rewarder of good and evil deeds, he writes, "A *good* deed has God as its debtor, just as an *evil* has too; for a judge is a rewarder of every cause."[19] Reward or punishment is due to human beings, respectively, for both good deeds and evil deeds. Both deeds are owed judgment, but God judges the evil negatively, the good positively. The principle of justice, which Tertullian invokes here, demands as much, in the sense that like determines like. Tertullian does characterize what one is owed in terms of duty, but duty, here, primarily functions in a moral valence. Sin, in this passage, is understood more in terms of individual acts rather than a state of being, which is why he can write that "no deed but an evil one deserves to be called sin, nor does anyone err by well-doing."[20]

Augustine likewise characterizes God as a debtor, not necessarily as subject to respond to good and evil deeds in kind but more generally in terms of the promises that God has made to those who put their trust in God. In one of his sermons, for instance, Augustine says, "[God] made the promise, put it in writing, made out the bond; you needn't worry at all. Read what you've got in your hand, you're holding God's bond;

---

18. For detailed discussions of this, see Anderson, *Sin*; Anderson, *Charity*; Brown, *Ransom of the Soul*.

19. Tertullian, *On Repentance* 2; emphasis in original.

20. Tertullian, *On Repentance* 2.

as your debtor you hold the one whom you have asked to cancel your debts."[21]

To characterize God as a debtor to human beings, whether in light of specific acts or deeds or more generally, does not, to be sure, mean that the relationship does not run the other way. Early theologians still use debt language to characterize the human condition qua sin, with human beings understood as debtors. Tertullian, for instance, also characterizes sin in terms of debt, which he likewise understands in terms of guilt.

> Debt is, in the Scriptures, a figure of guilt; because it is equally due to the sentence of judgment, and is exacted by it: nor does it evade the justice of exaction, unless the exaction be remitted, just as the lord remitted to that slave in the parable his debt; Matthew 18:21–35 for hither does the scope of the whole parable tend. For the fact withal, that the same servant, after liberated by his lord, does not equally spare his own debtor; and, being on that account impeached before his lord, is made over to the tormentor to pay the uttermost farthing—that is, every guilt, however small: corresponds with our profession that "we also remit to our debtors;" indeed elsewhere, too, in conformity with this Form of Prayer, He says, "Remit, and it shall be remitted you." Luke 6:37 And when Peter had put the question whether remission were to be granted to a brother seven times, "Nay," says He, "seventy-seven times;" Matthew 18:21–22 in order to remould the Law for the better; because in Genesis vengeance was assigned "seven times" in the case of Cain, but in that of Lamech "seventy-seven times."[22]

Augustine, too, conceives of human beings as debtors to God due to sin. Commenting on Matt 18:21–35, he notes, "For every man is at once God's debtor, and has also some brother a debtor to himself. For who is there who is not God's debtor, but he in whom there can be found no sin."[23]

I bring these examples up not to make a systematic point about God owing human beings or vice versa. The point is, rather, that the debt language used in the developing theological traditions is not even or systematic, meaning that it cannot be reduced to a singular apparatus. The notion of debt functions metaphorically in a variety of registers, as it does

---

21. Augustine, *Sermons* 177.11.
22. Tertullian, *On Prayer* 7.
23. Augustine, "Sermon 33 on the New Testament."

in the Gospels, referring to the relationship between human beings and God, with both, at times, taking on the attributes of the debtor.

But the use of debt to describe the relationship between human beings and God is not confined to them, as we see with the ransom theory of atonement. As discussed above, in the latter the debt that human beings owe through sin is not primarily held by God but by the devil. Augustine, for instance, notes that through sin, which he characterizes in terms of the debt of Adam and Eve, "the human race was delivered into the power of the devil."[24] Although the devil's enslavement of the human race is, Augustine emphasizes, made possible through "the justice of God in some sense," it is clearly the devil to whom we are subject as debtors.[25] Speaking of the manner in which Christ conquers the devil, thus releasing human beings from their bondage to him, Augustine writes:

> What, then, is the righteousness by which the devil was conquered? What, except the righteousness of Jesus Christ? And how was he conquered? Because, when he found in Him nothing worthy of death, yet he slew Him. And certainly it is just, that we whom he held as debtors, should be dismissed free of believing in Him whom he slew without any debt. In this way it is that we are said to be justified in the blood of Christ. For so that innocent blood was shed for the remission of our sin.[26]

It is because Christ is without debt that he can free us from the debt that we owe to the devil. However, as is also clear, debt here functions in tandem with sin; debt and sin go hand in hand, to the extent that it is impossible to draw a distinction between the two: debt is sin and sin is debt.

Two other prominent dramatic portrayals of atonement are helpful to understand what is at stake in such debt language vis-à-vis the devil or, in the case of Origen, flesh. Origen articulates the notion of ransom in his commentary on some of Paul's closing words in Romans, in which the apostle articulates his intent to go to Jerusalem:

> Now, however, I should set out for Jerusalem to minister to the saints. For Macedonia and Achaia have been pleased to take a collection for the poor among the saints who are in Jerusalem. For they were well pleased, and they are their debtors; for if they have become sharers in their spiritual matters, the Gentiles ought also to minister to them in fleshly matters. So, when I have

---

24. Augustine, *On the Trinity*, book 13.
25. Augustine, *On the Trinity*, book 13.
26. Augustine, *On the Trinity*, book 13.

> completed this, and have assigned to them this fruit, I should set out through you to Spain. For I know that when I come to you, I will come in the abundance of Christ's blessing. (Rom 15:26)

Origen reads "Gentiles" here in allegorical terms, as representative of "certain souls that are less perfect and require the instruction of the perfect."[27] He goes on to note that "if perchance they should become worthy to become sharers with them in understanding spiritual knowledge, they would be responsible to minister to them in fleshly things; that is, when their spirit begins to be steeped in loftier knowledge, the flesh likewise, taking the reins of self-control and chastity, ought to minister by spiritual commandments lest, perhaps, if it is still indulging in fleshly things, it should throw off its rider, the Word of God, having become heedless and unbridled."[28] Origen then divides the spiritual and fleshly in terms of debt. Whereas the spiritual is something that is "shared," the fleshly is "exacted as for a debt." Origen traces this indebtedness, which is related to the flesh, back to Adam.

> For we have become debtors according to him who originally lost the income he received of immortality and incorruptibility in Paradise by the serpent's persuasion. And for that reason we all become debtors, however many in the likeness of Adam become implicated in the fate of transgression. For that reason, then, commands are given, that we may pay off our debts.[29]

Origen thus maintains that it is possible that we can pay off such debts, so long as we follow God's commands. However, this in and of itself does not mean that one is in the spirit, so to speak, as opposed to in the flesh. God's commands, as the recompense for debts, address the flesh, in the sense that following them does not require anything beyond what is commanded. Origen quotes Luke 17:10 to solidify this point: "But when you have done all these things that I have commanded you, say: We are useless slaves; for we have done what we owed doing."[30] As we will discuss in the next chapter, Anselm's satisfaction theory will obviate any sense that we can alleviate our sin as debt via following God's commands. Indeed, one may, of course, do what is expected of one, but that does not remedy the affront sin poses to God's honor and sense of justice. Nevertheless,

---

27. As quoted in Origen, *Commentary of the Epistle to the Romans*, 283.
28. Origen, *Commentary on the Epistle to the Romans*, 286.
29. Origen, *Commentary on the Epistle to the Romans*, 286.
30. Origen, *Commentary on the Epistle to the Romans*, 286–87.

going beyond mere commands involves the spiritual and, for Origen, does not take the form of debt. Such is the case, for instance, with "virginity," which is "paid out not as a debt; for it is not demanded by a command but is offered as something beyond what is owed."[31] As I discussed in the last chapter, however, the logic of this excess increases the sense of indebtedness, in that it interiorizes the command.

Nevertheless, by far one of the most recognizable articulations of the so-called ransom theory of atonement is Gregory of Nyssa's, as he outlines it in his *Great Catechism*. Gregory maintains that God's nature is apparent in all things, as all things depends on their participation in the divine nature. As God's creation nature thus manifests God's presence, but the incarnation "transfuses" the divine nature specifically in us. Because Gregory holds that both refer to God's omnipresence, the difference in the mode of presentation is one of degree, not kind: we should read the condescension of God in us via the particularity of Christ's incarnation not in terms of a disjunction, but as an intensification of divine presence. Nevertheless, although the presence of God in Christ must be inherently recognizable due to God's overriding presence in all things, it also remains veiled or covert, due to sin. The incarnation, then, makes the recognizable unrecognizable, so that the unrecognizable can, once again, become recognizable. Or, to put it in other, dialectical terms, life takes the form of death so that death may, once again, take the form of life, specifically life eternal.

It is because the incarnation does not represent an absolute novelty with respect to God's presence in creation, however, that atonement can occur in the way it does for Gregory. The dialectical manifestation of God's presence in Christ is essential for actualizing atonement, which pivots the unrecognizable to the recognizable, death to life. That is, Christ, as the concentration of the divine in human form, enables the passage from one to the other. The passage itself occurs via the ransom Christ's death pays on behalf of humanity to the devil. The ransom is not and cannot be paid directly, in an above the board transaction or exchange. Given that through sin the devil holds humanity in his debt, it is inconceivable that he would willingly accept payment for that debt, thereby rendering us free from his control. The devil's power comes from that control, meaning that the acceptance of a ransom would simultaneously entail the end of his power, the emptying of its content. The devil,

---

31. Origen, *Commentary on the Epistle to the Romans*, 287.

then, had to be deceived, tricked into accepting the ransom. It's worth quoting two passages at length:

> For since, as has been said before, it was not in the nature of the opposing power to come in contact with the undiluted presence of God, and to undergo His unclouded manifestation, therefore, in order to secure that the ransom in our behalf might be easily accepted by him who required it, the Deity was hidden under the veil of our nature, that so, as with ravenous fish, the hook of the Deity might be gulped down along with the bait of flesh, and thus, life being introduced into the house of death, and light shining in darkness, that which is diametrically opposed to light and life might vanish; for it is not in the nature of darkness to remain when light is present, or of death to exist when life is active.[32]

> He who first deceived man by the bait of sensual pleasure is himself deceived by the presentment of the human form. But as regards the aim and purpose of what took place, a change in the direction of the nobler is involved; for whereas he, the enemy, effected his deception for the ruin of our nature, He Who is at once the just, and good, and wise one, used His device, in which there was deception, for the salvation of him who had perished, and thus not only conferred benefit on the lost one, but on him, too, who had wrought our ruin. For from this approximation of death to life, of darkness to light, of corruption to incorruption, there is effected an obliteration of what is worse, and a passing away of it into nothing, while benefit is conferred on him who is freed from those evils.[33]

Gregory uses the "hook and bait" metaphor elsewhere, mainly to describe the way in which evil inserts itself into humanity via impiety, vice, and sin. For instance, in a polemic against Eunomius, Gregory all but equates Eunomius with the "God-opposing tongue" of the devil; he transposes the metaphor onto Eunomius, noting that his teachings are nothing more than "bait to simple souls, to the end that the hook of impiety may be swallowed along with it."[34] Likewise, when discussing those who deny the impassibility of Christ's generation, he argues:

---

32. Gregory of Nyssa, *Great Catechism* 14.
33. Gregory of Nyssa, *Great Catechism* 16.
34. Gregory of Nyssa, *Against Eunomius* 2.7.

> Surely we may well complain, when we hear that even greedy fish avoid the steel when it comes near them unbaited, and take down the hook only when hope of food decoys them to a bait: but where the evil is apparent, to go over of their own accord to this destruction is a more wretched thing than the folly of the fish: for these are led by their greediness to a destruction that is concealed from them, but the others swallow with open mouth the hook of impiety in its bareness, satisfied with destruction under the influence of some unreasoning passion.[35]

Within the context of ransom, however, the devil takes the bait of flesh, without knowing that it is nothing but a cover for deity. Unbeknownst to the devil, Christ's deity, his perfection, penetrates sinfulness with sinlessness, darkness with light. Since the devil has no proper hold on the sinlessness and light—he only has dominion over sinful humanity—his capture of Christ's death effectively voids any claim he has, thereby obliterating the devil's hold. As mentioned above, Christ's actions here also often involve afterwards a descent into hell, where he literally defeats the devil and releases the latter's captives.

The notion that the devil holds our debt, from which Christ releases us, has political implications, in that it allows us to identity indebtedness with evil, with the power and rulers of the world, as it did in the Jubilee, Sabbath year, and usury traditions.[36] However, although the ransom theory has clear political application, it remains limited, to the extent that indebtedness becomes a feature of all humanity. Indebtedness becomes a generalized state of being; indebtedness may provide an ontological base from which to construct social relationships, but it remains abstract, that is, separated from the materiality of its economic valence. If all of us are, somehow, in debt to the devil (power, rulers, principalities, as the author of Ephesians puts it [cf. 6:12]), the real, material differentiations concerning asymmetrical relationships between debt and wealth fall away. It levels the playing field, so to speak, but the leveling, although using economic language, ignores real economic disparities, which deviates from the substance of some earlier, more economically focused texts, such as we find in the Sabbath year and Jubilee traditions and the Gospels.

We can see this difference clearly if we analyze, respectively, Tertullian's, Origen's, Augustine's, and Gregory's readings of the Lord's Prayer, which in chapter 2 I emphasized as important to understanding the logics

---

35. Gregory of Nyssa, *Against Eunomius* 4.4.
36. Kotsko, *Politics of Redemption*, 158.

of debt release. I focus on the Lord's Prayer rather than other aspects of their thought since, as I argued previously, the prayer condenses Jesus's call for debt forgiveness and, thus, remains essential for understanding the vagaries of debt throughout Christian thought.

READING THE LORD'S PRAYER

In chapter 2, I argued that the Lord's Prayer condenses Jesus's call for debt forgiveness, as it is expressed at the beginning of his ministry, at least as told in Luke's Gospel. The prayer certainly has economic debt in mind, given the materiality of images used throughout. Yet, as I also mentioned, the prayer tends to conflate sin and debt, to the point where the relationship between the two becomes undecidable. The prayer, for all its radicality when it comes to the release of debts, a radicality which hearkens back to the Jubilee tradition, risks emptying the prayer of its economic significance, even if the latter remains on its horizon. The equation of sin and debt refashions debt as a more general, moral concept, indicating a wrong or violation, a crossing of some drawn line.

The economic sense of debt, still present in Jesus's articulation of the Lord's Prayer, however, completely drops out in later readings of the prayer among the figures already mentioned in this chapter. Take Tertullian, for instance. For him the Lord's Prayer is comprehensive, in the sense that it not only exemplifies occasions of prayer (e.g., worship and petition) but also contains "a summary of the whole Gospel."[37] Tertullian, however, is clear that the prayer and, by extension, the gospel, concerns heavenly, rather than earthly things. This does not mean that the prayer does not address earthly concerns or needs, as is clear from the petition to God for "daily bread." Tertullian, however, interprets this more as allegory, meaning that he stresses the so-called spiritual sense of the petition over-against what to him is its mere earthly, and thus material, reference. He writes, for instance,

> Nonetheless, we should understand "Give us our daily bread" better in a spiritual sense. For Christ is our bread, because Christ is life and bread is life. "I am," he said, "the bread of life." And a little earlier, "The bread is the word of the living God who came down from the heavens" (Jn 6.48). Then, because his body is accounted bread: "This is my body" (Mt 26.26 and par.; 1 Cor

37. Tertullian, *On Prayer* 1.

11.24). Therefore, when we ask for our daily bread, we are asking that we should perpetually be in Christ and that we should not be separated from his body.[38]

He acknowledges that the clause is open to "carnal interpretation," but he goes on to emphasize that it applies more properly to "spiritual practice": "For he commands us to ask for the bread which is all that the faithful require, whereas the gentiles seek after other things."[39] Tertullian juxtaposes this petition for bread, for God's liberality when it comes to spiritual matters, with the next line, which concerns debts or, more precisely, the forgiveness of debts. Tertullian does not have material, economic debts in mind here, as I have argued the prayer does, but rather only sin, meaning that the appeal for forgiveness is a confession of wrongdoing and a concomitant request for pardon. Tertullian writes that

> a debt, in Scripture, is an image of a wrongdoing, because wrongdoing always owes a debt to judgment and is avenged by it; neither does it avoid the justice of restitution unless restitution be given, just as the master remitted the debt of his servant. For the lesson of the entire parable points this out. Our profession that we too "pardon our debtors" is consonant with the fact that the same servant, who was set free by his master but would in turn not spare his debtor, was on this account brought before his master and sent to torture until he should pay the very last cent (Mt 18.23–26), that is the very slightest wrongdoing.[40]

As I have already noted, debt does in the parable of an unmerciful servant Tertullian references function as a stand-in for sin, and so his reading of the parable itself is not wrong. Tertullian is mistaken, however, to label all instances of debt mentioned in the biblical texts as somehow indicative of wrongdoing, that is, sin. By the time of Tertullian debt is already one of the predominant metaphors through which to understand sin, but there are numerous places in the biblical texts where this is decidedly not the case. One only need look to the laws governing the Sabbath and Jubilee years as cases in point, which I discussed in detail in chapter 1. If anything, wrongdoing in the context of such legislation falls on the side of the creditor, rather than the debtor, meaning that the latter's debt cannot stand in for wrongdoing. Ignoring the very real, economic debt

---

38. Tertullian, *On Prayer* 6.
39. Tertullian, *On Prayer* 6.
40. Tertullian, *On Prayer* 6.

that the Sabbath and Jubilee legislation have in mind also cuts off the connection that Jesus himself makes with his gospel, at least if we take Luke's version as our guide. Tertullian would, of course, have us interpret Jesus's claims at the beginning of his mission in a "spiritual sense," but, as I have argued previously, Jesus has material concerns in mind, even if he is not consistent in their application (e.g., in the slippage between sin and debt in which he often engages). The Lord's Prayer, I have argued, still has economic debt in mind, meaning that our petition for debt forgiveness correlates with the forgiveness of the debts of others—not merely "spiritual" debts, that is, sins, but real, economic debts, which is consistent with Jesus's own understanding of his mission, as evidenced in numerous parables, albeit at times ambiguously.

Origen makes similar moves with respect to the prayer. Origen reads the phrase "forgive us our debts" in primarily moral terms. In his commentary on the prayer, he states that we "owe a certain disposition towards one another," without which we remain in debt. Such a debt applies, in the first instance, to family, which includes blood relationships but also fellow believers, those "who have been born again with us in Christ."[41] Origen states that we can "either pay them through discharging the commands of the divine law, or failing to pay them, in contempt of the salutary word, we remain in debt."[42] Second, we owe a debt "toward all men in common, in particular toward guests and toward men at the age of fatherhood, and another toward such as it is right that we should honor as sons or as brothers."[43] Third, we owe a debt to ourselves; that is, we owe a debt in personal matters: "to use the body in a certain way, so as not to wear out the flesh of the body through love of pleasure, and on the other hand to treat the soul with a certain care, and to take forethought for the keenness of the mind, and for our speech that it be without sting and helpful and not trifling."[44]

Failure to honor these sorts of personal debts, these debts to ourselves, results in the multiplication of debt or, more accurately, an increase in its burden. "Whenever we fail to perform what we owe, even to ourselves, the heavier does our debt become." We also owe God our love, our entire being, and "if we fail to achieve this we remain God's

---

41. Origen, *On Prayer* 18.
42. Origen, *On Prayer* 18.
43. Origen, *On Prayer* 18.
44. Origen, *On Prayer* 18.

debtors, sinning against the Lord."[45] Perhaps most of all, we owe a debt to Christ, "who bought us with His own blood, just as every house slave is also debtor to his purchaser for the sum of money given for him. We have also a certain indebtedness to the Holy Spirit: we are paying it when we do not grieve Him in whom we were sealed unto a day of redemption, and when, without grieving Him, we bear the fruits demanded of us, He being present with us and quickening our soul."[46]

What, then, is the upshot of outlining these debts? Or, as Origen puts it, "But what need is there, when readers of this writing select their own examples from the record, for me to speak of all the things we owe which we either fail to pay and so come to be restrained or else pay and come to be free?"[47] For Origen, to be in debt so understood is simply an unavoidable fact of life on this side of the divide and is a generalized, rather than specifically economic, condition. He writes, "Suffice it to say that it is impossible while in this life to be without debt at any hour of night or day. In owing, a man either pays or else withholds the indebtedness. He may either pay or withhold in this life. Some indeed owe no man anything; others pay off most and owe little; others pay little and owe more; and a man may conceivably pay nothing and owe everything."[48] For Origen, then, we owe a lot—our debts are spread out among numerous spheres of life, from the personal, the familial, the social, to the theological. The same logic applies to others as well; just as we owe much, others owe much as well, and that would include to us. The phrase from the prayer, "forgives us our debts, as we forgive our debtors," is not, then, about the abolition of debts per se but, rather, about our constant failure to uphold them in a consistent, loving manner. It is about acting charitably with one another in relation to debts, while still acknowledging the force of these debts: "Whenever, accordingly, any of our very numerous debtors have behaved too remiss in the matter of payment of their dues to us, our more charitable course will be to bear them no grudge and to remember our own indebtedness and how often we have failed to discharge them not only towards men but also towards God himself. Remembering what as debtors we have not paid but withheld during the time which it was our duty to have done this or that for our neighbor had run by, we shall be gentler toward those who have fallen in debt to us in turn and have

45. Origen, *On Prayer* 18.
46. Origen, *On Prayer* 18.
47. Origen, *On Prayer* 18.
48. Origen, *On Prayer* 18.

not paid their indebtedness, especially if we do not forget our transgressions against the Divine and the unrighteousness we have spoken against the Height either in ignorance of the truth or else in displeasure at the misfortunes that have befallen us."[49] If we do not show the sort of generosity envisioned in the prayer, then we are like that servant who, upon having his debts released by his master, fails to do the same with others who are indebted to him. Ultimately, we have an obligation to forgive to those who repent, to us and in general. "It is however on profession of penitence that we are to forgive those who have sinned against us, even though our debtor often does so; for He says: 'If your brother sin against you seven times a day and seven times turn and say, I repent,' you shall forgive him."[50] Origen uses the prayer not so much to reflect on forgiveness but on what we owe, on indebtedness.

Origen treats "forgive us our sins" in like fashion, noting that it refers to what happens when we fail to make good on our obligations, on the debts we owe to each other.

> When Luke says "forgive us our sins" he means the same as Matthew, since sins are constituted when we owe and do not pay, though he does not appear to lend support to him who would forgive only penitent debtors when he says that it is enacted by the Savior that we ought in prayer to add: for we ourselves also forgive everyone in debt to us. And it would seem that we have all authority to forgive the sins that have been committed against us as is clear from both clauses: as we also have forgiven our debtors; and for we ourselves also forgive everyone in debt to us.[51]

Debt for Origen, then, is not so much sin but obligation; failing to live up to these obligations is where sin seeps in. This failure is what Origen has in mind with the phrase "forgive us our debts." It is not a release from debt that he envisions but, rather, the perfect fulfillment of debt. He writes, "Suffice it to say that it is impossible while in this life to be without debt at any hour of night or day. In owing, a man either pays or else withholds the indebtedness. He may either pay or withhold in this life. Some indeed owe no man anything; others pay off most and owe little; others

---

49. Origen, *On Prayer* 18.
50. Origen, *On Prayer* 18.
51. Origen, *On Prayer* 18.

pay little and owe more; and a man may conceivably pay nothing and owe everything."⁵²

Augustine's reading of the Lord's Prayer also substitutes a moral understanding of debt for an economic one. As discussed in the previous chapter, although the prayer itself slides back and forth between a moral and economic reading of debt, the latter is not, thereby, lost. Otherwise put, although debt functions metaphorically, it also functions materially, which is condensed in asking for "bread." Augustine, however, obviates the material sense of the prayer. In a reading he gives in *The City of God*, he focuses primarily on the need to ask forgiveness of God, without reference to the material extension of the latter toward others. The prayer, thus, becomes an individual plea for forgiveness in the pursuit of righteousness. After quoting the line "Forgive us our debts," he writes, "In this, then, consists the righteousness of a man, that he submit himself to God, his body to his soul, and his vices, even when they rebel, to his reason, which either defeats or at least resists them; and also that he beg from God grace to do his duty, and the pardon of his sins, and that he render to God thanks for all the blessings he receives."⁵³ Augustine does, of course, discuss the other line of the couple elsewhere, but even here, the focus is on forgiving actions in general, rather than debt as a specific economic relationship. On the importance of also forgiving our debtors, he writes, "For, no doubt, whoever pardons the person who has wronged him does a charitable action."⁵⁴

That Augustine reads debt as sin in general is evident as well in the following passage, where he discusses the need to ask for forgiveness for sins committed.

> Then as to the daily prayer which the Lord Himself taught, and which is therefore called the Lord's prayer, it obliterates indeed the sins of the day, when day by day we say, "Forgive us our debts," and when we not only say but act out that which follows, "as we forgive our debtors"; but we utter this petition because sins have been committed, and not that they may be. For by it our Saviour designed to teach us that, however righteously we live in this life of infirmity and darkness, we still commit sins for the remission of which we ought to pray, while we must

---

52. Origen, *On Prayer* 18.
53. Augustine, *City of God*, 946.
54. Augustine, *City of God*, 1054.

pardon those who sin against us that we ourselves also may be pardoned.[55]

Augustine does not have in mind debt qua debt, here, but debt qua sin, that is, debt as a metaphor for sin, which can include any action that violates the commands of God.

In his commentary on the Lord's Prayer in his Fifth Discourse on the Lord's Prayer, Gregory also equates sin and debt. Debt is, for him, not an economic term, implying a real, material relationship but, rather, simply another name for sin. He states, "For the forgiveness of debts is a unique and special prerogative of God. It was said: 'No one can forgive sins but God alone' (Mark 2:7)." The conflation occurs at two levels simultaneously. On the one hand, there is the simple, linguistic substitution of "sins" for "debts." Gregory reads the phrase from the Lord's Prayer "Forgive us our debts" as "forgive us our sins," as is clear from his reference to Mark 2:7. On the other hand, he puts the possibility of such forgiveness in the hands of God alone, which we, in turn, may imitate.

The prayer, then, is "a request that God be forgetful of whatever offenses we have committed,"[56] which we in turn should extend to others. Granting forgiveness to others goes hand in hand with God's forgiveness of us; if the former is lacking, then we cannot have access to the latter. Thus, we should exercise no "hardness of heart" toward others since this separates us "from the love of God." Indeed, he goes on, "Whoever holds someone else in bitter bondage because of outstanding debts has by his own conduct excluded himself from divine love."[57] But the "outstanding debts," here, have nothing to do with material, economic relationships but, rather, refer to moral offenses or sins, which is why he can refer to them as "bitter."[58]

Our actions are, thus, to mirror God's. Although the notion of debt and sin are reversible here, it is interesting to point out that, for Gregory, our actions also make a claim on God. Otherwise put, our good deeds toward others, our release of their debts to us qua sin, also in a way makes God indebted to us. Gregory writes, "Just as God is an example to those who achieve goodness and seek to imitate Him according to the Apostle's words, 'Be imitators of me, as I am of Christ' (1 Cor 11:1), so conversely

---

55. Augustine, *City of God*, 1071.
56. Gregory of Nyssa, *Homily 5*.
57. Gregory of Nyssa, *Homily 5*.
58. Gregory of Nyssa, *Homily 5*.

God wants your disposition toward the good to be an example to Him! The order of things is somehow reversed! I dare propose that, just as the good is accomplished in us by imitating God, so also it is hoped that God himself will imitate our own deeds whenever we achieve anything good."[59] However, this is not just a hope but, rather, a petition we can make to God, one that, in effect, lowers God to our level, as does the incarnation. He goes on to say,

> Accordingly, you yourself can say to God: Do that which I have done. Lord, although You are the King of the universe, imitate Your servant, who is a poor beggar. I have forgiven the debts of others; do not Yourself cast away Your supplicant. I have sent away my debtor rejoicing; let Your debtor also depart in like manner. Do not make Your debtor sadder than I have made mine. Let both be equally grateful to their creditors. Let both of us ratify the same forgiveness to our debtors, Yours and mine. My debtor is so and so. Your debtor is myself. Whatever judgment I have passed over him, let Your judgment be the same over me. I have absolved, so also absolve. I have forgiven, so also forgive. I have shown much mercy to my fellow human being. Lord, imitate the mercy of Your servant.

It does not matter, for Gregory, if the weight of our sin is far graver to God than it is among others. God's goodness and love are greater as well, which entails a greater response. Gregory appeals to this in God, to solidify what God putatively owes us: "But my offenses against You are graver than those of my neighbor against me. I fully acknowledge this. Yet be mindful of how much You excel in goodness. You prove Your justice when You grant mercy to us sinners in proportion to Your exalted power. I have shown little love because my nature was capable of no more. But You can show as much love as You want because Your generosity is not curtailed by any lack of power."[60]

Now, for Gregory, this does not mean that the relationship is a one-way street, that we do not also owe things to God. After discussing how God can be said to owe us, he goes on to discuss what we owe God, simply because of our "human nature." He refers to that obligation as "debts owed by human nature."[61] Ultimately, the main debt we owe to God has to do with our falling away from God, our defection from God to God's

---

59. Gregory of Nyssa, *Homily 5*.
60. Gregory of Nyssa, *Homily 5*.
61. Gregory of Nyssa, *Homily 5*.

adversary, the devil. He writes, "The first penalty that man is obliged to pay to God is that he has revolted from His Creator and has defected to the adversary. Man became a deserter and apostate from his natural Lord. Second, he exchanged the liberty of free will with the wretched slavery of sin. Instead of communion with God, he preferred the tyranny of the power of corruption."[62] For these reasons we are guilty before God, that is, we owe God a debt, for which full repayment we are responsible.

Recognizing our responsibility and to act accordingly, both in prayer and outwardly, via our actions in and of themselves and toward others, can help us avoid becoming overly confident. Rather than being certain of ourselves, of our own goodness, we must fall back on God's mercy. He states,

> No one should be of this mind and exhibit the audacity of the Pharisee (Lk 18:10–42). The Pharisee did not know what he was by nature. For if he had understood that he was human, he would have been taught by Holy Scripture that human nature is in no way free from defilement. Scripture says: "It is not possible to live one day without finding a stain in man" (Eccl 7:20; Prov 24:16). In order that nothing of this sort may occur to the soul of a person who would approach God in prayer, the Divine Word directs that we should not look at our achievements. Rather, we should constantly be mindful of humanity's common debts in which every supplicant himself necessarily participates by being part of humanity, and should plead with the Judge to grant us release from offenses.[63]

Whereas we have seen that, in other places, distinctions can be made regarding sin, the phrase "forgive us our debts" serves a leveling function. It applies to everyone, no matter how pious one may appear. We are all, in some manner, prodigals, if only because we are descendants of Adam:

> Living in these conditions we are like the prodigal son who endured the long toil of tending to the swine. When we, as he did, come to our senses and remember the heavenly Father, we do well to pray the words: "Forgive us our debts." Whether one is another Moses or Samuel, or anyone else who has excelled in virtue, he should in no way think that this petition is less appropriate for himself. He, too, is human, sharing in Adam's nature and consequently sharing in the Fall. Since the Apostle

---

62. Gregory of Nyssa, *Homily 5*.
63. Gregory of Nyssa, *Homily 5*.

says, "in Adam we all die" (I Cor 15:22), the words of repentance appropriate to Adam are also suited to all those who died with him. Thus, by being granted forgiveness of sin, we in turn may be saved by grace, as the Apostle says (Eph 2:5).[64]

But, again, all of this requires that we act toward others the way that God can and will act toward us. We cannot expect God to extend to us God's mercy, if we do not do the same. God will not wipe our debts unless we do the same to others. Without these concrete acts, these manifestations of the love of God in and to others, prayer is, essentially, meaningless.

CONCLUSION

To conclude this chapter, it is worth pointing out that material, economic debt is not absent as a concern from someone like Gregory of Nyssa. He writes, for instance:

> But the Gospel tells us that this payment of debts was not effected by the refunding of money, but that the indebted man was delivered to the tormentors until he should pay the whole debt; and that means nothing else than paying in the coin of torment the inevitable recompense, the recompense, I mean, that consists in taking the share of pain incurred during his lifetime, when he inconsiderately chose mere pleasure, undiluted with its opposite; so that having put off from him all that foreign growth which sin is, and discarded the shame of any debts, he might stand in liberty and fearlessness. Now liberty is the coming up to a state which owes no master and is self-regulating; it is that with which we were gifted by God at the beginning, but which has been obscured by the feeling of shame.[65]

Notice, however, that the fault lies with the debtor, not the lender, which is the reverse of what we saw in chapter 1 with respect to the Sabbath and Jubilee years. Indeed, if we fold in Tertullian's, Origen's, and Augustine's understandings of atonement and their readings of the Lord's Prayer, fault must lie with the debtor, since indebtedness is ultimately related to sin. We saw an inchoate relationship between the two in the second chapter, even if the economic valence of indebtedness is not entirely absent, in that it marks Jesus's mission. Paul, as said in chapter 3, drops the economic valence in favor of a more abstract struggle between flesh and

---

64. Gregory of Nyssa, *Homily* 5.
65. Origen, *Contra Celsum*, book 7.

sin, on one side, and spirit and grace on the other. The authors discussed in this chapter continue that line of thought. Although the ransom theory of atonement and the notion that God owes us, articulated variously by Tertullian, Origen, Augustine, and Gregory of Nyssa, potentially harbor anti-debt politics, their non-material renderings of the Lord's Prayer tends to obviate this: all become spiritual debtors, whatever the economic disparities involved. Debt, simply put, is a matter of disposition, of the heart.

5

Anselm's Satisfaction Theory of Atonement

IN THE LAST CHAPTER I discussed the ransom theory of atonement and the notion that God owes us, articulated variously by Tertullian, Origen, Augustine, and Gregory of Nyssa. Although these articulations potentially harbor anti-debt politics, their immaterial renderings of the Lord's Prayer tend to obviate this: we all become spiritual debtors, whatever the real economic disparities among the subjects involved. Debt, simply put, is a matter of disposition, something of the heart, and does not occur via structural disparities between the material rich and poor.

In this chapter, I focus on the satisfaction theory of atonement, which, although articulated in various forms elsewhere, is largely synonymous with the work of Anselm of Canterbury. I focus on Anselm's satisfaction theory of atonement for three main reasons. First, as we have seen in previous chapters, Anselm is not the only or even the first thinker in the Christian theological traditions to employ the language of debt to understand the relationship between sin and forgiveness or, more properly speaking, atonement. As previous chapters have made clear, the use of the language of debt to describe sin and forgiveness is well established in the Greek New Testament and early Christian theology, even if early Christian articulations of salvation cannot be reduced to metaphors of commerce and exchange. To recall just one example from the last chapter, healing is another dominant metaphor; although still common in popular discussions of the extent of Christ's salvific work, such a metaphor would, eventually, take a back seat to more "rational" articulations of atonement, as is the case with Anselm. Anselm, nevertheless, grounds his theory of atonement in the language of debt in a more pronounced manner than his predecessors, so much so that, as Gary A. Anderson observes, "There is no thinker in the Christian tradition for whom debt and atonement come together in such integrated fashion."[1] Focusing on Anselm, then, provides a crucial case for understanding the theological elements at work in the creation of indebted subjects.

Second, Anselm's understanding of atonement has been the subject of intense criticism among modern and postmodern theologians. Such criticism has usually focused in one way or another on the interrelationship between honor and violence, but comparatively little attention has been paid to the language of debt. I hope that what follows, then, contributes to further criticisms of Anselm's theory. Third, and as I discuss below, numerous attempts have been made to rehabilitate Anselm's understanding of the atonement toward the development of the theological-political alternative to contemporary capitalism. The reading provided here at the very least complicates such attempts, in that I read the satisfaction theory as one of the apparatuses that buttresses capitalism, specifically in its neoliberal instantiation, as I discuss in more detail in the next chapter. Briefly put and continuing a line of thought developed in previous chapters, especially the last one, Anselm ontologizes debt as a basic structure of the human condition, from beginning to end.

ANSELM'S SATISFACTION THEORY AND THE LANGUAGE OF DEBT

Turning now to Anselm, in *Cur Deus Homo?*, he seeks to articulate the logic or necessity by which God assumed human form in order to restore a fallen humankind to its rightful place.[2] It is common among some critics and defenders to assume that his satisfaction theory of atonement departs significantly from the teaching of the early churches, but the picture is far more complicated. First, early on in *Cur Deus Homo?* Anselm articulates humankind's problem and solution in terms that would have been recognizable to many of the patristic theologians. Recapitulation

---

1. Anderson, *Sin*, 189.

2. Anselm, *Cur Deus Homo?* Subsequent quotations are given parenthetically in text, and reference paragraph section number.

and what Gustav Aulen labeled Christus Victor are clearly on display when, discussing the beauty and necessity of the incarnation against those who say it devalues God's being, Anselm writes:

> For it was appropriate that, just as death entered the human race through a man's disobedience, so life should be restored through a man's obedience; and that, just as the sin which is the cause of our damnation originated from a woman, similarly the originator of our justification and salvation should be born of a woman. Also that the devil, who defeated the man who he beguiled through the taste of a tree, should himself similarly be defeated by a man through tree-induced suffering which he, the devil, inflicted. (I.3)

Yet, such images, common to patristic theology, function for Anselm more at aesthetic, mythological levels. They are, Anselm's narrative interlocutor Boso notes, "beautiful notions, and are to be viewed like pictures" (I.4). Nevertheless, pictures can only go so far, and what both Anselm and Boso want is a "cogent reason which proves that God ought to have, or could have, humbled himself for the purposes which we proclaim" (I.4). Indeed, this is the guiding question of *Cur Deus Homo?*, around which all else oscillates: "By what logic or necessity did God become man and, by his death, as we believe and profess, restore life to the world, when he could have done this through the agency of some other person, angelic or human, or simply by willing it?" (I.4). At issue is the question of atonement, not forgiveness, and both want to get to the "physical reality" that underlines such "pictorial representations" (I.4). Anselm will thus portray his articulation of the atonement as a "logical" rather than dramatic solution to why God became human (I.2).

Second, one of the sticking points for Anselm, not to mention others, is the role that the devil plays in early Christian theologies, as the agent who holds humankind captive in debt to sin and death and whom God must deal with to liberate humanity. For Anselm such a view is problematic, to say the least, to the extent that it puts humankind under the jurisdiction of an agency that seemingly acts separately from God's rule, thereby giving the devil rights and powers that he does not—and should not—have. Dismissing such logic, Anselm states:

> For, supposing that the devil, or man, were his own master, or belonged to someone other than God, or was permanently in the power of someone other than God, then perhaps one could justly speak in those terms. However, given that neither the devil

> nor man belongs to anyone but God, and that neither stands outside God's power: what action did God need to take with, concerning, or in the case of, someone who has his own, apart from punishing this bondslave of his who has persuaded his fellow bondslave to desert his master and come over to join him, and had treacherously taken in the fugitive and, a thief himself, had received a thief along with the stolen property of his master. For they were both thieves, since one was stealing his own person from his master at the instigation of the other. Supposing God were to act in this way, could any action be juster? (I.7)

Simply put, dramatic theories of atonement, such as the ransom theory, give too much power to the devil over against God's sovereignty. The devil is not, in his person or representation, on par with God, being nothing more than a thief.

Because of Anselm's apparent dismissal of the devil, the devil plays a minor role in his theory, minor, at least, compared to the earlier dramatic theories, where he is the main antagonist. However, Adam Kotsko has convincingly argued that, although the devil appears on the surface to play little to no real role in Anselm's theory of atonement, the devil reappears structurally as "God himself."[3] Kotsko acknowledges that this claim comes across as "somewhat jarring," and he is by no means suggesting that Anselm made a conscious attempt to conflate what appears as separate in patristic theologies, the distinct roles of the devil and God in the history of salvation. But once we bracket the theological concerns that would in principle limit the structural identification of God and the devil, the conclusion, at least at a general level, seems unavoidable. Indeed, as Kotsko notes, "the inherent subject matter leads [Anselm], once he has downgraded the devil, necessarily to place God in an analogous role."[4]

That is, what remains constant among patristic theologies and Anselm's satisfaction theory of atonement is the notion that human beings owe a debt. For many of the patristic authors, this debt is owed, in one way or another, to the devil. Once the devil is effectively cut out of the picture, however, the debt that humanity owes does not disappear; rather, the holder of the debt changes, and in Anselm that holder is none other than God. Anselm flatly states that our "debt was to God, not to the devil" (II.19). As Kotsko notes, once "God is in the business of extracting payments for debts incurred, then that debt must ultimately and *really* be

---

3. Kotsko, *Politics of Redemption*, 269.
4. Kotsko, *Politics of Redemption*, 134.

paid: the abolishment of that system of debt, parallel with the abolishment of the devil's rule, is no longer an option once it is a matter of the divine nature."[5] We saw a similar logic at work in chapter 3, concerning the parable of the unforgiving servant.

Nietzsche, it is worth mentioning, came much to the same conclusion, at least in his own way. I discuss Nietzsche at length in the next chapter, but suffice it to say here that he writes of the "genius" of Christianity: "Suddenly we stand before the paradoxical and horrifying expedient that afforded temporary relief for humanity, that stroke of genius on the part of Christianity: God sacrifices himself for the guilt of mankind, God himself makes payment to himself, God as the only being who can redeem man from what has become unredeemable for man himself—the creditor sacrifices himself for his debtor, out of *love* (can one credit that?), out of love for his debtor!—"[6] God can only make payment to Godself, however, once the devil is out of the picture, once God takes on the attributes previously ascribed to the devil. Hence the irony of God's self-sacrifice, at least according to Nietzsche.

The "physical reality" present underneath the various pictorial representations that have been used to imagine atonement, then, is nothing other than debt, specifically the debt we owe to God. Human beings were, according to Anselm, created righteous, for the purpose of happiness (I.9). In addition to being created righteous, human beings were also created rational, which for Anselm in *Cur Deus Homo?* means that we were created with the ability to distinguish right from wrong and greater goods from lesser goods. Human beings, then, have the power of discrimination and judgment, and it is this power that allows human beings to attain happiness, which ultimately rests in the highest good, that is, God (II.1). Anselm writes that "rational nature was created righteous to the end that it might be made happy by rejoicing in the highest good, that is, God. Man, being rational by nature, was created righteous to the end that, through rejoicing in God, he might be blessedly happy" (I.1).

Although Anselm makes it clear that human beings should seek the highest good for its own sake—that is, of course, what rationality requires in his schema—it is also clear that we have an obligation or duty to do so, an obligation to God. Such is the nature of obedience, which God requires from God's creation, especially God's rational creations. Happiness, then,

---

5. Kotsko, *Politics of Redemption*, 135; original emphasis.
6. Nietzsche, *On the Genealogy of Morals*, 528 (II.22).

hinges on us seeking the highest good, but that entails a constant obedience to God. Anselm characterizes the obedience of human beings to God as a debt owed to God, as giving or rendering to God "what is owed to him" (I.2). He writes:

> This is the debt which an angel, and likewise a man, owes to God. No one sins through paying it, and everyone who does not pay it, sins. This is the righteousness or uprightness of the will. It makes individuals righteous or upright in their heart, that is, their will. This is the sole honour, the complete honour, which we owe to God and which God demands from us. (I.11)

On Anselm's account, then, the original condition of human beings is as debtors to God: we owe God our obedience and, in this sense, are "subject to the will of God" (I.11). Such obedience, if complete, would sustain human beings as righteous and satisfy God's honor. The prelapsarian, ontological condition of humanity—which is humanity's real, intended circumstance—is one of indebtedness to God, manifest in the form of obedience.

It is, of course, in reference to obedience that human beings run afoul, violating qua sin the relationship that human beings were meant to enjoy with God. Sin is, in this sense, not paying the debt of obedience that we owe to God. Anselm says explicitly that "to sin is nothing other than not to give to God what is owed to him" (I.11). Sin, then, is perhaps best understood as a default on the debt we owe to God; it is a violation of the terms that God our creditor or, in less sanguine terms, usurer, has set down for existence. Our failure to fulfill the terms on our end, however, does not just violate the initial arrangement of being subject to God. More seriously, Anselm takes our failure to pay what is due to God as a form of theft that offends God's honor, which means that the latter is inextricably bound up with the debt we owe to God. Anselm states, "Someone who does not render God this honour due to him is taking away from God what is his, and dishonouring God, and this is what it is to sin" (I.11).

Our failure to render to God the honor due to God, our theft of what rightly belongs to God, ultimately means that for Anselm, human beings are indebted at least twice over. In our initial, created state, human beings, as we have said, owe a debt of obedience to God to fulfill our own righteousness and satisfy God's honor. Our default on this initial debt, however, plunges us further into debt, so that we can speak of sin as an additional debt on top of the debt we owe to God or, perhaps, as interest compounded as original sin over the course of history. This addition to our original debt is crucial for understanding Anselm's articulation of the logic and necessity of atonement.

The way to make good on a debt is, of course, to repay it, and not repaying the debt we owe to God, Anselm states, keeps us "in a state of guilt" (I.11). However, it is not simply enough to repay what was first owed, that is, the principal or initial obedience owed to God. Repayment of the debt must exceed the principle and must be in proportion to the offense that the default caused. He writes:

> For just as, in the case of someone who injures the health of another, it is not sufficient for him to restore that person's health, if he does not pay some compensation for the painful injury which has been inflicted, similarly it is not sufficient for someone who violates someone else's honour, to restore that person's honour, if he does not, in consequence of the harmful act of dishonour, give, as restitution, to the person whom he has dishonoured, something pleasing to that person. One should also observe that when someone repays what he has unlawfully stolen, what he is under is an obligation to give is not the same as what it would be possible to demand from him, were it not that he had seized the other person's property. (I.11)

In other words, we owe more than our original debt, more than what we have taken from God. We owe God a type of interest. Human beings owe, in other words, recompense for the violation of God's honor, over and above the terms of the original agreement. Anselm writes "everyone who sins is under an obligation to repay God the honour which he has violently taken from him, and this is the satisfaction that every sinner is obliged to give to God" (I.11).

Forgiveness of the debt we owe to God without some sort of recompense is, for Anselm, out of the question, which is why I indicated in the last chapter that Christianity is first and foremost not a religion of forgiveness but one of atonement. God is certainly subject to no external law or compulsion, so there is no material force that constrains God from forgiving sins without requiring something in return. For Anselm, however, the problem is not ontological, in the sense of what God can do; the problem lies in what is fitting for God to do. Indeed, Anselm emphasizes, true freedom is not simply to act without constraint but to act in a manner that coincides with one's nature. God's freedom perfectly coincides with God's will, and God's will is to perform what is advantageous or fitting. Thus, the question is not whether God can forgive without recompense or retribution but whether it is right for God to do so.

Another way to put the matter is to say that God's mercy must coincide with God's justice, which latter, in reference to the debt that human beings owe to God, necessitates that God get what God is due. Indeed, the necessity of some form of recompense applies even if, as we will see below, we cannot pay off the debt we owe, since "it is impossible for God to lose his honour" (I.14). Mercy or forgiveness without satisfaction of God's honor is, Anselm states, "absolutely contrary to God's justice, which does not allow anything to be given in repayment for sin except punishment" (I.24). Thus, we either pay back of our own accord the debt we owe, or God takes it from us, in the form of punishment. Anselm states, "For either a sinner of his own accord repays what he owes or God takes it from him against his—the sinner's—will. This is because either a man of his own free will demonstrates the submission which he owes to God by not sinning, or alternatively by paying recompense for his sin, or else God brings him into submission to himself against his will, by subjecting him to torment, and in this way shows that he is Lord, something which the man himself refuses to admit voluntarily" (I.14).

Critics of Anselm have often zeroed in on this aspect of his theory, suggesting that it makes God out to be something of a tyrant with an arbitrary will, who takes human sin as a personal insult and punishes accordingly.[7] God comes across, to use a contemporary analogy, like King Joffrey Baratheon, the cruel, impetuous, and short-lived ruler of the Seven Kingdoms in HBO's *Game of Thrones*. What is at stake, however, is more than a personal slight. As Joerg Rieger has shown, the concept of honor that Anselm works with takes place within an "ontology of empire." For Anselm's medieval world, Rieger states, "Honor is what orders society and makes possible relationship in general. If the honor of a king is violated, this means the breakdown of order as a whole and the result is total chaos. Sin, interpreted as a violation of God's honor, is therefore not primarily a personal slight or insult of God but, rather, the destruction of the order of the world."[8]

A violation of God's honor, then, threatens the very order of things, personally, socially, and metaphysically. Anselm thus argues that "when

---

7. Rieger, *Christ and Empire*, 134–36. Rieger notes this line of critique in nineteenth-century liberal theology and contemporary feminist theology.

8. Rieger, *Christ and Empire*, 136.

a rational being does not wish for what is right, he dishonours God, with regard to himself, since he is not willingly subordinating himself to God's governance, and is disturbing, as far as he is able, the order and beauty of the universe" (I.15). This is why, for Anselm, God cannot "allow anything in his kingdom to slip by unregulated," meaning that "it is not fitting for God to forgive a sin without punishment" (I.12). To do so would disrupt the order that God has established and would invite further disorder by implicitly sanctioning future violations. The logic here is similar to that found, among others, in the United States criminal justice system, in which the punishment of crime functions as an ostensible deterrent against future crimes for both the offending individual and society as a whole.[9] Otherwise put, not punishing sin sets sinners and non-sinners on equal footing, thereby implicitly sanctioning a type of lawlessness that cuts against God's justice (I.12). Forgiveness without punishment, we could say, is antinomian, and thus not fitting for either God or humans.

Our choice, then, is between punishment or recompense, forced submission to God's will or freely repaying what we owe to God. Payment seems the better option, and it requires, as stated above, that what we pay be in proportion to the extent of our sin. It is here, however, that the problem arises. We can, Anselm states, undertake certain actions for the sake of God's honor. Thus, in response to Anselm's question about what is appropriate to give to God as recompense, Boso gives a litany of actions that would seem to render to God what is due: "Penitence, a contrite and humble heart, fasting and many kinds of bodily labor, the showing of pity through giving and forgiveness, and obedience" (I.20). Through such actions we make ourselves subject to God, which was and had been required from the get-go: it is exactly what God requires of us. Nevertheless, as Anselm points out, such acts should not and cannot be understood as recompense for sin, since we already owe God our entire being, which such acts make concrete. To put it in the terms outlined above, such acts have primary reference to the original debt we owe to God not to the additional debt that we have accrued through sin.

The problem is that there is really nothing we can do to make up for our sin, to repay the debt we owe to God, since the debt is infinite. Indeed, for Anselm, even the smallest sin, the slightest deviation from God's design, has an "infinite magnitude" (II.14), an emphasis that puts

---

9. For a discussion of the relationship between crime, punishment, and the satisfaction theory of atonement, see Gorringe, *God's Just Vengeance*.

him, as mentioned in chapter 2, in contrast to Jesus's practical demarcation of the severity of sins. Anselm states that

> one sin which we consider the most lightweight is of such an infinite magnitude that one ought not to take a glance contrary to the will of God, even supposing that an infinite number of universes, each full of creatures just as this one is, were to be laid out before one, and could not be kept from being reduced to nothing, except if someone were to take this glance. (I.14)

Even though we find ourselves in an infinite debt, a debt to God that by definition we will never be able to pay off on our own, we are still responsible for it. Indeed, in many ways, we are even more responsible for it, since through sin we knowingly offended God's honor and willfully took on a debt that we could never hope to pay. In other words, we are responsible for the debt that we owe but also for our incapacity to repay it.

> Thus, a person who has of his own accord bound himself by a debt which we cannot repay, has thrown himself into this state of incapacity by his guilt. As a result, he is unable to repay what he owed before his sin, that is, an obligation not to sin, and the fact that he is in debt as a consequence of sin is inexcusable. For the very fact of his incapacity is blameworthy: because it is something that ought not to have, no indeed, he is under an obligation to have it.... Consequently, a person's incapacity to repay to God what he owes—and incapacity which brings it about that he does not make repayment—does not excuse him, in the event that he does not make repayment. For the result of sin does not excuse a sin which brings it about. (I.24)

Human beings find themselves in what appears to be a no-win situation, then. We must pay the debt that we owe if we are to avoid punishment, but the debt is of such a magnitude that it is impossible for us to pay out of our own resources, meaning that punishment seems all but unavoidable. It is a situation not unlike that in which the servant finds himself in the parable of the unforgiving servant—his debt, too, is completely unworkable.

On a side note, we would be remiss not to note how this framing of the situation contrasts with some of the images we have explored in previous chapters. Take, for instance, the parable of the unforgiving servant (Matt 18:23–35). The king seeks to settle accounts with his slaves and summons one in particular who owes "ten thousand talents," which for all intents and purposes is an infinite amount of money. The servant appeals to the mercy of the king, who then, out of pity, forgives the debt—without any concern over a violation of honor. It is pure forgiveness out of mercy, without any attempt to balance it with a predetermined understanding of justice. The slave, ignoring the mercy extended to him, attempts to collect on his own debts, without any consideration of forgiveness. The king finds out and reneges the mercy extended to the slave, and "handed him over to be tortured until he would pay his entire debt" (Matt 18:35). The punishment involved, here, has nothing to do with the debt owed to the king, as in Anselm's theory. It rather has to do with the failure to extend the same grace to his fellow debtors. Only then is he punished, not for some original violation of debt but, rather, his relationship to his fellow debtors, his fellow human beings. The model in play, here, is not God's honor, but the Lord's Prayer, which requires the mutual forgiveness of debts because of God's forgiveness.

Moreover, if we go back to our earlier discussions of usury, the Sabbath year, and the Jubilee, Anselm's theory shifts the burden of debt to the debtor, rather than the creditor. That is, it is the creditor and his exploitation of others that are the focus of the prohibitions and manumissions surrounding these traditions. It is assumed, that is, that the debtor is always at a disadvantage and, because of this, their position as debtors and their debt is not moralized. This is contra Anselm who, in dropping the economic aspect of the term, can ascribe to them all kinds of moral failings, including guilt. The forgiveness of debts does not require atonement, in the case of the Sabbath and Jubilee years, but the regular, cyclical erasure of said debts.

Nevertheless, for Anselm, it is here that atonement and grace enter the picture. To preserve God's honor, God needs to collect on the debt owed to God, but God also desires to bring to completion the work begun in human beings and in creation entire. Someone, then, needs to pay the debt owed to God, but since the debt is infinite, only God can really pay it (II.7). God, however, is not responsible for the debt and, as we have seen, human beings cannot get out of their responsibility for their sin. Enter Christ, or the God-Man, who, as fully God and fully human, satisfies the basic conditions required for the repayment of the debt humanity owes. Anselm states the logic as follows:

> For God will not do it because it will not be his obligation to do it, and a man will not do it because he will not be able to. In order, therefore, that a God-Man should bring about what is necessary, it is essential that the same one person who will make

the recompense should be perfect God and perfect man. For he cannot do this if he is not true God, and he has no obligation to do so if he is not a true man. Given, therefore, that it is necessary for a God-Man to be found in whom the wholeness of both natures is kept intact, it is no less necessary for these two natures to combine, as whole, in one person, in the same way as the body and the rational soul coalesce into one human being. For otherwise it cannot come about that one and the same person my be perfect God and perfect man. (II.7)

Although the God-Man, in his being, satisfies the basic conditions for repayment, his death, understood in continuity with his life, is the means for actually making good on the debt we owe to God.

On the one hand, Christ's death, as the outcome of his life, serves as an example for humankind, but not in the sense that is commonly attributed to Abelard, that is, that Christ dies as an example of God's love for us.[10] Instead, Christ sets "an example to mankind, the purpose of which was that people would not turn aside, without the provocation of any perceptible discomforts, from which righteousness which they owe to God" (II.18). Because Christ suffers his death painfully and willingly, in perfect obedience to the Father, Christ's death embodies the type of original righteousness that all human beings owe to God. Christ could be said to be the perfect debtor. Others have, of course, done something similar—Boso, Anselm's interlocutor, notes John the Baptist as an example of dying "bravely for the sake of the truth" (II.18). But with Christ there is a qualitative difference that makes him unique in that he—and he alone—does not owe the debt that other human beings owe to God since he remains God; moreover, as human, he remains free from sin and not necessarily subject to punishment and death.

Interestingly, this claim blurs the line between the original debt we owe to God and the debt into which we fall due to sin. In Anselm's words, "No member of the human race except Christ ever gave to God, by dying, anything which that person was not at some time going to lose as a matter of necessity. Nor did anyone ever pay a debt to God which he did not owe. But Christ of his own accord gave to his Father what he was never going to lose as a matter of necessity, and he paid, on behalf of sinners, a debt which he did not owe" (II.18). Thus, although Christ's death serves as an example of obedience, of making good on the original debt we owe to God, Anselm also conceives it as "a great gift to God," a gift that satisfies

10. See Abelard, *Commentary on the Epistle to the Romans*.

God's sense of justice and honor (II.19). Christ's gift to the Father merits a reward or compensation, since to let such a gift go unrecognized would reflect negatively on God's character. An appropriate gift, in this context, would entail either giving Christ something he does not already have or excusing a debt. But neither is relevant in Christ's case, since "before the Son performed his supremely great action, all things which belonged to the Father belonged to him, and he had no debt which could be excused" (II.19).

What Christ does, in effect, is give over his merited reward to us, and it is through this gift that our salvation is accomplished, the elimination of the debt into which we have fallen through sin.[11] Anselm writes:

> On whom is it more appropriate for him to bestow the reward and recompense for his death than those for whose salvation, as the logic of truth teaches us, he made himself a man, and for whom, as we have said, he set an example, by his death, of dying for the sake of righteousness? For they will be imitators of him in vain, if they are not to be sharers in his reward. Again, whom is he with greater justice to make heirs of the recompense due to him, and of the overflowing of his bounty, than those who are parents and brothers to him, whom he sees, bound by so many and such enormous debts, wasting away with deprivation in the depths of misery? The debt that they owe for their sins would, as a result, be excused and they would be given what, because of their sins, they are deprived of. (II.19)

Because the whole transaction is, at every turn, free, subject to no compulsion (II.5), Anselm considers it the ultimate act of mercy and justice. There is, he says, nothing "more merciful than that God the Father should say to a sinner condemned to eternal torments and lacking any means of redeeming himself, 'Take my only-begotten Son and give him on your behalf,' and that the Son himself should say, 'Take me and redeem yourself'" (II.20). Likewise, there is nothing more just: "What also could be juster than that the one to whom is given a reward greater than any debt should absolve all debt, if it is presented with the feeling that is due?" (II.20). Such is the extent of God's love for us, the extent of God's unmerited grace, and for it, Anselm states that we owe God a "debt of gratitude" (II.5).

---

11. Kotsko, *Politics of Redemption*, 147, rightly notes that Christ does not perform a vicarious sacrifice as a means of satisfaction, as Anselm is sometimes read.

Anselm's satisfaction theory of atonement, then, begins, is shot through with, and ends in debt. Our initial condition is one of debt, taking the form of obedience to God; our disobedience, in turn, puts us further into debt, a debt that expresses itself morally as guilt and one that we cannot repay because it is infinite. Christ, through his obedience to the point of death, graciously redeems us from the debt that we owe. Because of Christ's meritorious act, we now owe God a "debt of gratitude" that takes the form of obedience, which brings us right back to the beginning. In this sense, God accomplishes or brings to completion God's original intent (II.5).

We should point out, then, that Anselm's entire discussion assumes we are, at root, debtors. Our condition—originally, fallen, and redeemed—is one of indebtedness, even if the content of that indebtedness shifts. The structure of the satisfaction theory of atonement is based on the notion of debt, albeit a highly moralized, metaphysically grounded conception of it. Anselm's understanding of atonement weighs human beings with an infinite debt and a corresponding sense of guilt, even *after* redemption, albeit expressed in the form of gratitude. Anselm's satisfaction theory of atonement is a theology of debt, of indebtedness, and for this reason, it resonates with and buttresses the subjectivity of debt that finds expression in neoliberalism, rather than challenging it, as some have argued. I return to these points in the next chapter, but for now we can focus on a few more contemporary positive readings of the satisfaction theory, to get at what is at stake.

BEYOND DEBT?

I turn now to some more positive readings of Anselm's satisfaction theory, ones that see in it the potential to dislodge the logic of debt we find expressed in neoliberal capitalism. For instance, in *The Economy of Desire: Christianity and Capitalism in a Postmodern World*, Daniel M. Bell Jr. engages in a critique of neoliberal capitalism, specifically the way in which it captures desire for the purposes of its own reproduction. Bell opposes to neoliberalism a theological-political alternative that urges Christians to live in accordance with "God's economy in the midst of worldly economies."[12] Bell, that is, seeks to draw out theological resources

---

12. Bell, *Economy of Desire*, 28. See also Bell, *Liberation After the End of History*.

for reorienting desire toward God and to articulate "the difference Christ makes to the economic life of those called as disciples of Christ."[13]

Bell's claims, in this respect, are not novel in certain contemporary theological circles, such as those associated broadly with postliberalism and radical orthodoxy. Our interest in Bell is the way he uses Anselm's satisfaction theory of atonement to attempt to articulate a christological difference in and for economic life, a life that, in its worldly form, is governed by distorted desire and debt.[14] For Bell, for our distorted desire to be healed and reoriented away from its neoliberal corruption, it first needs to be redeemed. Anselm's satisfaction theory, for Bell, provides the means for understanding our salvation. Bell, however, takes a view that on the surface comes across as diametrically opposed to the reading I provided in the last section, where I argued that Anselm's understanding of the atonement begins and ends with the logic of debt and, in this sense, functions as one of the subjective mechanisms that underpins and reinforces the indebted subject. Bell, in contrast, suggests that Anselm's reading of the atonement manifests an economy that is in excess of debt, and in this sense, it would ostensibly undercut and provide an alternative to the general sense of indebtedness that reigns in neoliberalism.

Bell, to be sure, acknowledges that, at first glance, Anselm's understanding of the atonement seems ill-suited to such a task, precisely because it appears to replicate the very logic that it seeks to oppose. Bell notes that "to the extent that Christ's work of redemption on the cross seems to work entirely within a logic of scarcity and debt, commutative exchange, equity, and strict accounting of what is due, it would appear to reinforce the material logic that underwrites that capitalist economy of desire."[15] From this perspective, it is hard to see how the satisfaction theory of atonement can do much good against the logic of debt, and neoliberal capitalism more generally, since Christ's death appears as little more than "an exchange accounted equivalent to our debt that settles the divine-human balance sheet."[16]

Yet, according to Bell, such a reading of the satisfaction theory is a "profound misreading," one that "reflects the way that our imaginations

13. Bell, *Economy of Desire*, 28.
14. Bell's reading of Anselm owes much to Hans Urs von Balthasar's reading of Anselm in *Glory of the Lord*, 211–59. A similar, more contemporary reading can be found in Hart, *Beauty of the Infinite*, 344–94.
15. Bell, *Economy of Desire*, 148.
16. Bell, *Economy of Desire*, 148.

have been so disciplined by the capitalist economy of desire that was beginning to emerge during Anselm's time."[17] Our distorted desire, for Bell, leads us to misunderstand Christ's salvific work as portrayed by Anselm, mistaking that work for one more economic exchange, albeit one writ large. The mistake is that we read back into the atonement the structure of capitalism and our own distorted desire. In contrast, Bell urges us to read things in the opposite direction:

> When understood rightly, the atonement is neither irrelevant to economy nor a tacit endorsement of the logic of the capitalist economic order. Rather, rightly understood, the cross reveals the gift of Christ as the incarnation of a divine economy that turns the capitalist order on its head. In particular, Anselm discloses how Christ's work on the cross cannot be correlated with a capitalist economic logic that revolves around scarcity, with its calculi of debt, equity, and death, but instead illuminates a divine economy of charity, an economic order characterized by plenitude and generosity that exceeds the strictures of capitalism as surely as Christ burst the bonds of death.[18]

Anselm's account of the atonement, then, is one in which Christ's death exceeds any sort of debt economy, and as such cannot be reduced to the logic of neoliberalism.

On this reading, Anselm's satisfaction theory is not primarily about the debt we owe to God and God's need to collect on it to preserve God's honor. It is, rather, about God's "making good on God's intention in creating humanity."[19] The debt that we owe to God's honor, in this sense, is not something God uses as a barrier to communication with God but the very means through which communion effects itself, once it has been lost through our original disobedience. "As such," Bell argues, "honor is the origin of God's free act to provide a path to renewed communion. God's honor demands not that one *pay* for thwarting God's intentions but *that* God's intentions for humanity *not* be thwarted."[20] Bell essentially reverses the priority here: the satisfaction theory is not about what we owe to God but what God desires for us.

So understood, the atonement is, for Bell, less a matter of debt and more a "matter of God's ceaseless generosity, of God's graceful

---

17. Bell, *Economy of Desire*, 148.
18. Bell, *Economy of Desire*, 149.
19. Bell, *Economy of Desire*, 150.
20. Bell, *Economy of Desire*, 150; original emphasis.

prodigality. It is a matter of donation, of divine donation for our sake."[21] Thus, "In Christ, God has refused to render to humanity what is due sin, but instead graciously endures humanity's rejection and extends the gift/offer of redemption and reconciliation in Christ."[22] For Bell, this reading of Anselm's satisfaction theory has direct economic import. Indeed, Christ's death is an "economic act," but one that undercuts and provides an alternative to neoliberal economic thinking and organizing, which includes the predominance of debt. Bell states, "It is a movement of the divine economy of plenitude, ceaseless generosity, and superabundance. As such it runs counter to every economy that operates on the basis of scarcity, debt, desert, and a strict accounting of what is due."[23]

Bell's reading is suggestive, but it ultimately fails to move beyond the logic of debt and, in this sense, likewise fails to provide an adequate theological alternative to neoliberalism. Bell is certainly correct to note that Christ's death functions as gift in excess of the debt we have accrued, which is why it can satisfy God's honor. Such excess, however, remains the correlate of debt, in the sense that Bell, following Anselm, still assumes that we do, in fact, owe a debt to God. God may, through Christ's death, refuse to render to humanity what is due, but it is *still* due, meaning that the refusal Bell plays up remains dialectically mediated through the condition of debt itself. The debt we owe to God, in Bell's reading, remains a precondition of excess, of restored communion with God, so there is no excess in and of itself. Bell himself says as much, when he refers to God's honor, the debt we owe to it, as the path to communion with God.

To recall Kotsko's claim mentioned above, this is the problem that arises once we become debtors to God rather than to the devil: the system of debt itself remains in place. Kotsko is right to note that "there is simply no way out of the economy of debt once God becomes the creditor. Even after Christ's superabundant fund of merit has been established, the debt economy is not abolished—God is still fundamentally a God who exacts payment, even if his demands have been fulfilled."[24] The problem of Bell's theory is the problem that Nietzsche caught onto in the logic of satisfaction:

---

21. Bell, *Economy of Desire*, 148.
22. Bell, *Economy of Desire*, 148.
23. Bell, *Economy of Desire*, 152.
24. Kotsko, *Politics of Redemption*, 138.

> God himself sacrifices himself for the guilt of mankind. God himself makes payment to himself, God as the only being who can redeem man from what has become unredeemable for man himself—the creditor sacrifices himself for his debtor, out of *love* (can one credit that?), out of love for his debtor!—.[25]

Bell's reading of Anselm's satisfaction theory, rather than moving beyond the logic of debt, intensifies it, in that our only way out is to acknowledge our essential indebtedness, an acknowledgment that becomes manifest before, in, and after our redemption.

Anselm's satisfaction theory is certainly the apex of debt-based thinking about atonement, and numerous streams follow from it. It is not my intention to analyze these here, since they all in one way or another repeat the logic of debt we originally find articulated in Anselm's theory.[26] Satisfaction, and later on in more properly penal substitution models, are inseparable from debt. I do, however, in addition want to take up a recent proposal put forward by Andrew Sutherland, concerning Catherine of Siena's own use of the notion of satisfaction.[27]

Sutherland shifts the emphasis of the satisfaction theory of atonement away from debt toward love or, more precisely put, debt as love and love as debt. What Sutherland emphasizes is that Catherine offers us a different form of "indebted subjectivity," one that, in identifying with the love of and for God, "suggests a politics of debt resistant to the politics of neoliberalism."[28] Sutherland ultimately wants to rehabilitate the language of debt through its complication: grounding debt in love—for God, our neighbors, and ourselves—"changes what debt *is* and thus changes the subjective possibilities for indebted life."[29] Debt is not, as I have suggested above, deleterious with respect to human relationships but, rather, salutary and, indeed, a precondition of redeemed life. Sutherland writes, "Humanity's essential indebtedness names a bond without bondage, a relationship that offers the bonded fuller life and whose obligations in fact empower her to deepen and expand her bonds with others."[30]

---

25. Nietzsche, *Genealogy of Morals*, 21 (528/II).

26. This is also Anderson's view in *Sin*, 189–202.

27. Sutherland, "Debt Resistance and Satisfaction?" Sutherland's rejoinder is to the original version of my argument, published in part in *Political Theology*.

28. Sutherland, "Debt Resistance and Satisfaction?," 13.

29. Sutherland, "Debt Resistance and Satisfaction?," 14.

30. Sutherland, "Debt Resistance and Satisfaction?," 14; original emphasis. This is, essentially, Ilsap Ahn's argument in *Just Debt*. Although Ahn wants to reconfigure debt

Sutherland does not deny, of course, that Catherine works with an Anselmian understanding of atonement, at least in its basic outlines. Sutherland quotes the following lines from Catherine's *Dialogue*, in which God speaks to Catherine:

> My divine justice demanded suffering in atonement for sin. But I cannot suffer. And you, being only human, cannot make adequate atonement.... Because you were so utterly handicapped, I sent the Word, my Son; I clothed him in the same nature as yours—the spoiled clay of Adam—so that he could suffer in that same nature which had sinned, and by suffering in his body even to the extent of the shameful death of the cross he could placate my anger. And so I satisfied both my justice and my divine mercy. For my mercy wanted to atone for your sin and make you fit to receive the good for which I created you.[31]

Commenting on this passage, Sutherland emphasizes that it is not suffering in and of itself which satisfies God but, rather, the soul's desire for God, which is manifest in contrition for sins. Such contrition, moreover, requires aligning our will with God's will and our desire with God's desire. So much is all well, good, and not surprising, given its consistency with the mainstream of Christian theological traditions and, more immediately, Bell's argument mentioned above concerning the righting of disordered desire. Nevertheless, when read in light of the satisfaction theory of atonement, it amounts to desiring our own suffering under the burden of sin. Sutherland makes this explicitly clear; as he writes,

> The soul that loves God wills what God wills, including God's honor and the neighbor's wellbeing, and thus genuinely grieves sin and desires the penalty that sin deserves according to God's justice.... Alignment of the will also explains the pleasure God takes from the soul's willingness to suffer for others; it is not that God wants humans to suffer, but that the desire to save souls demonstrates the alignment of one's will with God's. Thus, willingness to suffer, whether to atone for one's own sin or to help others, makes satisfaction insofar as it pays the debt of love that all creatures owe to God their Creator.[32]

---

along the lines of gift, he avers that any attempt to think outside the logic of debt leads us to a Hobbesian war of all against all.

31. Quoted in Sutherland, "Debt Resistance and Satisfaction?," 9.

32. Sutherland, "Debt Resistance and Satisfaction?," 9.

To be fair, Sutherland emphasizes that the alignment of our will with respect to putatively deserved suffering and punishment is corrective and restorative rather than punitive. We desire the penalty for our sins precisely because it draws us closer to God, because it literally atones for us. Such is what God offers us via Christ, whose suffering "does not placate God's anger but rather restores humankind in ways that recall the corrective nature of discipline."[33] Sutherland quotes Catherine on this point, as follows:

> Rebels that we were, we declared war on your mercy and became your enemies. But stirred by the same fire that made you create us . . . you gave us your only-begotten Son, your Word, to be mediator between us and you. He became our justice taking on himself the punishment for our injustices. He offered you the obedience you required of him in clothing him with our humanity, eternal Father, taking on our likeness and our human nature.[34]

Hence it is that, in accepting corrective punishment, "Christ demonstrates perfect obedience—marks of proper love for humankind's Creator. As human, then, Christ offers the love of God that satisfies humankind's debt."[35]

That which God requires of Christ, however, God also requires of us: "the same payment of debt." Such payment, as aligned with God's will and Christ's atonement, should not be considered a burden but, rather, an opportunity: the payment of legitimate debts—and debts to God are, for Sutherland, always legitimate—are something we should relish, to enjoy, because it moves us and others closer to God. Sutherland writes,

> To pay one's debt is to render love to God, neighbor, and self. Moreover, when guided by discretion, this payment does not operate on a zero-sum basis or extract goods, for rightly loving God requires loving self and neighbor in appropriate ways—that is, loving them as finite goods out of love for the infinite Good. If debt produces profit in this picture, it is not to the creditor. Rather, *debtors* benefit from paying their debts—and from *their neighbors'* payments of debt—as rightly loving God moves souls

---

33. Sutherland, "Debt Resistance and Satisfaction?," 9.
34. Sutherland, "Debt Resistance and Satisfaction?," 10.
35. Sutherland, "Debt Resistance and Satisfaction?," 10.

ever closer to their source of life and created end of union with God.³⁶

The love of God—God's love for us and our love for God, which translates into love of neighbor—does not so much abolish debt as change its meaning, above and beyond the calculated, contractual logic in neoliberalism. According to Sutherland's reading of Catherine, God's love changes "what debt *is* and thus changes the subjective possibilities for indebted life." He continues:

> Humanity's essential indebtedness names a bond without bondage, a relationship that offers the bonded a fuller life and whose obligations in fact empower her to deepen and expand her bond with others. This is the sense of debt on which Catherine's satisfaction theology doubles down. Rather than released from such debt, humanity is enabled and inspired by Christ, whose entire creaturely life rendered everyone their due for the benefit of all, to do the same—which is in fact the natural mode of creaturely existence. In short, to know oneself as indebted is to know bonds of love that drive a mode of being and relating opposed to that of neoliberalism's indebted subjectivity.³⁷

The essentialist language in this quotation (e.g., "essential indebtedness," "natural mode of creaturely existence") manifests, I think, a fear that the negation of indebtedness as a subjective mode of being dissolves social bonds. Sutherland emphasizes that indebtedness, reconfigured in terms of love, is all about "being" and "relating" to each other properly, as God intended and as we witness in Christ's incarnation and death. Sutherland is thus not against indebted subjectivity as such but, rather, encourages a different kind of indebted subjectivity, one that, to use the language of Bell, is "rightly understood." Given that the language of suffering pervades Catherine's understanding of atonement, however, Sutherland runs the risk of valorizing suffering as attendant to this putatively reconfigured mode of subjective indebtedness. To be fair, he is aware of this problem and wants to avoid it, but he quickly glosses over the issue.³⁸

Nevertheless, the fear that, without some form of indebtedness, social bonds would dissolve is a concern that Sutherland shares with Ilsup

36. Sutherland, "Debt Resistance and Satisfaction?," 10; original emphasis.

37. Sutherland, "Debt Resistance and Satisfaction?," 14.

38. As he puts it in Sutherland, "Debt Resistance and Satisfaction?," 15n89, "In Catherine's case, the obvious challenge remains that her language seems to valorize suffering. Space does not permit a thorough treatment of this issue."

Ahn. Ahn does not pull any punches in his support of debt. For instance, appealing to Hobbes, he states that "a debtless society is conceptually illustrated as a violent, unjust, and inhumane society. This society where no one is a debtor to anyone else appears to be far from being a utopia or the kingdom of God."[39] Indeed, it is to exist uncivilized, confined to a "state of nature."[40] Ahn argues against reductive conceptions of debt, such as we find in neoliberalism, and hyperbolic conceptions of debt, such as we see, for instance, in Nietzsche, to reconfigure debt as an original form of gift. Drawing on the work of David Graeber and Marcel Mauss, Ahn emphasizes that "debt was originally conceived in archaic society as part of the moral economy of gift to engender social and symbolic capital that made possible social cohesion and solidarity."[41]

Ahn wants to "radicalize" this anthropological insight via theology, specifically theological virtue ethics. Indebtedness, as both a material and subjective state, is not problematic as such. So long as it is free from exploitation and governed by the virtues of moderation, liberality, fortitude, and gratitude, debt can "serve humanity" rather than "subjugate it." The problem, however, is that situating debt in light of virtue ethics remoralizes debt, which, rather than challenging neoliberalism, only buttresses it and extends its logic, ultimately by conflating credit with debt. Or, in more theological terms, gift and debt become intertwined, where debt is gift and gift is debt. Ahn writes of this more "holistic" conception of debt, one based in and on "grace," "if we begin to regard debt as a form of gift in the economy of grace of God's giftfulness, then we also begin to consider that gratitude is not a due payment ('work') always owed by a debtor but an effect of the transformation ('labor') of the indebted soul, which is also the reflection of God's giftfulness."[42]

Although Ahn does not mention Anselm directly, his moralization of debt via virtue ethics clearly shares concerns over the binding function of debt, as does Sutherland. Debt is necessary because of the responsibility it putatively engenders to ourselves, others, and God, without which society would exist in a Hobbesian state of nature, a so-called war of all against all. But this is precisely Anselm's concern in *Cur Deus Homo?*, concerning why God cannot simply wipe the slate clean without some satisfaction of God's honor. To do so would give undue license to sin;

39. Ahn, *Just Debt*, 14.
40. Ahn, *Just Debt*, 14.
41. Ahn, *Just Debt*, 35.
42. Ahn, *Just Debt*, 156.

hence the need for satisfaction and/or the threat of punishment for violation of the obligations that God has established. Without satisfaction, there would be no social cohesion, which is the same assumption that Ahn works with concerning debt as gift and gift as debt, even if he avoids the language of satisfaction.

CONCLUSION

I want to conclude this chapter by flagging one more reading of debt-language, when it comes to central theological claims, that of Kathryn Tanner's. The fear present in the rehabilitations of debt I have discussed is that, without them, society would simply crumble. Tanner has emphasized the importance of debt to the functioning of finance capital, but her solution is to double-down, so to speak, on the language of debt. With regard to salvation, which she reads through a Protestant lens as entailing a radical break between the old and the new, she notes that salvation "might be likened to the release of cancellation of enslaving debt, one that is impossible to remit by way of one's own resources.[43]" In so doing, she equates "sin" with "unpaid debt in that one has failed to make good on what God has provided, defaulted on the obligation to act in accordance with God's good intentions, in ways that can no longer be remedied though one's own efforts, every such attempt bringing one into greater debt because of one's fundamental corruption."[44] Indeed, sin, so construed, is a type of "debt-slavery," which requires not gradual payoff but an abrupt transition out of debt via Christ's work. She writes that "Christ becomes the strange currency or treasure that allows one now to make good on one's obligations to God, and in that way Christ breaks one's bondage to sin."[45] The problem, here, is that, in her discussion of debt as a mechanism of finance-driven capital, any sort of "sin" lies squarely on the side of said capital. Human beings are quite literally trapped in debt, the fault of which lies squarely with financier debtors. She writes, for instance, that "Indefinite extension of debt until eventual default—at some point the diversion of funds might otherwise be used as food and shelter for people of limited means reaches its limit in default. Indefinite extension of that ultimate end—being chained to one's debt until defeated by

---

43. Tanner, *Christianity and the New Spirit of Capitalism*, 55.
44. Tanner, *Christianity and the New Spirit of Capitalism*, 55.
45. Tanner, *Christianity and the New Spirit of Capitalism*, 55.

it—seems endemic to the mechanism of profit generation here."[46] Debt, in this sense, has a "contractive and expropriating effect."[47]

But when she shifts to atonement theory, debt becomes a problem for individuals who need redemption via God who, it must be said, serves as the stand-in for financial capital. It is as if her theological commitments cannot allow her to conceive of debt language as problematic in and of itself; it only provides a solution by moralizing the problem to that of debtors. This is all contained in the assumption that sin equals debt; since sin is a problem for individuals, whatever their position on the side of the creditor-debtor relationship, sin names the condition of the debtor, not the creditor.[48] Or, rather, the creditor is the problem in her analysis of finance-driven debt mechanisms, but precisely not the problem when it comes to theological solutions. And this, it must be said, is endemic to theological analyses that ground atonement: all have sinned, to reference Paul, meaning that all bear responsibility.

Although Tanner, along with other critics of neoliberalism and the logic of debt, attempt to get out of the latter via their respective theologies—which, as I have shown above, overlap in significant ways—they simply recapitulate the logic of debt. The problem is not in the way we envision debt but in debt itself, as a concept and a subjective and material condition. To think beyond neoliberalism and the logic of debt it is not enough to rework that logic but think beyond debt itself. To do so, we must construct a different theology of debt, one that is critical of the notion of debt itself.

---

46. Tanner, *Christianity and the New Spirit of Capitalism*, 46.
47. Tanner, *Christianity and the New Spirit of Capitalism*, 46.
48. For this equation of sin and debt, see Tanner, *Christianity and the New Spirit of Capitalism*, 55.

6

Subjects of Debt

IN THE PREVIOUS CHAPTERS, I have followed some significant theological threads in the development of a subjective understanding of debt that identifies the latter as constitutive of the human condition. Whereas debt in the Sabbath and Jubilee traditions names an asymmetrical, material condition that sees it as an oppressive mechanism, debt gradually becomes an immaterial, morally charged ontological condition of individuals vis-à-vis God. Debt is sin and as such, needs atonement. But atonement never fully arrives since its accomplishment still entails our indebtedness. In this chapter I develop this idea, focusing on contemporary confluences of economic, moral, and theological valences of debt in relation to the subject. The main thread that runs throughout this chapter is that debt, understood in economic, moral, and theological senses, functions as a means of subjective control, a means that is rooted in Christianity because of its emphasis on debt and atonement. One can approach debt variously to make such a claim; and debt often functions on the subject via sheer force. I am, however, primarily interested in debt as a theological concept, specifically in its relationship to atonement. A theology of debt, then, must trace the contours of its development as a concept, as I have done in previous chapters, but also show how it relates to the moral and economic aspects of debt, especially considering the way in which the latter functions in neoliberal capitalism to generate value. A theology of debt, then, is a political and economic theology, which makes it salient to contemporary sociopolitical and economic concerns surrounding debt and indebtedness. Briefly put, the line that runs throughout the previous chapters regarding debt continues in modern valences of debt, both subjectively and objectively.

The first section of this chapter focuses on Nietzsche's discussion of how the moral sense of guilt originates in the creditor-debtor relationship. Nietzsche's genealogy of the power relationships that create a sense of guilt ultimately enters theological territory, where, as we have seen, he brings up the Christian doctrine of atonement, with Anselm always lurking in the background. Although the atonement takes the form of mercy, I argue again that it only increases the sense of indebtedness. The second section of this chapter takes up Walter Benjamin's extension of Nietzsche's ideas in his essay "Capitalism as Religion."[1] For Benjamin, Christianity and capitalism relate to each other parasitically and the relationship, moreover, hinges on guilt and debt. Capitalism increases the sense of the latter, but it does so in relationship to the doctrine of atonement. The third section of this chapter focuses on the way in which debt and the sense of indebtedness become a generalized, ubiquitous condition under neoliberal capitalism, a condition that is, ultimately, rooted in the notion of atonement. Drawing on the work of Louis Althusser, Gilles Deleuze, and Maurizio Lazzarato, among others, I highlight the shift from disciplinary societies to control societies. The latter, ultimately, depend upon debt and indebtedness for their maintenance. Under neoliberalism, the indebted subject is also a guilty subject, who owes their creditor not only what is borrowed but their very existence, life itself.

DEBT, GUILT, AND ATONEMENT

In the second essay of *On the Genealogy of Morals*, Nietzsche attempts to trace how the consciousness of guilt in human beings arises. The moral sense of guilt, of "bad conscience," is not for Nietzsche an innate characteristic but rather has its origins in the power differentials that constitute material, economic relationships. Specifically, Nietzsche notes that guilt, along with related concepts, finds its way into human consciousness—or, perhaps better put, becomes human consciousness—through the "contractual relationship between *creditor* and *debtor*."[2] So much is evident, Nietzsche famously suggests, in the linguistic relationship between the

---

1. Benjamin, "Capitalism as Religion."
2. Nietzsche, *On the Genealogy of Morals*, 499 (II.4); original emphasis.

concepts of guilt and debt: "the major moral concept *Schuld* [guilt] has its origin in the very material concept *Schulden* [debts]."³

The logic of this relationship is not natural or set in stone, so to speak; debt and guilt do not necessarily go hand in hand, as we saw in chapters 1 and 2. The relationship is, rather, attendant upon "the right of masters" that Nietzsche discusses in more detail in the First Essay. The origin of the moral concepts "good" and "bad" can be reduced to the "pathos of distance" separating the noble from the common, the powerful from the powerless, the creditor from the debtor. The former determines *their* actions as "good" because they consider themselves as good, in contradistinction to the actions of others of lower stature, meaning that moral judgement is really a species of the "will to power."⁴

The sphere of power so constituted determines obligations and what form they take, including the sphere of legal, contractual obligations. The latter give rise to a certain type of morality, and not the other way around. The legal relationship between creditor and debtor, the whole realm of "buying, selling, barter, trade, and traffic," turns the human being into a particular type of moral animal, one who is "necessary, uniform, like among like, regular, and consequently calculable."⁵ Indeed, such calculability, the delimitation of chance from necessity, breeds in the human being a memory and, as such, renders him capable of promising, of projecting his own security into the future over-against the present. Nietzsche argues that all this comes together within contractual relationships, specifically the relationship between creditor and debtor:

> It was [in contractual relationships] that *promises* were made; it was here that a memory had to be *made* for those who promised; it is here, one suspects, that we shall find a great deal of severity, cruelty, and pain. To inspire trust in his promise to repay, to provide a guarantee of the seriousness and sanctity of his promise, to impress repayment as a duty, an obligation upon his

---

3. Nietzsche, *On the Genealogy of Morals*, 498–99 (II.4).

4. Nietzsche, *On the Genealogy of Morals*, 460 (I.1). Nietzsche of course expresses the notion of "will to power" in various ways throughout his writings, where it functions as an explanatory concept for the biopolitical, non-moral origin of morality in internal and external operation of basic animal drives. He states in *Will to Power*, 359 (677), for instance, that "the ruling drives want to be viewed also as the highest courts of value in general, indeed as creative and ruling powers. It is clear that these drives either oppose or subject each other (join together synthetically or alternate in dominating). Their profound antagonism is so great, however, that where they *all* seek satisfaction, a man of profound mediocrity must result."

5. Nietzsche, *On the Genealogy of Morals*, 495 (II.2).

own conscience, the debtor made a contract with the creditor and pledged that if he should fail to repay he would substitute something else that he "possessed," something he had control over; for example, his body, his wife, his freedom, or even his life.[6]

A monetary relationship is certainly at issue here, as well as a moral one. But, in keeping with the "right of masters" which determines the shape of said morality, the creditor does not merely enter the relationship with the debtor for economic gain. The creditor also indebts their powerless counterpart for the sake of "*pleasure*—the pleasure of being allowed to vent his power freely upon one who is powerless, the voluptuous pleasure 'of doing evil for the pleasure of doing it,' the enjoyment of violation."[7] We see echoes of this in the asymmetrical relationship between creditor and debtor in the biblical laws on usury and the Sabbath and Jubilee traditions, discussed in chapter 1.

Through the contractual relationship, Nietzsche argues, human beings learn to measure themselves against others and learn to ascribe value. Indeed, it is here, he suggests, that human beings first learn to think and recognize their own putative superiority above the rest of the animal world. Nietzsche writes, "Setting prices, determining values, contriving equivalences, exchanging these preoccupied the earliest thinking of man to such a great extent that in a certain sense they constitute thinking *as such*; here it was that the oldest kind of astuteness developed; here likewise, we suppose, did human pride, the feeling of superiority in relation to other animals, have its first beginnings."[8] The act of determining value, however, also implies that human beings and things more generally have value, that they are susceptible, out there and ready for exchange; so it is not by any means a leap to move from valuation to the assumption that everything has value. Everything now "has its price; *all things* can be paid for."[9]

The creditor-debtor relationship thus provides the basis for interpersonal relationships, which are positively weighted toward the creditor and governed by a sphere of moral obligation that flows upward to said creditor. But it also, Nietzsche argues, provides the basis for understanding the social sphere, as the community stands in relationship to the

6. Nietzsche, *On the Genealogy of Morals*, 500 (II.5).
7. Nietzsche, *On the Genealogy of Morals*, 501 (II.5); original emphasis.
8. Nietzsche, *On the Genealogy of Morals*, 506 (II.8); original emphasis.
9. Nietzsche, *On the Genealogy of Morals*, 506 (II.8); original emphasis.

debtor as does the creditor. Members of the community, qua debtors, receive "the advantages of communality," but they must repay such debt through loyalty and obligation; they must, in other words, be members of the community in good standing, and that requires privileging one's relationship to it above all else, ultimately in the form of obedience. To put it differently, the individual qua debtor owes the community what Michel Aglietta refers to as a "life debt which defines the relationship between a society's members and this society as a whole, considered as a sovereign power."[10] Life debt is "inalienable," according to Aglietta, because it is the very thing that constitutes and maintains society, guaranteeing its power and permanence. To return to Nietzsche, the "lawbreaker," in this sense, is the one who has not made good on their debts to the community: to violate the law is to default on one's life debt and, thus, implies the negation of the social whole. "The lawbreaker is a debtor," Nietzsche writes, "a breaker of his contract and his word *with the whole* in respect to all the benefits and comforts of communal life of which he has hitherto had a share."[11]

Like in the interpersonal sphere, this exposes the bad debtor to the violence of being thrust out of the community's credit; but as communities gain power, the "violence" involved transforms itself, becoming more moderate, to the point where reserve with respect to the punishment involved becomes a sign of compassion. Nietzsche writes, "As the power and self-confidence of a community increase, the penal law always becomes more moderate; every weakening or imperiling of the former brings with it a restoration of the harsher forms of the latter. The 'creditor' always becomes more humane to the extent that he has grown richer; finally, how much injury he can endure without suffering from it becomes the actual *measure* of his wealth."[12] Indeed, the ultimate measure of such wealth, of such compassion, lies in *not* punishing the debtor, which reconfigures the violence of justice implied in the creditor-debtor relationship. Letting the debtor go free constitutes an act of mercy: "This self-overcoming of justice: one knows the beautiful name it has given itself—*mercy*; it goes without saying that mercy remains the privilege of the most powerful man, or better, his—beyond the law."[13]

10. Aglietta, *Money*, 71.
11. Nietzsche, *On the Genealogy of Morals*, 507 (II.9); original emphasis.
12. Nietzsche, *On the Genealogy of Morals*, 508 (II.10).
13. Nietzsche, *On the Genealogy of Morals*, 509 (II.10); original emphasis.

What does not disappear in mercy, however, is the *sense* of indebtedness, "the burden of still unpaid debts and of the desire to be relieved of them."[14] What Nietzsche isolates in his genealogical analyses of morality is the way in which the sense of indebtedness, which we can also understand as guilt, increases rather than diminishes with every instance of supposed relief. There is, in this sense, a paradoxical relationship between guilt and mercy: as indebtedness increases so too does the need for mercy, but mercy heightens the sense of indebtedness that it supposedly relieves. We see this relationship, especially, in the development of religion and, specifically, Christianity. If religion arises and is designed in large measure to alleviate humankind's sense of indebtedness, its guilt, then Nietzsche sees its apex in Christianity. He argues that the "guilty feeling of indebtedness to the divinity continued to grow for several millennia—always in the same measure as the concept of God and the feeling for divinity increased on earth and was carried to its heights. . . . The advent of the Christian God, as the maximum god attained so far, was therefore accompanied by the maximum feeling of guilty indebtedness on earth."[15]

The irony, here, is that the attempt to reverse the sense of indebtedness actually perpetuates it, to the point that it will ultimately rule out the "prospect of a final discharge."[16] As Deleuze puts it in his reading of Nietzsche, any sort of redemption in this schema involves not a "discharge" of debt but its "deepening."[17] Unless, that is, both positions—debtor and creditor—can coincide, since that would alleviate the strain between the two that allows the increase in indebtedness, which is, arguably, at play in the materialist reading of the Lord's Prayer. It is at this point, of course, that we confront the "genius" of Christianity, which as I argued in the last chapter is expressed most cogently in Anselm's satisfaction theory of atonement. Nietzsche writes that

> suddenly we stand before the paradoxical and horrifying expedient that afforded temporary relief for humanity, that stroke of genius on the part of Christianity: God sacrifices himself for the guilt of mankind, God himself makes payment to himself, God as the only being who can redeem man from what has become unredeemable for man himself—the creditor sacrifices himself

14. Nietzsche, *On the Genealogy of Morals*, 526 (II.20).
15. Nietzsche, *On the Genealogy of Morals*, 526 (II.20).
16. Nietzsche, *On the Genealogy of Morals*, 528 (II.21).
17. Deleuze, *Nietzsche and Philosophy*, 141.

for his debtor, out of *love* (can one credit that?), out of love for his debtor!—.[18]

The problem, however, is that the entire process that culminates in Christianity is based on pathologizing or, what amounts to the same thing, moralizing what are essentially "ineluctable animal instincts."[19] This is, to be sure, Nietzsche's entire critique of morality, that it turns us into "tame domestic animals," which also means "modern men."[20] The category "human" is designed to separate its subject from its animal nature and counterparts, but it cannot do so without also creating all those categories (guilt, responsibility, obligation, sin, etc.) that subject us to an external force, or will to power. The need for redemption, which is also redemption from our animal nature, irretrievably condemns us at the same time: redemption creates the conditions that then need redeeming. Nietzsche states that the human being, individually and collectively, "apprehends in 'God' the ultimate antithesis of his own ineluctable animal instincts; he reinterprets these animal instincts themselves as a form of guilt before God (as hostility, rebellion, as insurrection against the 'Lord,' the 'father,' the primal ancestor and origin of the world)."[21] Such, Nietzsche takes it, is an "absolutely unexampled . . . madness of the will."[22]

Nietzsche's analysis of the development of the sense of debt and guilt does not rest on its anthropological or historical facticity, even if David Graeber deems it mostly "insane" from these vantage points.[23] Nietzsche's genealogy is not concerned with history per se, though it is certainly not ignorant of it; rather, its concern is to trace a conceptual problematic back from its present. Genealogy, then, delves into the past to illuminate the present and, in this sense, should be understood as concerned with the contemporary. From this perspective, Nietzsche's genealogy remains a salient resource, since we have not moved on from the problems it highlights with respect to the creditor-debtor relationship. Moreover, in many ways, Nietzsche's investigation of the development of debt is overdetermined by his critique of Christianity, which here focuses on the way in which the narrative condenses in the idea of atonement.

18. Nietzsche, *On the Genealogy of Morals*, 528 (II.22).
19. Nietzsche, *On the Genealogy of Morals*, 528 (II.22).
20. Nietzsche, *On the Genealogy of Morals*, 502 (II.7).
21. Nietzsche, *On the Genealogy of Morals*, 528 (II.22).
22. Nietzsche, *On the Genealogy of Morals*, 529 (II.22).
23. Graeber, *Debt*, 78.

THE RELIGIOUS NATURE OF CAPITALISM

In his short, exploratory essay "Capitalism as Religion," Walter Benjamin points to the ambiguous relationship between guilt and debt to which Nietzsche draws attention to frame the religious nature of capitalism. For Benjamin, Nietzsche's philosophy provides us with the "paradigm of capitalist religious thought," which rests ultimately on the relationship among debt, guilt, and atonement.[24]

Benjamin is certainly not the first to draw attention to the relationship between religion, and specifically Christianity, and capitalism to explain and critique capitalism as somehow internal to Christianity itself. For example, Marx, as is well known, understands the commodity fetish along these lines, when he refers to the fetishistic characteristics of commodities. The latter's abstraction from concrete social relationships as things in themselves via the processes of exchange shrouds commodities in "metaphysical subtleties and theological niceties."[25] Benjamin's more immediate reference, however, is Max Weber. Weber wanted to understand the role that religious forces played in the development of contemporary, secular culture. Weber, to be sure, does not deny the influence of other historical, social, and cultural factors in shaping capitalism. Nor does he suggest that capitalism could only have arisen out of Christianity, specifically the Protestant Reformation, as if the ideas and practices contained therein constituted a necessary link between the two. He is, rather, interested in the "elective affinities between certain forms of religious belief and a vocational ethic."[26] In this sense, Weber is interested in the question of influence without, however, reducing that influence either to explicit motivations or to a straightforward and even development.

For Weber the development of capitalism entailed a shift in what he refers to as the "natural relationship" between human beings and economic activity. As Weber points out, this relationship subordinates economic activity to material needs; the acquisition of material wealth, that is, is only a means to an end, and not the end in and of itself. Capitalism, however, reverses this relationship: under capitalism economic activity is not a means to an end but the end itself, the *summum bonum* of life, as Weber puts it. This end, moreover, takes the form of an ethical obligation or duty, a "calling" that human beings must "feel" and, thus, internalize.

24. Benjamin, "Capitalism as Religion," 289.
25. Karl Marx, *Capital*, 1:163.
26. Weber, *Protestant Ethic and the Spirit of Capitalism*, 97.

In turn, the individual must then actualize this sense of vocation in relation to professional and economic activities.

Weber locates the "background of ideas" that enabled this shift in two main Protestant notions, the Lutheran idea of calling and the Calvinist doctrine of election. The monasticism of the medieval period had thought of calling in terms of the renunciation of worldly pursuits and obligations, but Luther flattens this conception. Calling is not located uniquely in the religious practice of asceticism but, rather, applies across the board, to all peoples, in their normal, day-to-day activity. Calling, that is, takes the form of the obligations that the world imposes on individuals and, thus, "the fulfillment of one's duties in the world constitutes, under all circumstances, the only way to please God. This fulfillment, and only this, is God's will."[27]

Luther's idea of calling thus grants legitimacy to worldly activity for its own sake, but Weber notes that the effect of this shift was largely negative: it detached the notion of calling from a specifically religious notion of vocation but did not, in and of itself, foster the practices that would coincide with capitalism. The Calvinist doctrine of election, or predestination, is a more apt contender here. Weber speculates that, at some point, the doctrine of predestination—the idea that God sovereignly predetermines the fate of individuals in terms of salvation and damnation, irrespective of proclivities—raises questions concerning one's election. Weber writes, "A particular question must arise immediately for every single believer. It forces all such this-worldly interests into the background: Am *I* among the predestined who have been saved? How can *I* become certain of my status as one of the chosen?"[28]

For Calvin himself, such a question is inconsequential: it is enough for him to maintain faith in the goodness of God's plan, no matter how mysterious it may look from our own, partial, and sin-laden perspective. Weber notes that, for his followers and the "mass of ordinary men," such faith was impossible and, thus, unsustainable. The "feelings of religious anxiety" that the doctrine evoked had to be met with some form of worldly assurance. Such assurance, Weber argues, would be found in worldly activity itself, in "good works" and one's relationship to them. Good works, it is crucial to emphasize, do not function as a means of attaining salvation, since salvation is entirely up to God. They are, rather,

---

27. Weber, *Protestant Ethics and the Spirit of Capitalism*, 90.
28. Weber, *Protestant Ethics and the Spirit of Capitalism*, 110.

"technical means, but not ones that can be used to purchase salvation. Rather, good works serve to banish the anxiety surrounding the question of one's salvation."[29] Ultimately, assurance could be had through the means of economic security and success. Success in the pursuit of these, combined with frugality, prudence, and reserve, or what Elettra Stimilli calls "inner-worldly asceticism," could be interpreted as signals of God's favor. But it is the pursuit itself that, Weber argues, drives the sort of economic activity that would be necessary to the emergence and later development of capitalism. Such pursuit initially does not aim at wealth for its own sake but, rather, functions sacrificially, in the sense that renunciation of immediate desire translates into this- and otherworldly-success. Hence Stimilli refers to Weber's thesis as adopting a "sacrificial paradigm" to explain the emergence of capitalism out of Protestantism.[30]

In contrast to Weber, who only emphasizes the religious influence on capitalism, Benjamin argues for the religious nature of capitalism itself. That is, for Benjamin the relationship between Christianity and capitalism is not epiphenomenal but, rather, parasitical, in the sense that, once established, both require each other for their continued existence. Benjamin thus notes, "One can behold in capitalism a religion, that is to say, capitalism essentially serves to satisfy the same worries, anguish, and disquiet formerly answered by so-called religion."[31]

The cult of capitalism has three salient characteristics. First, Benjamin argues that it is a "pure religious cult, perhaps the most extreme there ever was. Within it everything only has meaning in direct relation to the cult: it knows no special dogma, no theology."[32] Second, and relatedly, capitalism is a cult of "permanent duration": "Here there is no 'weekday,' no day that would not be a holiday in the awful sense of exhibiting all sacred pomp—the extreme exertion of worship."[33] Taking these two features together, capitalism flattens the common distinction between the sacred and the profane, the division between the religious realm of pure, unadulterated experience and calculated, utilitarian logic. Capitalism, that is, knows no punctuation, allows for no sacred interruption of the mundane. Capitalism does not so much dissolve the sacred to prioritize the profane but, rather, renders the distinction between the

29. Weber, *Protestant Ethics and the Spirit of Capitalism*, 113.
30. Stimilli, *Debt of the Living*, 1.
31. Benjamin, "Capitalism as Religion," 259.
32. Benjamin, "Capitalism as Religion," 259.
33. Benjamin, "Capitalism as Religion," 259.

two insubstantial and transposable: the sacred becomes profane and the profane, in turn, is sacralized.

Third, Benjamin notes that capitalism is a cult of blame, a cult of universalized, unrequited guilt. "An enormous feeling of guilt not itself knowing how to repent, grasps at the cult, not in order to repent for this guilt, but to make it universal, to hammer it into consciousness and finally and above all to include God himself in this guilt, in order to finally interest him in repentance," Benjamin writes of it.[34] Nevertheless, in capitalism, there is no escape from this guilt via atonement in the classical sense but, rather, only its multiplication and acceleration. For this reason, capitalism is not a religion of salvation or redemption but, rather, one of destruction, of the eternal torments of hell on earth or, better put, as earth. "Therein lies the historical enormity of *capitalism*: religion is no longer the reform of being, but rather its obliteration. From this expansion of despair in the religious state of the world, healing is expected. God's transcendence has fallen, but he is not dead. He is drawn into the fate of man."[35]

Christianity and capitalism cross-pollinate each other, in a way that cannot be chalked up to mere influence, as Weber argues. For Benjamin, capitalism lies in utero in Western Christianity until the point where it shifts position with its host: now Christianity feeds on capitalism, from which it is inseparable. Indeed, at the point of the emergence of capitalism proper, Christianity's history becomes "essentially that of its parasite—that is to say, of capitalism."[36] What is common to both, as Benjamin points out, is debt as guilt and guilt as debt. The difference lies in the expectation of atonement: it is that expectation, Benjamin argues, that capitalism dissolves into permanent despair, permanent guilt and debt. Lacking atonement, capitalism is, as Agamben points out, a "religion entirely founded on faith; it is a religion whose adherents live *sola fide*, by faith alone."[37]

I have suggested in the previous chapters that even the expectation of atonement functions to increase guilt, meaning that atonement, understood as providing the conditions for the forgiveness of sin as debt, always remains outstanding. This is exactly what it means to owe a "debt of gratitude," as Anselm would put it. The doctrine of atonement, in this

---

34. Benjamin, "Capitalism as Religion," 259.
35. Benjamin, "Capitalism as Religion," 260; original emphasis.
36. Benjamin, "Capitalism as Religion," 289.
37. Agamben, *Creation and Anarchy*, 60.

sense, works in tandem with capitalism, especially in its contemporary, neoliberal variety, to sediment the sense of indebtedness. Nevertheless, to conclude this section it is important to emphasize at this point the parasitical nature between capitalism and Christianity to which Benjamin draws attention. Much contemporary theological literature devoted to understanding and providing an alternative to capitalism often sets the two in opposition to each other. In *The Enchantments of Mammon*, for example, Eugene McCarraher tries to take seriously Benjamin's claim that capitalism is religion in its own right. Proceeding from this assumption allows McCarraher to argue against Weber's notion of disenchantment and insist that capitalism is itself a form of enchantment. However, McCarraher ignores other aspects of Benjamin's argument, particularly when it comes to the relationship between capitalism and Christianity. For McCarraher capitalism does not work out the inner logic of Christianity, as Benjamin suggests by positioning the two internal to each other via the notion of parasitism. Rather, for McCarraher, capitalism is a "*mis*enchantment, a parody or perversion of our longing for a sacramental way of being in the world."[38] Capitalism can only issue "counterfeit promissory notes, for the love of money misdirects our sacramental desire to know the presence of divinity in our midst."[39] For McCarraher, there is no need to cast a light on the complicity of theological assumptions and concepts, since the problems lie elsewhere. Christianity, albeit in a modern, more romantic guise, is the solution, not part of the problem in and of itself. When Christianity does appear to lend support to the capitalist project, it does so not through any internal logic of its own but via external forces. Hence the need for a reorientation of our desire back to God via redemption, repentance, and renewal—a claim that coincides with attempts to rework Anselm's theory to more salutary ends that I discussed in the last chapter.

DEBT AND CONTROL

In the last section I mentioned that, for McCarraher, Christianity is part of the solution, not the problem with which we are currently dealing, that of indebtedness. Both Nietzsche and Benjamin provide a way to understand the fundamental relationship between debt or guilt, on the one hand, and religion (Christianity) and capitalism, on the other.

---

38. McCarraher, *Enchantments of Mammon*, 5; original emphasis.

39. McCarraher, *Enchantments of Mammon*, 5.

Capitalism is, Benjamin says, a religion all its own, but one that emerges out of Christianity as the culmination of the latter's internal logic. That logic can be found in Nietzsche's claim that the sense of guilt and debt track upwardly with redemption: an increase in the former entails a more fervent necessity for the latter. Benjamin, as I pointed out, pits the difference between the two in terms of atonement, in the sense that capitalism dissolves any hope for the latter in the immanence of its rituals, its economic demands, its debt. Debt then, for Benjamin, becomes a ubiquitous, generalized condition, one whose very immanence seems to close off any possibility of relief, any straining toward some external hope that would remedy indebtedness. We should understand this claim subjectively and economically, with both coinciding as one to create a generic sense of indebtedness that circulates throughout life under capitalism. Debt, under late or neoliberal capitalism, becomes an apparatus of control.

The language of "apparatus" comes from Louis Althusser, and his famous essay "Ideology and Ideological State Apparatuses."[40] Analyzing how the means of production reproduce themselves, Althusser famously makes a distinction between the Repressive State Apparatus (RSA) and Ideological State Apparatuses (ISAs). The RSA, as the name indicates, functions primarily through repression or violence, in the sense that it forms a unified, centralized whole as a means of maintaining order over-against the otherwise disparate elements of society. So understood, the RSA includes, among other things, "the Government, the Administration, the Army, the Police, the Courts, the Prisons, etc."[41] ISAs, in contrast, function primarily through ideological means as "distinct and specialized institutions."[42] Such institutions, as ISAs, tend to be more private than public, as is the RSA, and Althusser gives a list of the more crucial kinds, including the religious ISA, the educational ISA, the family ISA, the legal ISA, the political ISA, the trade union ISA, the communications ISA, and the cultural ISA.[43] The ISAs function separately, in terms specific to them, but in concert with each other to reproduce the means of production, which also means that the ruling class to a large extent controls them, at least in terms of ideology. Indeed, Althusser notes that it is virtually impossible for the ruling class to hold state power for an

---

40. Althusser, "Ideology and Ideological State Apparatuses."
41. Althusser, "Ideology and Ideological State Apparatuses," 142–43.
42. Althusser, "Ideology and Ideological State Apparatuses," 143.
43. Althusser, "Ideology and Ideological State Apparatuses," 143.

extended period without also exercising hegemonic control over the ISAs. Althusser writes:

> Each of them contributes towards this single result in the way proper to it. The political apparatus by subjecting individuals to the political State ideology, the "indirect" (parliamentary) or "direct" (plebiscitary or fascist) "democratic" ideology. The communications apparatus by cramming every "citizen" with daily doses of nationalism, chauvinism, liberalism, moralism, etc, by means of the press, the radio and television. The same goes for the cultural apparatus (the role of sport in chauvinism is of the first importance), etc. The religious apparatus by recalling in sermons and the other great ceremonies of Birth, Marriage and Death, that man is only ashes, unless he loves his neighbour to the extent of turning the other cheek to whoever strikes first. The family apparatus . . . but there is no need to go on.[44]

Nevertheless, because of the role ISAs play in the reproduction of the means of production, they can also, Althusser notes, be "the *site* of class struggle, and often of bitter forms of class struggle."[45] This is a point I return to in the next chapter, where I work out a theoretical basis for debt resistance at both the subjective and economic levels.

The multitude of ISAs function in tandem, reinforcing each other in their relatively separate spheres, but one usually plays a predominant role. For Althusser the educational ISA, or the system of public and private schools, predominates. The State, Althusser writes,

> takes children from every class at infant-school age, and then for years, the years in which the child is most "vulnerable," squeezed between the Family State Apparatus and the Educational State Apparatus, it drums into them, whether it uses new or old methods, a certain amount of "know-how" wrapped in the ruling ideology (French, arithmetic, natural history, the sciences, literature) or simply the ruling ideology in its pure state (ethics, civic instruction, philosophy). Somewhere around the age of sixteen, a huge mass of children are ejected "into production": these are the workers or small peasants. Another portion of scholastically adapted youth carries on: and, for better or worse, it goes somewhat further, until it falls by the wayside and fills the posts of small and middle technicians, white-collar workers, small and middle executives, petty bourgeois of all kinds. A last

---

44. Althusser, "Ideology and Ideological State Apparatuses," 154.
45. Althusser, "Ideology and Ideological State Apparatuses," 147; original emphasis.

portion reaches the summit, either to fall into intellectual semi-employment, or to provide, as well as the "intellectuals of the collective labourer," the agents of exploitation (capitalists, managers), the agents of repression (soldiers, policemen, politicians, administrators, etc.) and the professional ideologists (priests of all sorts, most of whom are convinced "laymen").[46]

Portions of Althusser's analysis, here, are obviously particular to his context, France in the 1960s and '70s. Nevertheless, the basic point is that the educational system functions to impart the "know-how" required to reproduce the means of production via labor. Simply put, school prepares people for work. To quote him again:

They go varying distances in their studies, but at any rate they learn to read, to write and to add—i.e. a number of techniques, and a number of other things as well, including elements (which may be rudimentary or on the contrary thoroughgoing) of "scientific" or "literary culture," which are directly useful in the different jobs in production (one instruction for manual workers, another for technicians, a third for engineers, a final one for higher management, etc.).[47]

As Althusser also makes clear in these passages, the school system interpellates individuals into the reigning ideology unevenly or, perhaps better put, differentially. The overall function of the system is ideological, but since the sphere of production and the various apparatuses that support it depend upon a division of labor, the latter must also be incorporated into the educational ISA. Otherwise put, up to a certain point, schools do not teach all individuals the same thing, the same "know-how." The educational ISA divvies up its ideologically determined knowledge and necessary skills based on the interplay of aptitude, class, and social need.

Beyond specific "know-how," students also learn the various affective components necessary to be a "good worker" and, hence, productive member of society.

But besides these techniques and knowledges, and in learning them, children at school also learn the "rules" of good behaviour, i.e. the attitude that should be observed by every agent in the division of labour, according to the job he is "destined" for: rules of morality, civic and professional conscience, which actually means rules of respect for the socio-technical division

46. Althusser, "Ideology and Ideological State Apparatuses," 155.
47. Althusser, "Ideology and Ideological State Apparatuses," 155.

of labour and ultimately the rules of the order established by class domination. They also learn to "speak proper French," to "handle" the workers correctly, i.e. actually (for the future capitalists and their servants) to "order them about" properly, i.e. (ideally) to "speak to them" in the right way, etc.[48]

All in all, the purpose of schooling is to teach the sets of "necessary" skills and values required to reproduce the means of production.

The same could be said of the other ISAs as well. Although they may do so differently and, at times, haphazardly, their function individually and collectively is to reproduce the means of production through ideological means. ISAs are, in this sense, ideological training grounds but, because of this, they do not have or produce value in and of themselves. Rather, they point away from themselves, as they externalize their value in the means of production, in the constant, circular reproduction of the means of production.

A state that exercises its power primarily through ideological state apparatuses can be understood as primarily disciplinary in nature. However, in "Postscript on the Societies of Control" Gilles Deleuze draws a distinction between disciplinary societies and control societies. The difference between the two, moreover, hinges on debt; he notes that in control societies, "a man is no longer a man confined but a man in debt."[49] The significance of debt to control societies no doubt corresponds to its mobility and ubiquity. Deleuze points out that in disciplinary societies, discipline is more contained and static, in that it is confined to the specific sphere of its influence, as Althusser maintains happens with ISAs. Discipline, of course, is one of the common threads that links institutions together, but it does so analogously: the school and the factory, for instance, are both disciplinary sites, but separately. No doubt they share a common denominator, and shape individuals accordingly, but they do so differently. The differences among domains may indeed and often do resonate to produce a whole, but the whole produced will always remain unstable, for the simple reason that individuals can and do move in and out of specific domains. As Deleuze puts it, in disciplinary societies "individuals are always going from one closed site to another, each with its

---

48. Althusser, "Ideology and Ideological State Apparatuses," 155.
49. Deleuze, "Postscript on the Societies of Control," 181.

own laws"; that is, "you were always starting over again (as you went from school to barracks, from barracks to factory)."⁵⁰

Another way to put the matter is to say that although in disciplinary societies discipline is widespread, it flounders on its inconsistency across domains and the gaps present in the passage among the latter. Confining discipline to discrete domains means that discipline is not all-confining, which is one of the reasons that Althusser can aver that ISAs may function as sites of class struggle. Debt fills in the gaps, rendering the distinction between disciplinary sites ultimately insignificant. In control societies, one still moves among the sites formerly marked as disciplinary. One still, in other words, passes from, between, and among family, school, work, and a host of other apparatuses, which gives the appearance of the gap that Deleuze considers essential to disciplinary societies. But debt moves with individuals, floating above the various passages we make between institutions as a sort of general equivalent that loops back on said institutions, shaping them in its own image.

Given that debt functions as a general equivalent, Deleuze notes that the difference between disciplinary and control societies is best expressed in money. He writes that "discipline was always related to molded currencies containing gold as a numerical standard, whereas control is based on floating exchange rates, modulations depending on a code setting sample percentages for various currencies."⁵¹ The difference between money understood hierarchically as grounded in a stable unit of account versus understood as determined immanently through its very ungroundedness correlates with the difference between discipline and control. That difference, moreover, extends throughout society as a whole, reshaping the way that institutions fashion individuals according to the demands of capital. Deleuze notes, for instance:

> In the prison system: the attempt to find "alternatives" to custody, at least for minor offenses, and the use of electronic tagging to force offenders to stay at home between certain hours. In the school system: forms of continuous assessment, the impact of continuing education on schools, and the related move away from any research in universities, "business" being brought into education at every level. In the hospital system: the new medicine "without doctors or patients" that identifies potential cases and subjects at risk and is nothing to do with any progress

---

50. Deleuze, "Postscript on the Societies of Control," 177, 179.
51. Deleuze, "Postscript on the Societies of Control," 180.

> toward individualizing treatment, which is how it's presented, but is the substitution for individual or numbered bodies of coded "dividual" matter to be controlled. In the business system: new ways of manipulating money, products, and men, no longer channeled through the old factory system. This is a fairly limited range of examples, but enough to convey what it means to talk of institutions breaking down: the widespread progressive introduction of a new system of domination.[52]

Thus, as Steven Shaviro summarizes the difference between the two, "the disciplinary society is closed and hierarchical, [whereas] the control society is open, fluid, and rhizomatic."[53] Byung-chul Han uses the image of the snake in contrast to the mole as representative of the neoliberal regime, to mark how the control society operates. Whereas the mole "moves within a closed system," the snake "does not move in closed spaces. Rather, *it makes space by means of its own movement.*"[54] The snake, moreover, "embodies the guilt and debts (*die Schuld, die Schulden*) that the neoliberal regime employs as instruments of domination."[55]

Two things are important to emphasize here. First, the passage from discipline to control should not be understood in terms of replacement. Institutions may reshape themselves according to a new and different logic, but it is still those institutions that are being reshaped, and some of their former functions remain. Han reads the passage to control societies as an "intensification" of capitalism. He writes, for instance, that the "passage from the mole to the snake—from subject to project—does not amount to setting out for an entirely new way of life; instead, it represents a mutation, indeed an intensification, of capitalism, which remains one and the same."[56] Second, although control may not function top-down, concentrated in particular, socially sanctioned institutions, it still exercises a type of sovereignty over the individual—or dividual, to use Deleuze's term—and it does so via debt. Disparate institutions may, at first glance, function in terms of their own, disciplinary laws, but debt renders any sort of autonomy they once had null and void. Debt moves among domains, is always with the individual, as a sort of supplement to identity.

---

52. Deleuze, "Postscript on Societies of Control," 180.
53. Shaviro, "Bitter Necessity of Debt."
54. Han, *Psycho-Politics*, 17–18.
55. Han, *Psycho-Politics*, 18.
56. Han, *Psycho-Politics*, 18.

Or, as Maurizio Lazzarato has argued, debt is identity itself, at least as it is conceived under neoliberalism.[57] The identity of the subject under the auspices of finance-driven capitalism is mediated through the creditor-debtor relationship. Neoliberalism, obviously, does not invent this relationship; indeed, the argument of this book rests on the assumption that the asymmetry of the creditor-debtor dyad is a form of control that runs through history, although it is articulated concretely in various ways. The antagonism found within the creditor-debtor relationship is one way to mark the centrality of class struggle or, what is more often the case, control as a driver of social organization. Neoliberalism does, however, intensify this relationship, specifying it to the point at which it becomes the primary driver of the economy economically, socially, morally, and theologically. It is in this sense that, according to Lazzarato, the base of social relationships under neoliberalism is the creditor-debtor relationship.[58]

The easiest way to specify, albeit briefly, what we mean by neoliberalism here is to distinguish it from the political economy of classical liberalism. As Adam Kotsko points out, classical liberalism certainly upheld the virtues of laissez-faire capitalism, but it did so while staying in its own lane, so to speak. Capitalism and the state in this model can and should coexist, so long as each maintains its own domain, without unnecessary interference from the other. Such is the condition of state power in classical liberalism, at least as an ideal. Neoliberalism seeks to break down the imagined border between the two, by insisting that capitalism should not and cannot remain confined to its own domain because it is essentially without domain. Neoliberalism, in this sense, seeks to subject other, formerly off-limit social spheres to a market logic, refashioning these according to its image. However, as Kotsko emphasizes, neoliberalism does not do this through a limitation of state power, pushing it to the point where it merely cowers in the corner and is left almost impotent. Rather, neoliberalism transforms state power itself, so that it can then be deployed "against the institutions of the welfare state, to reshape society in accordance with market models."[59]

One component of this shift, at least economically speaking, is the rise and subsequent dominance of finance capitalism as the main generator of value over and above the so-called real, material economy. In the

57. Lazzarato, *Making of the Indebted Man*, 13–36.
58. Lazzarato, *Making of the Indebted Man*, 13–36.
59. Kotsko, *Neoliberalism's Demons*, 5.

United States that distinction has often been marked popularly in the contrast between "Wall Street" and "Main Street" or the "1%" and the "99%."[60] Although such pithy contrasts have rhetorical value in political struggle, the distinction between the two is ambiguous at best, especially given the fact that the so-called real economy increasingly relies on its financial counterpart and vice versa. Nevertheless, Lazzarato suggests that it is better and more accurate to speak of "finance" in terms of "debt" and "credit" or "interest." He writes, "Debt is finance from the point of view of the debtors who have to repay it. Interest is finance from the point of view of creditors, security-holders who guarantee they benefit from debt."[61] What we call the "finance economy," then, is really the "debt economy," in the sense that its production and continuous reproduction depends on the simultaneous production and reproduction of debt, in both monetary and subjective terms.

CONCLUSION

Although politicians and the media often rail against debt as somehow inimical to economic security and growth, the fact is that under neoliberalism debt is an essential ingredient to the generation of value, and, if the argument is at all salient in previous chapters, to atonement itself. Debt does not impede growth but, rather, creates the conditions for its creation. Lazzarato notes that debt "represents the economic and subjective engine of the modern-day economy. Debt creation, that is, the creation and development of the power relation between creditors and debtors, has been conceived and programmed as the strategic heart of neoliberal politics. If debt is indeed central to understanding, and thus combating, neoliberalism, it is because neoliberalism has, since its emergence, been founded on the logic of debt."[62] Without debt, there is no neoliberalism, which means that debt props up neoliberalism as an economic program and mode of government. Nevertheless, in line with Marx's claim that capitalism creates the conditions for its own demise and destruction, Lazzarato points out that because it is foundational, debt provides the means to combat neoliberalism.

---

60. The Occupy Wall Street Movement organized itself around this notion. For an overview of the movement, see Gitlin, *Occupy Nation*.

61. Lazzarato, *Making of the Indebted Man*, 24.

62. Lazzarato, *Making of the Indebted Man*, 25.

Debt thus creates value, but it only does so via an initial capture of value, a capture that, like Marx's notion of primitive accumulation, must remain unacknowledged, hidden, or naturalized in the subsequent operation of the system it maintains and creates. Debt is, according to Lazzarato, an "extraction machine" that uses the whole of society as its resource. In so doing, debt captures the generic value present in society and redistributes it asymmetrically, along the lines of the creditor-debtor relationship. But it can only do so as long as it exercises subjective control as well; that is, subjects must experience and identify themselves as indebted. Such a claim brings us back to Nietzsche's identification of guilt and debt and, ultimately, the satisfaction theory of atonement: the indebted subject is also a guilty subject, who owes their creditor not only what is borrowed but their very existence—life itself.

Conclusion—The Unsavable Life

IN THE LAST CHAPTER, I attempted broadly to outline from a critical, philosophical perspective the way in which modern individuals are indebted subjects, economically, morally, and theologically. The wager of this book is that the economic needs the moral and theological to keep running, to keep extracting resources via the creation and extension of debt. This is why I have primarily devoted attention in the previous chapters to moral and theological issues related to the subjectivity of debt. The point of the argument I make is not, in the end, an economic analysis but is, rather, concerned with debt, with the experience of debt, for it is the latter, I think, that makes the former possible through its theological and moral legacies. Individuals who conceive of themselves as morally and theologically indebted pave the way for economic debt, allowing it to function, allowing it to capture individuals as indebted subjects.

I have traced these subjective conditions through certain theological texts because theology still remains with us, still remains salient when it comes to discussions of and practices related to debt. Another way to put the matter is to say that indebtedness is a form of political theology, which means that its so-called secular functioning in the economic realm is inseparable from its theological and moral valences, as these continue to operate in the present. Carl Schmitt's famous claim about political theology is, thus, relevant here: "All the significant concepts of the modern theory of the state are secularized theological concepts not only because of their historical development—in which they were transferred from theology to the theory of the state, whereby, for example, the omnipresent became the omnipotent law maker—but also because of their systematic structure, the recognition of which is necessary for a sociological considerations of these concepts."[1]

1. Schmitt, *Political Theology*, 36.

Nietzsche, in his own way, knew this all too well, when he claimed that "suddenly we stand before the paradoxical and horrifying expedient that afforded temporary relief for humanity, that stroke of genius on the part of Christianity: God sacrifices himself for the guilt of mankind, God himself makes payment to himself, God as the only being who can redeem man from what has become unredeemable for man himself—the creditor sacrifices himself for his debtor, out of *love* (can one credit that?), out of love for his debtor!—"[2] Drawing on Nietzsche, Benjamin too sees the connection between debt as guilt and debt as economic, which grounds capitalism as a religion. Benjamin saw capitalism as a religious cult of permanent duration, one that universalizes guilt. As he puts it, "An enormous feeling of guilt not itself knowing how to repent, grasps at the cult, not in order to repent for this guilt, but to make it universal, to hammer it into consciousness and finally and above all to include God himself in this guilt, in order to finally interest him in repentance."[3]

Benjamin saw capitalism as a religious cult that refuses the possibility of atonement, and this lack of forgiveness is what make capitalism unique qua religion. Benjamin's argument assumes that at one time atonement operated, but in contrast I see the promise of atonement as a trap, a façade that only increases the sense moral and theological indebtedness in tandem with economic indebtedness, even if this, in the end, takes the form of a debt of gratitude for grace.

The atonement, central to Christian faith and practice, rather than releasing subjects from debt only increases it, creating perpetually indebted subjects. This is, I have argued, on display in the satisfaction theory of atonement, which grounds and systemizes debt in theological terms, terms that would influence later theories of atonement. But the basic idea of Anselm's theory—that we are debtors to God, that we owe God gratitude for salvation—are contained in various ways and to greater or lesser degrees throughout biblical and theological sources, as I have shown in the previous chapters. The satisfaction theory atonement, along with its progeny, far from offering pure forgiveness, indebts subjects even further, through a debt of gratitude that hearkens back to our putative original state as debtors to God via obedience to God's commands.

The problem, then, as I have pointed out repeatedly, is not to rework atonement theory for contemporary sociopolitical issues but abandon atonement itself. My wager is that political theology in its constructive

2. Nietzsche, *Genealogy of Morals*, 528 (II.22).
3. Benjamin, "Capitalism as Religion," 259.

mode should abandon the idea of atonement, which amounts to abandoning what is often taken as a central component of the Christian faith. Abandoning atonement, however, does not mean that we cannot draw on theological and other sources to construct a quasi-religious or theological response to debt. It is the burden of this conclusion to show how this might be the case, although my attempt to do so is somewhat partial, piecemeal, and unabashedly ideal or utopian rather than systematic. Indeed, as Fred Moten and Stefano Harvey argue, which I discuss in detail below, systematization is part of the problem, hence the need for an approach that relies more on vignettes than tight, philosophical presentation.

If the idea is to abandon atonement as traditionally conceived, then it is essential to discuss the work of Adam Kotsko, who has done much to reconsider the idea of atonement, especially as it is present among early and medieval Christian thinkers, including Gregory of Nyssa and Anselm. I discussed Kotsko's critique of atonement theory in chapter 5, so I will not repeat it here. But Kotsko sees political potential in atonement theories that ground the devil as the evil infecting humanity, as we see it in earlier, ransom accounts of Christ's atonement. In other words, the devil, read metaphorically in the present, provides us with a concrete image to fight against: the devil's rule of this world.

Devils are everywhere, and I'm sympathetic to Kotsko's attempt to rehabilitate the ransom theory for political, theological ends. Nevertheless, I want to take a different line of thought, one that attempts to marshal biblical and theological sources against the creditor-debtor relationship. The problem with atonement theories, even ones that attempt to rehabilitate them, is that they still assume debt as a fundamental condition that must be resolved. I want to challenge this assumption, mining resources to think about the human condition beyond indebtedness.

THE CALL FOR JUBILEE

In *Debt: The First 5000 Years*, David Graeber calls for a Jubilee-style politics focused on debt forgiveness. He writes,

> It seems to me that we are long overdue for some kind of Biblical-style jubilee: one that would affect international debt and consumer debt. It would be salutary not just because it would relieve so much human suffering, but also because it would be

our way of reminding ourselves that money is not ineffable, that paying one's debts is not the essence of morality, that all these things are human arrangements and that if democracy is to mean anything, it is the ability to all agree to arrange things in a different way.[4]

Andrew Ross has expressed a similar sentiment when he notes, "In the jubilee tradition, freedom from debt bondage is intrinsically bound up with the idea of citizenship. This is one of the reasons why societies have chosen to ban usury, whether through religious proscription or as a matter of civil, even natural law."[5] Richard Dienst has also written positively about Jubilee, noting that the biblical tradition keeps "returning to inspire revolutionary political movements."[6]

One of the compelling aspects of the Jubilee tradition, which I outlined in chapter 1, is its legal codification. As I mentioned there, debt forgiveness or release was not an uncommon practice in the ancient world, but it was, for the most part, left up to the prerogative of the ruler. Debt release, in this sense, is pragmatic and at the whim of individuals, as a way to reset social relationships to keep the peace, so to speak. Debt forgiveness, here, is not really about altruism as it is the consolidation of power, for what better way to garner the support of the people than to cancel their debts.[7]

The Sabbath and Jubilee years certainly have such practices in mind in the background, but what is interesting, as Michael Hudson notes, is that it is part of the covenant. Debt forgiveness is codified in the law and, thus, not subject to the whims of the ruling class. In other words, what makes Israelite debt cancellation unique is that it is worked into the law, as a ritualized part of covenantal obligations. To what extent such programs were put into practice is, of course, up for debate, but the ideal remains salient for rethinking the role that debt plays in society and the individuals that it both enriches and harms.

Barring any whole-scale rearrangement of the economy, which I take as desirable but not currently sociopolitically feasible, the significance of the Sabbath and Jubilee years becomes important. The point of these institutions does not reside in a one-off cancellation of debts but,

4. Graeber, *Debt*, 390.
5. Ross, *Creditocracy and the Case for Debt Refusal*, 94.
6. Dienst, *Bonds of Debt*, 179.
7. These arguments are made by Michael Hudson in . . . *And Forgive Them Their Debts*.

rather, in their periodic cancellation of debts, codified into law. If the law is taken seriously and followed, the Sabbath and Jubilee years are not left up to the whim of any individual ruler but are, rather, worked into the substance of the law itself. Debt release is, in this sense, automatic, designed to manumit debts without reliance on vagaries and subjective whim.

Thus, calls for Jubilee cannot limit themselves to one-off debt cancellations. To call for Jubilee is to instantiate a regular, non-personal legal mechanism that would release debts periodically, thereby resetting economic arrangements to a base level. Granted, the conditions that created debt and debtors would remain the same in such an arrangement, but the automatic, periodic release of debt may open a space to rethink said conditions from the ground up.

Similar things could be said about the prohibition of usury as discussed in chapter 1, which limits the extent to which individuals can go into debt in the first place. Nevertheless, what remains interesting about these two streams of thought is that they clearly side with the debtors, over against the creditors. Debt relationships are, in this sense, not yet moralized or conceived as sinful but, rather, the result of unjust economic arrangements and practices. If anyone comes under fire it is the creditor, and not the debtor. Of course, this emphasis on the creditor as sinful and the debtor as receiving the short end of the stick would change and reverse relationships, as I have outlined in the previous chapters. Whereas sin with regard to financial arrangements did not attach to the debtor, in both his person and his practices, gradually the emphasis shifts to the creditor, with the debtor cast out into the realm of sin for his debt and debt for his sin.

One of the problems, however, with calls for Jubilee-style politics is that it still places that onus of debt forgiveness on those holding the debt. In other words, it is an appeal to the powerful to wield their power for the common good but, given our current sociopolitical and economic realities, there appears to be little hope in any sort of mass forgiveness, although partial and piecemeal proposals can no doubt be pointed to.[8] Debt is, simply put, a form of power.[9] If we are going to have significant, lasting debt-release policies, these have to come from the ground up,

---

8. The Biden-Harris Administration's Student Debt Relief Plan is a good example at such partial proposals, though aspects of it have repeatedly been blocked.

9. Di Muzio and Robbins, *Debt as Power*.

using tactics against those in power, those who hold and make profit from our debt and indebtedness.

INSOLVENCY

A more ground-up means to tackle debt release is to shift the discussion away from forgiveness (which is ultimately a Christian concept predicated on atonement, as least when it comes to indebtedness), toward refusal and resistance. Granted, what this would look like on the ground is up for debate, but we can outline some theoretical parameters to begin to think in terms of debt resistance. One such proposal comes from Franco "Bifo" Berardi, in his claim that we declare "the right to insolvency," which means "We're not going to pay the debt."[10] The phrase "We're not going to pay the debt" is not merely a catchy, activist slogan but, rather, a set of words designed to shift social perceptions about debt and its putatively irrevocable control. As Berardi writes, "These words are meant to change the social perception of the debt, creating a consciousness of its arbitrariness and moral illegitimacy."[11] The notion of insolvency, then, implies not only a refusal to pay debts but, rather, "a refusal to submit the living potency of social forces to the formal domination of the economic code."[12] "Insolvency means," for Berardi, "disclaiming the economic code of capitalism as a transliteration of real life, as a semiotization of social potency and richness."[13]

Roberto Esposito, writing in the context of economic-political theology, has expressed similar ideas regarding debt. Indeed, because of the position that debt holds over individuals in contemporary societies, he has expressed concerns that we should begin talking about economic theology, rather than simply political theology per se. According to Esposito's reading of Benjamin, the latter "situates the concept of guilt in the orbit of the law, economic theology as he conceived of it appears to reproduce the same exclusionary effect as the political-theological machine."[14] He goes on to note that "in the same way that original sin, in spite of Christ's intercession, is paid for by all human beings with the ultimate punishment

10. Berardi, *Uprising*, 55.
11. Berardi, *Uprising*, 57.
12. Berardi, *Uprising*, 58.
13. Berardi, *Uprising*, 58.
14. Esposito, *Two*, 205.

of mortality, the liability of the *nexus* to the arbitrary will of the creditor tends to become generalized in a condition of universal indebtedness."[15] Modern debtors, in such a schema, remain formally free, but they are subject to the debt that has seized—and therefore determined—their very lives. Lazzarato makes this point as well: one is only free to the extent that one buys into the system of credit-debt, having a subjectivity created by the condition of indebtedness.[16] Echoing Nietzsche, Esposito notes that, "despite the critical function that Christianity performed toward Roman cruelty, the idea of original sin, with the eternal punishment that came as a consequence of it, ended up reinforcing the notion of the debtor's irredeemable guilt."[17] To translate into the terms that I have been using, atonement increases the sense of indebtedness, meaning that we cannot talk about atonement without also confronting the way in which it buttresses and reinforces debt language and a debtor subjectivity.

Esposito, however, does not think that we can get rid of debt language entirely, but that we can, perhaps, implode it from within. Writing about sovereign debt, which affects individuals as well via austerity measures, he writes that we can "reverse its meaning." He continues, "Instead of trying to stop what is by now an unstoppable dynamic, we can speed it up, pushing it to its limit point, until it implodes. The fact that we are all debtors, or are becoming ones, means that there are no more real creditors. Every creditor is a debtor to another, in a chain whose first link has been lost. The problem we are facing is to transform this oppressive chain into a circle of solidarity."[18]

Transforming such oppressive chains into circles of social solidarity is precisely and what Stefano Harney and Fred Moten have in mind with their notion of "bad debt." They write, "It is not credit we seek nor even debt but bad debt which is to say real debt, the debt that cannot be repaid, the debt at a distance, the debt without creditor, the black debt, the queer debt, the criminal debt. Excessive debt, incalculable debt. Debt for no reason, debt broken from credit, debt as its own principle."[19] What would it mean to have debt as its "own principle"? What would it mean to detach debt from credit? Crucial here is the distinction they make between debt and credit along the lines of privatization and socialization.

15. Esposito, *Two*, 205–6.
16. Lazzarato, *Making of the Indebted Man*, 31.
17. Esposito, *Two*, 205.
18. Esposito, *Two*, 209.
19. Harney and Moten, *Undercommons*, 61.

"Credit is a means of privatizing debt and debt a means of socialization." They continue:

> So long as they pair in the monogamous violence of the home, the pension, the government, or the university, debt can only feed credit, debt can only desire credit. And credit can only expand by means of debt. But debt is social and credit is asocial. Debt is mutual. Credit runs only one way. But debt runs in every direction, scatters, escapes, seeks refuge. The debtor seeks refuge among other debtors, acquires debt from them, offers debt to them. The place of refuge is the place to which you can only owe more and more because there is no creditor, no payment possible.[20]

Harney and Moten call this space of "bad debt" the "fugitive public." They make it clear, however, that bad debt is a sort of justice that circulates among the populace, thereby posing a danger to creditors and their methodical extraction of capital. They write, for instance:

> Debt cannot be forgiven, it can only be forgotten to remember again. To forgive debt is to restore credit. It is restorative justice. Debt can be abandoned for bad debt. It can be forgotten for bad debt, but it cannot be forgiven. Only creditors can forgive, and only debtors, bad debtors, can offer justice. Creditors forgive debt to offer credit, to offer the very source of the pain of debt, a pain for which there is only one justice, bad debt, forgetting, remembering again, remembering it cannot be paid, cannot be credited, stamped, received.[21]

They continue:

> Credit can be restored, restructured, rehabilitated, but debt forgiven is always unjust, always unforgiven. Restored credit is restored justice and a restorative justice is always the renewed reign of credit, a reign of terror, a hail of obligations to be met, measured, meted, endured. Justice is only possible where debt never obliges, never demands, never equals credit, payment, payback. Justice is possible only where it is never asked, in the refuge of bad debt, in the fugitive public of strangers not communities, of undercommons not neighborhoods, among those who have been there all along from somewhere. To seek justice through restoration is to return debt to the balance sheet and

---

20. Harney and Moten, *Undercommons*, 63.
21. Harney and Moten, *Undercommons*, 63.

the balance sheet never balances. It plunges toward risk, volatility, uncertainty, more credit chasing more debt, more debt shackled to credit. To restore is not to conserve, again. There is no refuge in restoration. Conservation is always new. It comes from the place we stopped while we were on the run. It's made from the people who took us in. It's the space they say is wrong, the practice they say needs fixing, the homeless aneconomics of visiting.[22]

There is, to be sure, much going on in these paragraphs. But to summarize for our purposes, the language we often use to describe debt—such as forgiveness, restoration, restructuration, rehabilitation—contribute to a politics of debt that primarily has the creditor in mind. What Moten and Harney call "bad debt" is an immanent communal concept, one that is on the side of the debtors rather than the creditors. It is, as they say, an "aneconomics." Bad debt is thus a space outside of atonement, outside of salvation, outside of sin. It is the space of insolvency, or the refusal to pay because payment always flows upward to the creditor.

I do not want to reduce the radical potential of Moten and Harney's notion of "bad debt," but it is interesting to read it in the context of the Lord's Prayer. To reiterate the prayer:

> Our Father in heaven,
> may your name be revered as holy.
> May your kingdom come.
> May your will be done
> on earth as it is in heaven.
> Give us today our daily bread.
> And forgive us our debts,
> as we also have forgiven our debtors.
> And do not bring us to the time of trial,
> but rescue us from the evil one. (Matt 6:9–13)

The assumption of the prayer, along with the various parables that support the idea, is that we are entangled in a web of mutual indebtedness, one that blurs the lines between creditor and debtor. To forgive one's debts is, simultaneously, to receive forgiveness from one's debts from God. The problem, here, is that the wires between sin and debt remain crossed in the Lord's Prayer, not to mention elsewhere, as we have seen, thereby reinforcing the very sort of subjectivity that we intend to interrupt.

22. Harney and Moten, *Undercommons*, 63.

To overcome the subjectivity of indebtedness is to reshape identity without reference to indebtedness or, at the very least, to instantiate a sort of negative indebtedness, wherein debt cannot gain a hold. This is what I take Harney and Moten to be up to. Although they do not drop the language of debt, "bad debt" translates debt into something else, into a space outside the creditor-debtor relationship. Their use of the language of bad debt recalls Alain Badiou's notion of forcing language toward the construction of new truth procedures. For Badiou, truth procedures must be conducted in the language circulating in any situation, but a truth procedure will twist and rework that language into something new.[23] By using the language of "bad debt," Harney and Moten are doing something similar, using bad debt as a means to foster different types of communities, or "undercommons," as they prefer to say. Bad debt is a space outside of atonement, outside of salvation, outside of sin. It is the space of insolvency, or the refusal to pay, because in the creditor-debtor model payment always flows upward to the creditor.

This space outside sin is explored by Agamben, in his reading of a particular passage on limbo from St. Thomas Aquinas. In the Supplement to the *Summa Theologica*, Thomas discusses the so-called limbo of children. As Thomas points out, the limbo of children is not the same as what is referred to as the limbo of the fathers, the liminal place and state reserved for the just who had died in a state of original sin prior to Christ's redemption. Children who die without receiving the sacrament of baptism likely die in a state of original sin, but as Thomas points out, that state is not exactly the same in the two cases, since unbaptized children stand in a different relation to original sin than the fathers. Thomas notes that "in the Fathers original sin was expiated in so far as it infected the person, while there remained an obstacle on the part of nature, on account of which their satisfaction was not yet complete."[24] Unbaptized children, however, present "an obstacle both on the part of the person and on the part of nature."[25] Because of this, the "quality of punishment or reward" must differ, thereby necessitating that the fathers and unbaptized children be assigned "different abodes," with the limbo of the fathers "placed higher than the limbo of children."[26] The difference, however, also relates to a difference in expectation. Whereas the limbo

23. Badiou, *Being and Event*, 391–409.
24. Aquinas, *Summa Theologica*, suppl. 69, 6.
25. Aquinas, *Summa Theologica*, suppl. 69, 6.
26. Aquinas, *Summa Theologica*, suppl. 69, 6.

of the fathers is a temporary state, a state that has as its ultimate goal future redemption, the same cannot be said for the limbo of children. Since, unlike the fathers, unbaptized children are doubly burdened with personal and natural sin, "they have no hope of the blessed life."[27] The limbo of children is, then, a permanent state, a state that carries no hope for redemption.

Agamben has interpreted Thomas's discussion of the limbo of children in an interesting, though certainly heterodox, way. Agamben's reading, I suggest, provides us with a theological trope for thinking beyond the logic of debt, one that is in line with the authors mentioned above. Agamben notes that, for Thomas, the "punishment" of those consigned to the limbo of children is not afflictive but privative: it is based on lack, rather than direct action and, as such, is without pain. Such punishments, if they can even be called that, differ in kind rather than the degree to which it is inflicted on the damned. Agamben writes:

> The inhabitants of limbo, in the contrast to the damned, do not feel pain from this lack: Since they have only natural and not supernatural knowledge, which is implanted in us at baptism, they do not know that they are deprived of the supreme good or, if they do know (as others claim) they cannot suffer from it more than a reasonable person is pained by the fact that he or she cannot fly.[28]

Unlike the damned, then, the children of limbo suffer no penalty as such; to deal with them punitively, to inflict pain on them, would, according to Agamben, be unjust. To be sure, the children persist in their condition without hope of the blessed life, but he turns this relatively benign divine abandon into a virtue. Agamben writes, "The greatest punishment—the lack of the vision of God—thus turns into a natural joy: Irremediably lost, they persist without pain in divine abandon. God has not forgotten them, but rather they have always already forgotten God; and in the face of their forgetfulness, God's forgetting is impotent."[29] Since they are neither blessed nor punished, neither elected nor damned, they exist in a liminal state outside the law, "infused with a joy with no outlet."[30]

---

27. Aquinas, *Summa Theologica*, suppl. 69, 6.
28. Agamben, *Coming Community*, 5.
29. Agamben, *Coming Community*, 6.
30. Agamben, *Coming Community*, 6.

Agamben certainly takes some liberties with Thomas's treatment of the issue and the tradition of limbo more generally. Nevertheless, the logic he draws out serves to underline an important notion, one that dovetails with Berardi's, Lazzarato's, and Esposito's calls to reject debt and its legitimacy: the unredeemable or unsavable life. Limbo, for Agamben, represents neutrality with regard to salvation, which also means neutrality with regard to any sort of condition that would create the need for salvation. Of course, this flies in the face of orthodox theological reflection and, if taken seriously, threatens the Christian theological apparatus of debt and atonement. Agamben thus states, "The truly unsavable life is the one in which there is nothing to save, and against this the powerful theological machine of Christian *oiconomia* runs aground."[31] But its heterodoxy is also what makes it theologically, economically, and politically potent, since it denies the very conditions that work to create the indebted subject. Perhaps it is only when we realize that we do not need to be redeemed because there is nothing to save—that is, as Berardi and Lazzarato claim, we owe nothing—that we can begin to think anew, beyond the logic of debt and atonement. Thinking in such a manner would likewise be a potent resource against neoliberalism, in the sense that it would undercut that on which it feeds: the indebted subject.

The limbo of children may seem a hopelessly heterodox image, but its basic assumptions dovetail with other biblical passages as, for instance, Jesus's comments concerning children in Luke: "People were bringing even infants to him that he might touch them, and when the disciples saw it, they sternly ordered them not to do it. But Jesus called for them and said, 'Let the children come to me, and do not stop them, for it is to such as these that the kingdom of God belongs. Truly I tell you, whoever does not receive the kingdom of God as a little child will never enter it'" (Luke 15:17–18). When it comes to disrupting the sovereignty of debt over the creation and maintenance of subjectivity, perhaps we should all take a lesson from children, who remain blissfully unaware of their supposed debts. At the very least, doing so incites us to think otherwise than and outside of the creditor-debtor relationship, morally, theologically, and economically. It incites us, that is, to rethink community and put into practice a form of life together—one unburdened of debt.

---

31. Agamben, *Coming Community*, 6.

Bibliography

Abelard, Peter. *Commentary on the Epistle to the Romans*. Translated by S. R. Cartwright Washington, DC: Catholic University of America Press, 2011.

Agamben, Giorgio. *The Coming Community*. Translated by Michael Hardt. Minneapolis: University of Minnesota Press, 1993.

———. *Creation and Anarchy: The Work of Art and the Religion of Capitalism*. Translated by Adam Kotsko. Stanford: Stanford University Press, 2019.

———. *Homo Sacer: Sovereign Power and Bare Life*. Translated by Daniel Heller-Roazen. Stanford: Stanford University Press, 1998.

———. *Profanations*. Translated by Jeff Fort. New York: Zone, 2007.

———. *The Time That Remains: A Commentary on the Letter to the Romans*. Translated by Patricia Dailey. Stanford: Stanford University Press, 2005.

Aglietta, Michel. *Money: 5,000 Years of Debt and* Power. Translated by David Broder. London: Verso, 2018.

Ahn, Ilsup. *Just Debt*. Waco, TX: Baylor University Press, 2017.

Alfeyev, Hilarion. *Christ the Conqueror of Hell: The Decent into Hades from an Orthodox Perspective*. Crestwood, NY: St. Vladimir's Seminary Press, 2009.

Althusser, Louis. "Contradiction and Overdetermination." In *For Marx*, translated by Ben Brewster, 87–128. London: Verso, 2006.

———. "Ideology and Ideological State Apparatuses." In *Lenin and Philosophy and Other Essays*, translated by Ben Brewster, 127–87. New York: Monthly Review, 1971.

Anderson, Gary A. *Charity*. New Haven: Yale University Press, 2013.

———. *Sin: A History*. New Haven: Yale University Press, 2010.

Anselm of Caterbury. *Cur Deus Homo?* In *Anselm of Canterbury*, edited by Brain Davies and G. E. Evans, 260–356. Oxford: Oxford University Press, 2008.

Aquinas, Thomas. *Summa Theologiae*. 2nd rev. ed. Translated by Fathers of the English Dominican Province. 1920. https://www.newadvent.org/summa/.

Aristotle. *Nicomachean Ethics*. In *The Basic Works of Aristotle*, edited by Richard McKeon, 935–1126. New York: The Modern Library, 2001.

———. *Politics*. In *The Basic Works of* Aristotle, edited by Richard McKeon, 1127–324. New York: The Modern Library, 2001.

Arthur, Chris. *Financial Literacy: Neoliberalism, the Consumer, and the Citizen*. Rotterdam: Sense, 2012.

Augustine. *The City of God*. London: Penguin Classics, 2004.

———. *On the Trinity*. In *Nicene and Post-Nicene Fathers*, First Series, vol. 3, edited by Philip Schaff and translated by Arthur West Haddan. Buffalo, NY: Christian Literature, 1887. https://www.newadvent.org/fathers/130113.htm.

———. "Sermon 33 on the New Testament." In *Nicene and Post-Nicene Fathers*, First Series, vol. 6, edited by Philip Schaff and translated by R. G. MacMullen, 6:762–67. Buffalo, NY: Christian Literature Publishing Co., 1888.

———. *Sermons*. Edited by John E. Rotelle. New Rochelle, NY: New City, 1992.

Aulen, Gustav. *Christus Victor: An Historical Study of the Three Main Types of the Idea of Atonement*. Translated by A. G. Herbert. Eugene, OR: Wipf & Stock, 2003.

Badiou, Alain. *Being and Event*. Translated by Oliver Feltham. London: Continuum 2005.

———. *Saint Paul: The Foundation of Universalism*. Translated by Ray Brassier. Stanford: Stanford University Press, 2003.

Balthasar, Hans Urs von. *The Glory of the Lord: A Theological Aesthetics, Volume 2*. Translated by Louth A. McDonagh and F. B. McNeil. San Francisco: Ignatius, 1982.

Barclay, John. *Paul and the Gift*. Grand Rapids: Eerdmans, 2017.

Barth, Karl. *The Epistle to the Romans*. Translated by Edwyn C. Hoskyns. London: Oxford University Press, 1968.

Bataille, Georges. *The Accursed Share*. Translated by Robert Hurley. New York: Zone, 1991.

Bell, Daniel M., Jr. *The Economy of Desire: Christianity and Capitalism in a Postmodern World*. Grand Rapids: Baker, 2012

———. *Liberation After the End of History: The Refusal to Cease Suffering*. London: Routledge, 2001.

Benjamin, Walter. "Capitalism as Religion." In *Walter Benjamin: Selected Writings*, edited by Marcus Bullock and Michael W. Jennings, 1:288–91. Cambridge: Harvard University Press, 1996.

Berardi, Franco "Bifo." *The Uprising: On Poetry and Finance*. Los Angeles: Semiotext(e), 2012.

Biddle, Mark E. *Missing the Mark: Sin and its Consequences in Biblical Theology*. Nashville: Abingdon, 2005.

Birnbaum, Philip. "Prozbul." In *A Book of Jewish Concepts*, 513. New York: Hebrew Publishing, 1975.

Blanton, Thomas R., IV. *A Spiritual Economy: Gift Exchange in the Letters of Paul*. New Haven: Yale University Press, 2017.

Blanton, Ward. *Displacing Christian Origins: Philosophy, Secularity, and the New Testament*. Chicago: University of Chicago Press, 2007.

———. *A Materialism for the Masses: Saint Paul and the Philosophy of Undying Life*. New York: Columbia University Press, 2014.

Bloch, Ernst. *Atheism in Christianity*. Translated by J. T. Swann. London: Verso, 2009.

Boer, Roland. *The Sacred Economy of Ancient Israel*. Louisville: Westminster John Knox, 2015.

Breton, Stanislas. *A Radical Philosophy of Saint Paul*. Translated by Joseph Ballan. New York: Columbia University Press, 2011.

Brondos, David. *Fortress Introduction to Salvation and the Cross*. Minneapolis: Fortress, 2007.

Brown, Peter. *The Ransom of the Soul: Afterlife and Wealth in Early Western Christianity*. Cambridge: Harvard University Press, 288

Calvin, John. *Letter on Usury*. In *Usury: A Scriptural, Ethical, and Economic View*, by Calvin Elliot, 73–78. Millersburg, OH: The Anti-Usury League, 1902.
Caputo, John D., and Linda Martín Alcoff, eds. *Saint Paul Among the Philosophers*. Bloomington: Indiana University Press, 2009.
Catherine of Siena. *The Dialogue*. Translated by Suzanne Noffke. Mahwah, NJ: Paulist, 1980.
Concannon, Cavin W. *Profaning Paul*. Chicago: University of Chicago Press, 2021.
Crary, Jonathan. *24/7: Late Capitalism and the Ends of Sleep*. London: Verso, 2014.
Deleuze, Gilles. *Nietzsche and Philosophy*. Translated by Hugh Tomlinson. New York: Columbia University Press, 1983.
———. "Postscript on the Societies of Control." In *Negotiations*, translated by Martin Joughin, 177–82. New York: Columbia University Press, 1997.
Derrida, Jacques. *The Gift of Death*. Translated by David Wills. Chicago: University of Chicago Press, 2005.
———. *Given Time: Counterfeit Money*. Translated by Peggy Kamuf. Chicago: University of Chicago Press, 1992.
Dienst, Richard. *The Bonds of Debt: Borrowing Against the Common Good*. London: Verso, 2011.
Di Muzio, Tim, and Richard H. Robbins. *Debt as Power*. Manchester: Manchester University Press, 2016.
Duchrow, Ulrich, and Franz J. Hinkelammert. *Property for People, Not for Profit*. Translated by Elaine Griffiths et al. London: Zed, 2004.
Esposito, Roberto. *Immunitas: The Protection and Negation of Life*. Translated by Zakiya Hanafi. London: Polity, 2011.
———. *Two: The Machine of Political Theology and the Place of Thought*. New York: Fordham University Press, 2015.
Federal Reserve Bank of New York. "Household Debt and Credit Report (Q2 2024)." https://newyorkfed.org/microeconomics/hhdc.
Foucault, Michel. *The Birth of Biopolitics*. Translated by Graham Burchell. New York: Picador, 2008.
Geisst, Charles R. *Beggar Thy Neighbor: A History of Usury and Debt*. Philadelphia: University of Pennsylvania Press, 2013.
Gitlin, Todd. *Occupy Nation: The Roots, The Spirit, and the Promise of Occupy Wall Street*. New York: It, 2012.
Gorringe, Timothy. *God's Just Vengeance*. Cambridge: Cambridge University Press, 1996.
Graeber, David. *Debt: The First 5,000 Years*. Brooklyn: Melville House, 2011.
Gregory of Nyssa. *Against Eunomius*. In *Nicene and Post-Nicene Fathers*, Second Series, vol. 5, edited by Philip Schaff and Henry Wace, eds. Buffalo, NY: Christian Literature, 1893. https://www.newadvent.org/fathers/290105.htm.
———. *The Great Catechism*. In *Nicene and Post-Nicene Fathers*, Second Series, vol. 5, edited by Philip Schaff and Henry Wace, eds. Buffalo, NY: Christian Literature, 1893. https://www.newadvent.org/fathers/2908.htm.
———. *Homily 5*. Translated by Theodore G. Stylianopoulos. 2003. https://www.orthodoxprayer.org/Articles_files/GregoryNyssa-Homily5%20Lords%20Prayer.html.
Gutiérrez, Gustavo. *Essential Writings*. Edited by James B. Nickoloff. Maryknoll, NY: Orbis, 1996.

———. *A Theology of Liberation*. Translated by Sister Caridad Inda and John Eagleson. Maryknoll, NY: Orbis, 1971.

Han, Byung-chul. *Psycho-Politics: Neoliberalism and New Technologies of Power*. Translated by Erik Butler. London: Verso, 2017.

Harney, Stefano, and Fred Moten. *The Undercommons: Fugitive Planning and Black Study*. London: Minor Compositions, 2016.

Hart, David Bentley. *The Beauty of the Infinite: An Aesthetics of Christian Truth*. Grand Rapids: Eerdmans, 2004.

Harvey, David. *A Companion to Marx's Capital*. London: Verso, 2018.

Henry, Michel. *Words of Christ*. Translated by Christina M. Gschwandtner. Grand Rapids: Eerdmans, 2012.

Hudson, Michael. *. . . And Forgive Them Their Debts: Lending, Foreclosure, and Redemption from Bronze Age Finance to the Jubilee Year*. Glashütte: ISLET-Verlag, 2018.

Irenaeus. *Against Heresies*. In *Irenaeus of Lyons*, edited by Robert M. Grant. London: Routledge, 1997.

Kierkegaard, Soren. *Fear and Trembling*. In *Fear and Trembling/Repetition*, translated by Howard V. Hong and Edna H. Hong, 1–124. Princeton: Princeton University Press, 1983.

Konstan, David. *Before Forgiveness: The Origins of a Moral Idea*. Cambridge: Cambridge University Press, 2010.

Kotsko, Adam. *Neoliberalism's Demons*. Stanford: Stanford University Press, 2018.

———. "The Persistence of the Ransom Theory of Atonement." In *T&T Clark Companion to Atonement*, edited by Adam J. Johnson, 277–94. London: Bloomsbury, 2017.

———. *The Politics of Redemption: The Social Logic of Salvation*. London: T&T Clark, 2010.

Lacan, Jacques. *The Four Fundamental Concepts of Psychoanalysis: The Seminar of Jacques Lacan, Book XI*. Translated by Alan Sheridan. New York: Norton, 1978.

Lazonby, David. "Apply the Jubilee to Contemporary Socio-Economic and Environmental Issues." *Journal of European Baptist Studies* 16 (2016) 30–50.

Lazzarato, Maurizio. *The Making of the Indebted Man*. Translated by Joshua David Jordon. Los Angeles: Semiotext(e), 2012.

Le Goff, Jacques. *Your Money or Your Life*. Translated by Patricia Ranum. New York: Zone, 1990.

Martin, Craig. *A Critical Introduction to the Study of Religion*. London: Routledge, 2012.

Marx, Karl. *Capital, Volume 1*. Translated by Ben Fowkes. London: Penguin, 1990.

———. *Capital, Volume 3*. Translated by David Fernbach. London: Penguin, 1993.

McCarraher, Eugene. *The Enchantments of Mammon*. Cambridge: Harvard University Press, 2019.

McClanahan, Annie. *Dead Pledges: Debt, Crisis, and Twenty-First-Century Culture*. Stanford: Stanford University Press, 2017.

Meeks, Douglas M. *God the Economist*. Minneapolis: Fortress, 1989.

Miranda, José Porfirio. *Communism in the Bible*. Translated by Robert R. Barr. Eugene, OR: Wipf & Stock, 1982.

———. *Marx and the Bible: A Critique of the Philosophy of Oppression*. Translated by John Eagleson. Maryknoll, NY: Orbis, 1974.

Nietzsche, Friedrich. *On the Genealogy of Morals*. In *On the Genealogy of Morals and Ecce Homo*, edited by Walter Kaufmann, 24–163. New York: Vintage, 1989.
———. *The Will to Power*. Translated by Walter Kaufmann and R. J. Hollingdale. New York: Vintage, 1967.
Noonan, John T., Jr. "*Tokos* and *Atokion*: An Examination of Natural Law Reasoning Against Usury and Against Contraception; Note." *Natural Law Forum*, Paper 109 (1965).
Oakman, Douglas E. *Jesus, Debt, and the Lord's Prayer*. Eugene, OR: Cascade, 2014.
———. *The Political Aims of Jesus*. Minneapolis: Fortress, 2012.
Origen. *Commentary on the Epistle to the Romans*. In *Commentary on the Epistle to the Romans Books 6–10*, translated by Thomas P. Scheck, 1–310. Washington, DC: Catholic University of America Press, 2002.
———. *Contra Celsum*. In *Ante-Nicene Fathers*, vol. 4, edited by Alexander Roberts, James Donaldson, and A. Cleveland Coxe. Buffalo, NY: Christian Literature Publishing Co., 1885.
———. *On Prayer*. Translated by William A. Curtis. Nottingham: Nottingham Publishing, n.d.
Petrella, Ivan. *Beyond Liberation Theology: A Polemic*. London: SCM, 2008.
Phelps, Hollis. *Alain Badiou: Between Theology and Anti-Theology*. London: Acumen, 2013.
———. *Jesus and the Politics of Mammon*. Eugene, OR: Cascade, 2019.
Ramsey Solutions. "Debt Help That Actually Works." *Ramsey Solutions*, Apr. 2, 2024. https://www.ramseysolutions.com/debt/the-truth-about-getting-debt-help.
Rieger, Jeorg. *Christ and Empire: From Paul to Postcolonial Times*. Minneapolis: Fortress, 2007.
Ross, Andrew. *Creditocracy and the Case for Debt Refusal*. New York: OR Books, 2013.
Ruprecht, Louis A. *Afterwards: Hellenism, Modernism, and the Myth of Decadence*. Albany: State University of New York Press, 1996.
Schmitt, Carl. *Political Theology*. Translated by Georg Schwab. Chicago: University of Chicago Press, 2005.
Schweitzer, Albert. *The Quest of the Historical Jesus*. Translated by W. Montgomery. Mineola, NY: Dover, 2005.
Serres, Michel. *The Natural Contract*. Translated by Elizabeth MacArthur and William Paulson. Ann Arbor: University of Michigan Press, 1995.
——— *The Parasite*. Translated by Lawrence R. Scheher. Minneapolis: University of Minnesota Press, 2007.
Shaviro, Steven. "The Bitter Necessity of Debt: Neoliberal Finance and the Society of Control." http://www.shaviro.com/Othertexts/Debt.pdf.
Singh, Devin. *Divine Currency: The Theological Power of Money in the* West. Stanford: Stanford University Press, 2018.
Sobrino, John. *No Salvation Outside the Poor: Prophetic-Utopian Essays*. Maryknoll, NY: Orbis, 2008.
Sölle, Dorothee. *Christ the Representative*. London: SCM, 1997.
Stimilli, Elletra. *Debt and Guilt: A Political Philosophy*. Translated by Stefania Porcelli London: Bloomsbury Academic, 2019.
———. *The Debt of the Living: Ascesis and Capitalism*. Translated by Arianna Bove, Albany: State University of New York Press, 2017.

Sutherland, Andrew W. "Debt Resistance and Satisfaction? Notes from Catherine of Siena toward a Theology of Redemption Against Neoliberal Capitalism." *Modern Theology* 38 (2022) 3–18.

Tanner, Kathryn. *Christianity and the New Spirit of Capitalism*. New Haven: Yale University Press, 2019.

Taubes, Jacob. *The Political Theology of Paul*. Translated by Dana Hollander. Stanford: Stanford University Press, 2004.

Tertullian. *On Prayer*. In *Ante-Nicene Fathers*, vol. 3, edited by Alexander Roberts et al. and translated by S. Thelwall. Buffalo, NY: Christian Literature, 1885. https://www.newadvent.org/fathers/0322.htm.

———. *On Repentance*. In *Ante-Nicene Fathers*, vol. 3, edited by Alexander Roberts et al. and translated by S. Thelwall. Buffalo: Christian Literature Publishing Co., 1885. https://www.newadvent.org/fathers/0320.htm.

Trueba, Elena. "Life or Debt: Dave Ramsey's Capitalist Theology." *The Bias* (Dec. 10, 2020). https://christiansocialism.com/dave-ramsey-debt-capitalism-socialism/.

Van der Heiden, Gert-jan, et al., eds. *Saint Paul and Philosophy: The Consonance of Ancient and Modern Thought*. Berlin: De Gruyter, 2023.

Weaver, Taylor. *The Scandal of Community*. Minneapolis: Fortress, 2021.

Weber, Max. *The Protestant Ethic and the Spirit of Capitalism, with Other Writings on the Rise of the West*. 4th ed. Translated by Stephen Kalberg. Oxford: Oxford University Press, 2009.

Wykes, Michael. "Devaluing the Scholastics: Calvin's Ethics of Usury." *Calvin Theological Journal* 38 (2003) 27–51.

Žižek, Slavoj. *The Fragile Absolute: Or, Why is the Christian Legacy Worth Fighting For?* London: Verso, 2000.

———. *The Ticklish Subject: The Absent Figure of Political Ontology*. London: Verso, 2009.

Index

Abelard, Peter, 96, 98, 132
Abraham (Abram), 32, 51, 78–80
Abrahamic covenant, 32
abundance, 5, 31–33, 45, 62–64, 70, 83, 106, 137
Adam, 82, 85, 105–6, 118–19, 139
Adam's disobedience, 82n21, 83–85, 123
Agamben, Giorgio, 27n45, 71n1, 76–77, 89n31, 93–94, 155, 175–77
Althusser, Louis, 45n2, 146, 157–61
animality, as feature of human nature, 147–48, 151
Anselm of Canterbury, 6–7, 60, 89, 98, 101–2, 106, 121–44, 146, 150, 155–56, 167
anti-philosophy, 77
apocalypticism, 99
Aquinas, Thomas, 23–25, 33–34, 43, 175–77
Aristotle, 17–23, 26, 33
asceticism, 21, 153–54
asymmetry, in relationships, 46, 57, 62, 64, 163
atonement, 4–7, 44, 78–79, 95–97, 119–20, 144–46, 150–52, 155, 164–77
    Christus Victor, 99–100, 123
    dramatic theories, 97–101, 105, 123–24
    moral influence theory, 98
    objective theories, 97–100
    penal substitution, 138
    ransom theory, 49–50, 69n35, 99–109, 120–21, 124, 168
    recapitulation, 82, 122
    satisfaction theory, 6, 43, 60, 92, 98, 101–2, 106, 121–44, 147, 150, 165, 167, 175
    subjective theories, 97–100
Augustine, 6, 97, 103–5, 109, 115–16, 119–21
Aulen, Gustav, 97–100, 123

Badiou, Alain, 71n1, 73–74, 76–79, 85, 89, 175
bad debt, as a form of social solidarity 172, 174
baptism, 54, 78, 96, 175–76
Barth, Karl, 76
Benjamin, Walter, 146, 152, 154–57, 167, 172
Berardi, Franco, 171, 177
blessings, Jesus' pronouncement of, 50, 52–53
Bloch, Ernst, 15, 37
blood, of Christ, 78, 81, 105, 113
borrowing, 1, 7, 13–15, 24–25, 32–34, 42, 66, 146, 165
Breton, Stanislas, 71n1, 73

Calvin, John, 16–17, 153
Catherine of Siena, 138
charity, 16–17, 68–69, 91, 94, 103, 136
circumcision, 75, 80, 93
class conflict, 28, 36, 157–63, 169

commerce, 31–32, 121
commercial transaction, 20, 29–30
commodity fetishism, 152
community, 4, 8, 18, 27–28, 39–40, 77–78, 148–149, 176–78
control societies, 161–63
covenant, with Israel, 27, 29–30, 32, 36, 169–70
creation, doctrine of, 107, 126, 131
credit, 2, 27, 35, 62, 64, 68–69, 125, 138, 142, 151, 167, 172–74

death, of Christ, 78–83, 96, 100–102, 105–9, 123, 132–41, 158
death, law of, 84–90
death drive, 75, 85, 90
debt cancellation, 27, 35–38, 48, 61–62, 70, 169
debt forgiveness, 44, 55, 62, 110, 112, 169–70, 173
debt slavery, 28
Deleuze, Gilles, 146, 150, 160–62
Derrida, Jacques, 67–68, 80
descent into hell, Christ's, 100–101, 109
desire, as theological concept, 19–20, 82, 85, 134–37, 139–40, 154, 156
Deuteronomic history, 37
devil, the, 48–50, 54, 99, 101–2, 105, 107–9, 118, 123–25, 137, 168
differentiating wealth, 31–32, 41, 53
disciplinary societies, 160–62
disenchantment, 156
disobedience, to God, 134, 136
dualism, 99

economy, 2, 12–13, 33, 35, 56, 63–64, 67–68, 92, 134–37, 142, 163–64, 170
election, doctrine of, 153
empire, ontology of 128
enjoyment, 20, 51–52, 148
entrepreneur of the self, 14
Esposito, Roberto, 102, 171–72, 177

eternal life, 26, 52, 54, 61, 69, 70, 76, 80, 82–84, 103, 107,
eternal punishment, 17, 54, 133, 155, 172
exchange, 1, 18–27, 31–33, 51, 57, 68, 75–77, 107, 118, 121, 135–36, 148, 152, 161
exchange-value, 18, 51
Eve, 105
event, the, 75–79, 89
evil, 24, 53, 56, 66, 84, 99–100, 103, 108–9, 148, 168

fall, Christian doctrine of, 75
financial literacy, 12–14
flesh, 5, 35, 72, 79, 84, 87–91, 94–95, 105–6, 108–9, 112, 119
forced choice, 34, 44
Foucault, Michel, 13–14
free will, 24, 118, 128
friendship, 13–14, 25, 60

general economy, 63
gentiles, 73–74, 79–80, 105–6, 111
gift, 69, 79–80, 83–84, 87, 133, 136–37, 142–43
glory, 49, 53, 63, 75–76, 78, 81, 135
good life, 18–20
grace, 5, 58, 60–61, 72, 77–79, 81–84, 87, 90–91, 95, 115, 119–20, 131, 133, 136, 142, 167
gratitude, debt of, 133–34, 142, 155, 167–68
Gregory of Nyssa, 6, 97, 101, 103, 107–9, 116–21, 168
guilt, 4, 7, 11–12, 35, 40, 44, 82, 85, 87, 98, 104, 118, 125, 127, 130–31, 134, 138, 146–47, 150–52, 155–57, 162, 165, 167, 172
Gutiérrez, Gustavo, 15n8, 29n52, 51

Harney, Stefano, 172–175
honor, 6, 14, 76, 106, 112, 122, 126–31, 133, 137, 139, 142
household management, in Aristotle, 17–19

incarnation, 48, 107, 117, 123, 136, 141
indebtedness, as behavioral problem, 12–15
ideological state apparatus, 157–61
ideology, 157–60
idolatry, 75–76
immortality, 75–76, 106
immunity paradigm, 102
insolvency, 36, 171, 174–75

Irenaeus, 82
Isaac, 80
Israel, 27–33, 36–37, 41, 48–49, 72, 79–80, 169

jubilee, 33–42, 44–49, 55, 70, 109–12, 119, 131, 145, 148, 169–70
justice, 11, 14, 16–17, 21–23, 25, 33–34, 36, 42, 51, 54, 62, 79, 82, 87, 103–6, 111, 117, 128–29, 131, 133, 139–40, 149, 173, 174
justification, 47, 79, 81, 83, 123

kenosis, 101
Kierkegaard, Søren, 80
kingdom of heaven, or God, 50–55, 57, 63–66, 128–29, 142, 174, 177

land, 38, 30, 32, 36, 38–41, 59, 62
law, 5, 17, 21–25, 27, 30–31, 36–40, 52, 62, 65–66, 68, 70, 72–91, 104, 111–12, 127, 129, 148–49, 161–62, 167, 169–80, 172, 177
Lazzarato, Maurizio, 2–3, 14, 146, 163–65, 172, 177
Le Goff, Jacques, 16–17, 25–26
lending, 15, 24, 26, 29, 30, 32–33, 39, 42, 68–69, 103
liberation theologies, 8, 15, 50–51
limbo, 175–77
loans, personal, 1–2, 13, 20, 28, 30, 38, 67–68
love, 13–14, 30, 59, 61, 64, 66–67, 72–73, 81, 91–92, 94, 98, 100, 112, 116–17, 119, 125, 132–33, 138–41, 151, 156, 158, 167
Luther, Martin, 153

mammon, 61–62, 64, 83, 90, 94, 156
Marx, Karl, 18, 27–28, 51–52, 152, 164–65
means of production, 27, 157–160
mercy, 51–53, 57–58, 100, 117–19, 128, 131, 133, 139–40, 146, 149–50
messianism, 48, 77, 93–94
Miranda, José Porfirio, 31–32, 53
money, 1, 13, 16–30, 33–34, 58, 61–62, 67, 113, 119, 131, 156, 161–62, 169
mortality, 172
Moses, 51, 82, 118
Moten, Fred, 168, 172–75

neoliberalism, 2–7, 11, 13, 43, 122, 134–38, 141–46, 156–157, 162–64, 177
Nietzsche, Friedrich, 125, 137–38, 142, 146–52, 156–57, 166–67, 172
non-reciprocity, in relationships, 5, 45, 67–70

obedience, 68, 82–85, 92, 123–129, 132–26, 140, 149, 168
obligation, 1–3, 25, 35–36, 66, 68–69, 80, 87, 90–92, 114, 117, 125, 127, 130–32, 138, 141, 143, 147–53, 170, 173
Occupy Wall Street, 164
omnipotence, God's, 99, 167
omnipresence, God's, 107–67
Onesimus, 91–92
Origen, 6, 97, 101–9, 112–15, 119–21
original sin, 75, 127, 172, 175

parables, 5, 45, 56, 70, 112, 175
  of the rich fool, 62–63
  of the rich man and Lazarus, 50–52
  of the two debtors, 58–59

parables (*cont.*)
   of the unforgiving servant,
     60–61, 81, 125, 130, 173
parasitism, 27n4, 57, 156
patron-client relationship, 92
personal finance, 13
power, 1–3, 13, 16, 28, 49, 51, 56, 67,
   75, 81, 99–102, 105, 107–9,
   117–18, 123–25, 138, 141,
   146–51, 157, 160, 163–64,
   169–71, 177, 179
preferential option for the poor, 51
primitive accumulation, 165
profanation, 193–94
prohibitions against usury, biblical
property, 2, 18, 26, 36, 40–41, 60, 62,
   124, 127
protestant work ethic, 152–56
prozbul, 37–40
punishment, 54, 76, 86, 103, 124,
   128–32, 140, 143, 149, 172,
   176–77

Ramsey, Dave, 12–14
rationality, as feature of human
   nature, 21, 23, 38, 102,
   123–26, 129, 132
Reciprocity, 5, 21, 27, 45, 65–70, 80,
   82, 86, 103
Reconciliation, with God, 81–82, 96,
   98–99, 137
repentance, 54–55, 96, 103, 114,
   119, 155–56, 167
repressive state apparatus, 157
responsibility, 12–15, 25, 33–35,
   42–44, 52, 67, 76, 118, 131,
   144, 151
restrictive economy, 63
resurrection, 5, 74, 77–80, 83, 96,
   100
reversal of values, 50

sabbath year, 4, 11, 35–41, 47, 70,
   109, 111–12, 119, 131, 145,
   148, 169–70
sacrifice, 78–80, 125, 133, 138, 150,
   154, 167

salvation, 97–99, 108, 121, 123, 133,
   143, 153–55
salvation history, 96
scarcity, 5, 36, 45, 62–64, 70, 77,
   119, 135–37, 155
Schmitt, Carl, 166
sermon on the mount, 50–56, 66
slavery, 28, 31, 72, 84, 89–94, 118,
   143
Stimmili, Elettra, 85–87, 91, 94, 154
structural inequity, 53, 70, 121
suffering, 78–79, 99, 123, 139–41,
   149, 169
supersessionism, 72
symbiosis, as a form of relationship,
   56–57

Tertullian, 6, 97, 103–4, 110–12,
   119–21
Thomas of Chobham, 25

undercommons, the, 173–75
universalism, 73, 77
use-value, 18
utopianism, 4, 168

value, 2, 7–8, 18, 26–33, 47, 51–53,
   63, 67, 72, 123, 145, 147–48,
   160, 163–65
violence, 1, 6, 58, 122, 149, 157, 173
virtue, 18–22, 51–53, 61, 74, 78, 118,
   142, 163, 176
vocation, 93, 152–53

wage relationship, 76
wealth, 13, 17–20, 27–28, 31–35, 38,
   41–43, 52–53, 61–64, 69, 92,
   109, 149, 152–54
Weber, Max, 152–56
woes, Jesus' pronouncement of,
   50–53
wrath, of God, 76, 80–81

Yom Kippur, Day of Atonement, 40

Žižek, Slavoj, 66

www.ingramcontent.com/pod-product-compliance
Lightning Source LLC
Chambersburg PA
CBHW031432150426
43191CB00006B/477